YASSMIN'S
Story

FEARLESS, FUNNY AND INSPIRING

YASSMIN ABDEL-MAGIED

VINTAGE BOOKS
Australia

Some of the names of people in this book have been changed to protect their privacy.

A Vintage book
Published by Penguin Random House Australia Pty Ltd
Level 3, 100 Pacific Highway, North Sydney NSW 2060
www.penguin.com.au

Penguin
Random House
Australia

First published by Vintage in 2016
This edition published by Vintage in 2017

Addresses for the Penguin Random House group of companies can be found at global. penguinrandomhouse.com/offices.

National Library of Australia
Cataloguing-in-Publication entry

Abdel-Magied, Yassmin, author
Yassmin's story / Yassmin Abdel-Magied

ISBN 978 0 85798 617 7 (paperback)

Abdel-Magied, Yassmin
Abdel-Magied, Yassmin – Influence
Muslim women – Australia – Biography
Determination (Personality trait)
Role models – Australia

A920.720994

Cover images © Simon Hewson/fa tog'ra fi
Picture section: all images care of Yassmin Abdel-Magied
Cover design by Luke Causby/Blue Cork
Typeset by Peter Guo/LetterSpaced Typesetting
Printed in Australia by Griffin Press, an accredited ISO AS/NZS 14001:2004 Environmental Management System printer

Penguin Random House Australia uses papers that are natural, renewable and recyclable products and made from wood grown in sustainable forests. The logging and manufacturing processes are expected to conform to the environmental regulations of the country of origin.

Contents

I once asked my mum what her expectations of me were
and she said:
'Do the best you can in everything you can.
Do your absolute best.'

This is for you, Mama (and you, Baba and Yasseen).
This is for my family.

This is for all the teachers who have made me who I am today.
(Mrs Lepp, Mr Henderson, Mr Stumpf, Mr Carlil).

For the mentors, informal teachers and those who took a
chance on me.
(Lorraine Collins, Julianne Schultz, Julie McKay,
Barbara Piscitelli, Michael Rose).

For all my 'habibs'.
You know who you are; thank you for always keeping
me grounded.

For all the sisters.
We've got this.

Prologue

I'm sitting on a helideck in the middle of the ocean, hundreds of kilometres away from any land. It's the dead of night, the only time I find peace and the chance to be alone on an oil rig full of – well, mostly – men. When you live with over a hundred not-quite-strangers for weeks at a time, sharing accommodation, bathrooms, meals and work, you do become family, but those precious moments of being alone with your thoughts are few and far between. This helideck is my refuge.

The surface of the dark green landing pad is rough; I sit cross-legged in the middle of the brightly lit 'H' that marks the touchdown spot in the centre of the octagon. This raised platform was never meant for human lounging but I am always one for repurposing.

Why am I here? This is my day job. I work as a drilling engineer on oil and gas rigs and my career so far has taken me to remote rigs on land and in the ocean, around Australia and the world. I am sometimes on call, sometimes on a roster of one month on, one month off. A day job, however, doth not a woman make. I have the privilege and blessing of taking on multiple identities. Yes, I am a mechanical engineer; I am also a practising Muslim woman (*Alhamdulillah*), a founder of a youth-led organisation, a former race car Team Principal, a Sudanese-born member of the Arab-African diaspora, a Queenslander, a boxer, a doer and, hopefully, also a thinker who is able to add value, to be *useful*. I care about leaving this world a better place, so I spend my time advocating and agitating for that positive change.

Why am I here, typing up my story under the moonlight, with the never-ending din of machinery in the background? The rig derrick shines brightly in front of me, a forty-metre-high beacon of industrialisation in an unforgiving and terribly beautiful landscape. Why tell this tale at all?

When I was growing up, I didn't see stories about people with lives I could relate to. There were no stories centring on young women, people of colour or Muslims. There were definitely no stories of young migrant Muslim women who grew up eating *mahshi* and listening to Avril Lavigne. The stories being told *about* people like me are often told by people who are not like me, and often without permission. It is exhausting to forever be talked about without being involved in the conversation in a meaningful manner. Yes, some people do try, but it is not enough to be invited to speak only when spoken to. Also, I have never been one to wait my turn. This book is about reclaiming the narrative, redefining it to my lived experience and the varied experiences of the strong women and mentors in my life. In doing so, I hope to provide some insight into a different world: one that has always existed but has not often been acknowledged by the society I live in, the West.

I am writing this to share my story, but I am not arrogant enough to believe it is particularly remarkable, or unique. This is not about teaching, as I still have so much to learn. It is about sharing experiences and the lessons learnt along the way, as well as asking the questions those experiences continue to raise. It is clear that we are facing immense challenges as a global society and will continue to in the decades to come. Creating effective responses to these challenges will only happen through a combination of critical thought and fully considered action, a balance I have been searching for throughout my life. I am grateful to have been involved in a lot of 'doing' for someone my age – a healthy 24 years. This book is about some of the doing, but also some of the thinking that lay behind those actions. Hopefully, these stories will add texture and context to a different perspective – the perspective of a young Muslim post 9/11, of a girl who grew up seeing the strong women around her all wearing hijabs and being confused as to why the world was telling her those same women were oppressed. Hopefully, they will encourage thought and discussion around why we, as Australians and global citizens, are at the crossroads we are, and what needs to change to move us to where we could be: a place where we learn from and respect each other's choices and experiences.

This isn't just my story. This is the story of so many other young people, so many other women, and so many other people of faith and colour. My story may seem unique because it does not fit in with what you expect from a young Australian Muslim woman, but there are many stories of young Muslims, women and people of colour that challenge, question and inspire, without tokenism or self-doubt. The difference is that a lot of these stories never see the light of day, don't make it into our newsfeeds or the morning television shows because not everyone has a ready platform from which to share their story. *Alhamdulillah*, I have been blessed with access to a microphone and as such it's my responsibility and my duty to make the most of it – for myself, and for the many others who don't yet have that space.

I write this story – my story and the story of the people around me who have created who I am – so that I can open a window into another world, the world of an Arab-African Muslim migrant woman who calls Australia home, of a chick on a rig, of a motorsport maniac, of a lady who lifts, of a smart mouth in a hijab. This world isn't so far away, though, and any partition can so easily be dismantled, bit by bit. After all, we're just drops in the same ocean. What are we waiting for?

Chapter 1:

Where the Blue and White Nile Meet

'Yassmin was born in a world of her own!' The phrasing made the statement sound dramatic, as Arabic's poetic language is wont to do. 'She was so impatient to join the world that she didn't even wait to come out properly! She slid out in a bubble and the nurse used a needle to pop the sac because it wouldn't break.' My mum mimed the situation as she told the story, holding her hand out in front of her as though she was the nurse, wearing an irritated expression and poking at the surface of the balloon with exasperation. I was born en-caul, or in the 'water bag', as our family calls it. It has always quietly pleased me to hear that, even at the very beginning, I did things unconventionally.

That story is not nearly as good, though, as the story of how my parents actually *got* to the hospital that night. They dodged army personnel who were out roaming the streets, enforcing the 11 pm state-imposed curfew, and they braved this alone – an extremely unusual situation for the first-born-of-the-first-born in Sudanese culture. The rest of the family wasn't expecting me for another week and were caught up at another hospital supporting an ill aunt. When my mother started feeling something in her belly as she got into bed that night and suggested to my father that they drive to the hospital, they got into the car quietly and without the usual fanfare, unaware of what lay ahead – nothing to do with an oppressive regime, but all to do with an addition to the family. Sure, I was not due for another week, but I guess I was too excited to wait. Bubble or no bubble, Yassmin was coming out to get amongst it.

I was born in Sudan in 1991, in the aftermath of the coup by Omar Hassan Ahmad al-Bashir, a man who, decades later, still runs (and ruins) the nation.

We – my mother, father and I – lived in an apartment above my paternal grandmother's house. This is still the traditional thing to do in Khartoum, the capital of Sudan. Typically, the main family grows up in one house and as the children mature the family builds apartments above. This allows the extended family to have some space yet all share the same building, in the spirit of communal living that is the bedrock of Sudanese culture. We inhabited a modest flat with two small rooms as well as a dining room, lounge and kitchen, with my cousins on the same level next door, in a different but similarly sized apartment. After we left Sudan, my other aunt's family moved into our old place and so although we never lived in the apartment again, we were regular visitors, returning from Australia to visit Sudan every two years. My other aunt's family extended our old apartment from two rooms to three, in an attempt to contain the rowdiness of the kids to a separate area. The apartments were built for multiple families to be closely connected, so the bathrooms connected bedrooms, and the kitchen in our apartment had a window above the sink that opened into the front corridor of the apartment next door – an early, Sudanese version of intercom. The parents would use it to discuss family trips or coordinate school pick-ups, and, as the kids grew older, the window was a portal we whispered important information through, like what time we were going to be allowed outside to play, or making plans to meet up during our mandated hours of afternoon naptime without having to leave the house and risk the wrath of the parents.

The aunt who moved into our apartment had a daughter only a few months younger than me – my cousin and first best friend, Aya. We grew up together, briefly in the same country, then on opposite sides of the world, literally taking baby steps at the same time. Aya and I are similar in many ways; we are both loud and social, and the firstborn in our families. We also both have a slightly rebellious streak, although it manifest itself in different ways in each of us. Her laugh is infectious; she is always up for an adventure and was always game to play. On our family visits to Sudan, Aya was my Partner in Crime (PIC), although sometimes we disagreed on what was fun. While I really wanted to play with things like the rock polisher I found in the cupboard, she thought that was lame and, to be fair, most of the cousins agreed. It would take at least sixteen hours to polish a rock, so their reluctance was understandable, but I loved the idea of creating something beautiful out of something so raw – at that time, every rock around me had the potential to be a thing of great value, no matter what it looked like. The rock polisher (a contraption owned by my father as a young boy) was like a mini tumble dryer chamber powered by a small electric motor. You would load a few 'gems' (rough rocks from the garden) into it, along with some polishing powder. The chamber would then be placed on a spindle and switched on, allowing it to slowly smooth the rocks into fabulous gems. The pictures on the front of the box were entrancing: gleaming quartz and cobalt globules placed against a blue background, juxtaposed against the 'before' photos of rocks. Aya and the other cousins were never quite convinced, though, so we didn't polish any rocks on my visits. What we did both agree on was the fun value of cops and robbers, or *Agbud Alharami!* as it is called in Arabic. This was a game all the cousins could play, from the youngest who could barely walk, through to Aya and me, the leaders of the rabble. We would hide outside the house, in alcoves on the outer walls, and chase one another around the ground floor, past the lemon tree, smashing leaves pungent with the scent of citrus, the plastic of our thongs making slapping sounds against the tiles as we sped. The corridor on the right-hand side of the house was always full of activity; there was a door to the kitchen so my paternal grandmother would constantly pop her head out, reminding us to slow down and checking if we'd been fed. This area also had an outside kitchen workspace, a concrete basin covered in white tiles to form a sink. My grandmother and the maids would sit around it on small stools, cleaning rice and meat or washing clothing under the bright Sudanese sun, day in and day out. This was the place where I would later learn to braid intestine for the *Mararah*, a traditional Sudanese salad made from fresh offal, and also where we would wash our faces and feet before we went back into the house if the play had become a little too rambunctious. We would continue running past the washing line, in focused pursuit of the *Harami* (robber), typically a younger cousin. After we turned the corner, it was time to slowly sneak past the back of the house where the maids slept (all of us trying to be respectful, as we were taught this was their space), then as soon as we cleared their rooms we would pick up speed, bolt around the last corner of the house, and sprint!

Growing up alongside Aya has given me a comparable Sudanese yardstick against which to gauge my life. We are from the same family tree so blossomed in environments with similar values. When we reconnect, our life stages feel familiar yet we are on such different paths, partly due to opportunity and partly due to expectation. How different would Aya be if she'd grown up with me in Australia? How different would I be if I'd grown up in Sudan? Of course, there's the nature and nurture debate to keep in mind, but it is startling to be reminded so clearly of a potential alternative reality through the life of a family member. Like me, Aya is well educated and has a degree from one of the best universities in her country. She performed exceptionally at university and is a young, empathetic, independent woman. Unlike me, Aya married shortly after graduating, as many Sudanese ladies do (or are expected to). She is no longer working in her field either. Typically, Sudanese women will continue to work after getting married, but as Aya moved to Saudi Arabia to follow her husband's career that was not really an option.

Aya still lives in Saudi and we stay in each other's lives via phone apps that work in the region. Every time we speak, I am keenly reminded that my cousin, who started out just like me, now lives a life so completely different to mine.

Photos of me as a baby look a lot like those of my father at the same age: plump arms, short, curling hair and a pointed chin, with one obvious difference being the giant pearl earrings that droop from my earlobes, demanding attention. As tradition in Sudan dictates, my ears were pierced pretty much as soon as I was born, to let people know I was a little girl, the sign of femininity bold and clear. It was important to my family from the beginning that my gender was so obviously defined; this set the scene for the expectation of the clear visual definition of gender roles that continues throughout a person's life in Sudan. Of course, my family would not have imagined that piercing my ears could be considered a political act or that it could be viewed as limiting or oppressive. It's just what people do when a young girl is born in Sudan, to make her 'beautiful'. It might be a simple cultural tradition, but it is also emblematic of an attitude that exists more broadly in Sudanese culture; one that assumes girls should aim to make themselves beautiful and adorn themselves with lovely things. This tradition sets a standard for how women should present themselves, which is not just as a 'female' and as an expression of their biology, but more than that, as a 'lady'.

In Sudan there are clear, though usually unspoken, rules that dictate what it means to be a 'lady', and they often start with your family members reinforcing a particular gendered expectation. Whether the expectations are around jewellery, your hairstyle (even if you are wearing a hijab), how loudly you laugh or who makes the tea, they define a way of being that is tough to defy. It is even more difficult when religion is brought into the mix, because these expectations are then bestowed divine legitimacy. Discussions that challenge gendered expectations become much more complicated when some view them as sacrilegious. However, Islam is far more nuanced than that, and it is galling to see a beautiful religion used in a rigid and inflexible manner when the essence of the faith is anything but.

It is not just Sudan or other countries in the East that have issues with strict gender structures. Countries like Australia still battle to define what a 'good woman' or a 'good man' looks like, acts like and *is* like. If anything, our discussions in the West are more complex, cloaked behind a screen of superficial equality, when the reality is far from it. In Australia, the gender pay gap is growing, violence against women is rife and bias still limits the future of half the population. There has been progress; we have significant legislative change and a public discourse that we can engage in. However, if we are to continue to improve we would do well to listen to other cultures and learn from their experiences.

My time in Sudan was short-lived. A year and a half after my ungraceful entry into the land of the living, my folks made the brave decision to travel to the other side of the globe and raise their family in the land down under.

Australia.

Migrant parents do not often talk about why they made the move to a new country, and mine are no exception. Most of what I know about the reasons and motivations behind our move was learnt from listening to stories relayed to others – to family friends and at public forums and dinner parties.

My father tells a few stories but only ever shares them when asked directly why he moved to Australia.

Well, he says, they were the kindest people he met on his travels around the world. Dad lived for four years in the United Kingdom (UK), a year in Rugby training with GEC and the other three living in London and completing a PhD in electrical engineering at Imperial College. On his return from his studies in the UK he taught at the University of Khartoum for a number of years; he was one of the youngest academics in the university. It was during his years in Europe that he met Australians and found them welcoming, a scarce trait in England in the 1980s.

While positive experiences with Australians led my father to favour this nation out of all the possible places to migrate to, my mother has a much more concrete reason for picking the lucky country, although it took some digging on my part to uncover the details.

Sometime in 1982 or 1983, a ten-year-old Queenslander placed an advert for a penpal in a British educational magazine at the encouragement of his father, Ian Hamilton. Ian thought it would give his son some writing practice and expose him to the experience of others around the world. The advertisement garnered four or five responses, some well written and others not. Ian, seeing his son's reluctance to pen his own messages, resorted to replying to three of the letters himself. One didn't respond, but the other two did: a girl on Christmas Island and a university student in Sudan. Ian eventually lost contact with the girl on Christmas Island but kept in touch with the architecture student, Faiza, my mother. The exchange of letters continued throughout my mum's university degree, first job and engagement to my father. Eventually, Ian and his wife sent my parents the migration forms to help us move to the land down under, and gave us a roof over our heads until we found our feet. The Hamiltons were a large Jehovah's Witness family and their love of community connected with the Sudanese experience and helped forge a truly international friendship. It turned out that although writing wasn't his son's forte, at least half of Ian's plan worked. His family didn't just get exposure to different communities; they took it a step further and welcomed the people with those experiences into their home.

★ ★ ★

On 30 June 1989, Colonel Omar Hassan Ahmad al-Bashir overthrew the government of the democratically elected Prime Minister, Al-Sadiq Al-Mahdi. With the support of the National Islamic Front (NIF), Bashir claimed to be saving the country from the six-year civil war between the ethnically Arab north and the tribal south. The war, which scored a bloody rift into the nation, crippled the economy and left hundreds of thousands dead, became Africa's longest civil battle and gave birth to a generation now known as the 'lost boys'. The war ended in 2005.

Initially, Bashir's new government was known as the Revolutionary Command Council for National Salvation (RCC). It was later, in 1993, that Bashir abolished this body and appointed himself President of the nation. After the coup, Bashir instituted a version of the common law that governs Muslims, a destructive form of Sharia law that warped its true form.

'Sharia', as a word and as a concept, is globally misinterpreted and misunderstood. It is important to understand the notion of Sharia to understand the flaws in Bashir's implementation, and appreciate why the fear of Sharia law in Western countries is unfounded.

The word 'Sharia' is Arabic for 'path or road to a watering hole or place of salvation'. The five objectives of Sharia are protection of life, mind, religion, property and offspring; rulings in Sharia law are based around the protection and promotion of these areas. Logically, decisions that lead to their degradation are considered fundamentally unIslamic.

In practical terms, traditional Sharia is quite unlike any legal system in the modern West. Rather than law referring to a number of acts and legislation sitting in a library, Sharia is actually what is known as a common law structure: a constantly changing and evolving process aimed at ensuring society operates intelligently and ethically, although it should be noted that Sharia has an unchanging core; the protection of the five areas a constant that underpins all rulings. With that core in mind Sharia was meant for constant revision and improvement. Like a computer user too busy to update their systems, however, governments and religious institutions have simply been unable to adequately update Sharia to today's context, perhaps finding the version they are using more politically convenient or simply more comfortable. It is tremendously important that the rulings of Islam are interpreted to fit the framework in which we live because that is what makes religion relevant and powerful. If this does not happen, we stagnate and stagnation only serves to breed disease.

What is often forgotten is that the foundation of Islamic law was not linked to a state's authority, because when it was introduced in the seventh century the 'nation-state' as we know it today didn't exist. Islamic law was about finding a balance for society through rational thinking and religious morality, determined by scholars of Sharia rather than any government or rulers. Today, however, many governments and political rulers use the guise of Sharia law to bestow divine legitimacy to their actions – regardless of how true they are to the core tenets of the faith.

Because Sharia relies on a large element of interpretation, finding an answer to any one question can be very difficult. At any particular time there can be a number of different interpretations of the same set of facts – but this interpretive element allows Sharia the flexibility to be relevant to all times and places, as long as it adheres to Islam's original principles and the protection of life, mind, religion, property and offspring.

Bashir's move to 'Arabise' Sudan, which meant that the public institutions would now operate in Arabic rather than English, was about discarding the remnants of British colonialism, and was an effort to make the nation more 'Islamic' by employing superficial changes the government believed were significant. These changes included the policing of women's clothing, switching the language of education and encouraging polygamy, rather than focusing on deeper, more socially impactful Islamic measures like charity and integrity within governance.

These shifts in society affected my family deeply and were the catalyst for our eventual migration. My father is a practising Muslim, but he believed the political Islam that was being touted by the new government was destructive. Baba also believed teaching classes in Arabic would mean preventing Sudanese students from accessing global education and institutions. It was more difficult for a Sudanese student who studied in Arabic to be accepted into a leading university in England or the USA, much less awarded a scholarship, and thus Arabising education made the Sudanese less competitive on the world stage. My father wanted his nation and his students to be the best engineers possible, so to him, this move seemed regressive.

From the government's point of view, Arabising their universities was part of challenging the West in a postcolonial push as they focused on finding an independent identity for the nation. In attempting to remove the Western education and thinking processes entirely, though, they indiscriminately dismantled many of the institutions that the British had created, rather than preserving the good and removing the bad. Decolonisation is an unimaginably difficult and delicate process to navigate; there are few countries that have been able to successfully recover from this destructive form of oppression.

However, not all aspects of the Western education system in Sudan would have necessarily been oppressive. It takes nuance and courage to see the benefits in a system that is associated with so much pain.

My father is a man who always sticks to his principles and he vehemently disagreed with the Arabising process. It was his vocal protest and subsequent actions that eventually had consequences for us as a family.

'There were eighty others. Eighty-one of us lecturers signed a petition refusing to set exams in protest against the Arabising movement,' my dad said. 'United, we were fine, but when I came back from holiday, seventy-eight of those lecturers had set exams. They got to seventy-eight of them. Only three of us stood against the university, and we were fired.

'None of us worked as engineers again. One of these academics was brilliant; he was a world leader in his area and now he's tutoring A-Level students. The other academic, also an authority in his field, now runs a building services company installing lighting fixtures. I moved to the other side of the world. But I would never do anything differently, and don't regret it, not one bit. Someone has to stand up for what is right.'

My mother has her own stories of rebellion. She studied architecture in a politically volatile time, and her college experience was full of demonstrations, strikes and unrest. It gives her a different perspective on 'tough times during university', one that my grumbles about too much assessment don't quite stack up against.

The first I heard of my mother's student action at university was over the traditional Sudanese breakfast we had every Saturday morning as a family, after I had begun my first semester of engineering and was talking about the upcoming exams. We were sitting under the pergola in the backyard, the weekend papers covering the large timber table, eating *fool-u-bayd* (broad beans and eggs, garnished with tomato). I asked my mother about the architecture exams she sat at university and unwittingly opened a can of worms.

'When I was at the University of Khartoum we didn't have exams for the first two years!'

'How, Mama? What are you talking about?'

The conversation then became less about assessments and more about making change, the Sudanese way.

'It seemed like every time there was an exam, something would be happening with the government and people would start to riot. They would have to shut down the university. It was great, until we had to do the exams for first, second *and* third year all in one year so we could catch up!'

I laughed, imagining the chaos that would ensue if we tried to shut down the University of Queensland because we disagreed with the government.

Mum continued, a piece of Lebanese bread in her hand, using it to punctuate her passion as she schooled my brother and me on our lack of radical action. 'You're all so quiet and tame here; you need to be vocal. Protest and riot more!'

'Mama, that's crazy! Right?' I looked at my father and brother for support but Dad just shook his head slightly and returned to reading the newspaper; this was not a conversation he was going to get involved in.

My father, for all his love of Noam Chomsky, Robert Fisk and conspiracy theories, is at heart a conservative man. He likes order, systems, and for things to follow due process. 'It's all about the process, following the process!' he would say to me in frustration when venting about situations where he felt the correct procedure had been flaunted, like nepotism in his workplace. He would regularly deny me a last-minute favour because I hadn't followed due process and asked at dinner, where we discussed important family matters. We reckon his love of order and discipline came from being brought up by a German nanny for the first four years of his life (the side effect of being born in a communist nation just after the war). My mother once said that my father used up his risk-taking quota on the big move to Australia, so once we arrived he retreated into a more conservative way of thinking, which is why he was strict in our upbringing. Honestly, though, I don't mind. Not everyone has a large enough risk-taking quota to throw everything up in the air and hope it doesn't break when it lands, like my parents did when they chose to migrate.

Whatever the reason for his conservativeness, the chaos and risk a public protest would entail was too much for my father to entertain and so he tended to retreat and allow my mother to stand in the spotlight, as she did at breakfast that day, regaling us with stories of a truly tumultuous university experience and implicitly reminding us that Muslim women were powerful and would stand for what they believed in.

It was Mum who first showed me that my religion was revolutionary and that her family had lived that story, the women in her family all bucking the cultural Sudanese norms in some way but always maintaining their Islamic faith. When I was growing up, Mum would tell me stories of the famous female scholars in Islamic history, stories of women doing things that today some Muslims would incorrectly say is impermissible. These women were strengthened by their faith, Mama would tell me, rather than weakened or oppressed by it. That was at the heart of my mother's activism: an Islam that radically strengthened women despite their oppressive and often patriarchal environments. It belies the perception often touted in Western media. The public commentary about Islam is often so far removed from my actual experience of it that sometimes I forget they are talking about *me, my mother, my family,* the faith I hold dear and the values by which I live my life. My mother is a woman who fights inequality where she sees it, regardless of culture, and uses her faith and religious values to back her up. She has never accepted 'cultural norms' as an excuse for injustice, something I inherited. It also meant all the things I did that I expected would be culturally challenging for my mother did not even cause her to bat an eyelid.

Many years later, when I asked whether she was okay with me flying the coop to follow my engineering career she answered, 'Anything you've done, the women in our family have done already.'

They had!

My mother was one of eight: four girls and four boys who grew up in a nation that was finding its feet in independence from the British. While my mother was growing up, Sudan had not yet become an Islamised nation ruled by a government with roots in the Muslim Brotherhood as it is now, so in some ways it was a more open-minded society. Education was highly valued and of an internationally recognised standard, so scholars would travel around the world and exchange ideas, bringing back knowledge to improve Sudan. Policy making was thorough and based on global best practices, and companies brought investment into a nation that they saw as full of potential. Women were largely free to wear what they chose, and so there were fewer hijabs than there are today. In fact, photos of my grandmother, aunts and mother showed them wearing outfits that wouldn't have looked out of place in Europe at the time, knee-length skirts and short coiffed hair all the rage.

My mother's eldest sister is a tall, fierce, almost Amazonian doctor who apparently used to entertain the family with stories of dissection and disease from her medical studies, whether they liked it or not. Gorgeous curls abound in her graduation photos as she chose not to wear a hijab until she was older; none of the sisters did until they were mothers themselves. Some of my aunts became more traditionally religious with age, putting on the hijab to demonstrate this. Others felt that if they were not visibly observant in their dress, how could they ever hope their children might be? For each individual it was a personal choice and journey. However, in Sudan there is also an element of social pressure around what is deemed appropriate, taken from the language used by scholars on TV through to what the neighbours might think. These days it is sometimes simply easier to err on the side of caution. This echoes the reality all over the MENA region; after the decolonisation process, the sweep of Islamised governments (which, I remain staunch in believing, do not represent or implement Islam as it was intended to be) began to slowly restrict the freedoms and rights of their constituents, particularly women, and this is felt in different countries in varied ways.

The next daughter was even more radical. Super stylish, she wore skirts and shoes that were the latest European fashion and studied Nile River fish at the University of Khartoum. Her PhD took her to Norway: a small Sudanese woman wandering naively into a cold northern winter.

'I had no idea what I was getting into,' my aunt told me. 'People said it was going to be cold, so I took a cardigan.'

The cardigan wasn't enough. I can only imagine the shock

that must have rocked my aunt's body as she walked out of the airport for the first time, given that twenty degrees is considered quite cool in Sudan.

My last aunt is the only one of the sisters to stay with the family in Khartoum, holding the fort. The youngest daughter, she studied architecture like my mother and is currently a lecturer at the University of Sudan, submitting her third or fourth thesis. Just, you know, the traditional thing to do.

Mum was the third daughter, a tomboy by all accounts, ganging up with her brother to play pranks on the other siblings. She was also independently minded and took risks she thought had a high pay-off, like moving with her family to the other end of the world with nothing but a suitcase and a couple of thousand dollars.

I'm by no means suggesting that my mother's experience is the norm, rather highlighting the terrific range of diversity within the Sudanese and Muslim experience.

Mum often talks about how her father's passion for education came from watching the English kids he saw heading to schools run by the church. He would tell them stories about how the children wore new clothes, polished shoes, looked well fed and like they lived a good life. My grandfather didn't have that growing up, but he knew that he wanted it for his children. He believed that if they could get that education, his kids would have a chance at living life with the comforts of the British. My grandfather didn't want to *become* British, he just wanted his children to be afforded the same opportunities and so worked every possible job to make that dream a reality.

My mother's heritage is mixed. Her father was part Egyptian (maternal) and part Sudanese (paternal), which meant that he was able to identify as Sudanese from the Ja'afari tribe (tribal affiliations are passed through the father). My maternal grandmother is even more of a mix, part Turkish, Moroccan and Sudanese. Unlike my mother, my father's family was from a line of merchants and businesspeople who migrated from Egypt and so they have no tribal Sudanese affiliation. Nonetheless, they played a role in Sudan's politics, economics and social fabric. There was apparently a time you could say 'I am an Abdel-Moneim' to a taxi driver at the airport and they would know where to take you.

My full name is Yassmin Midhat Abdel-Salam, Abdel-Magied, Hassan Bey Abdel-Moneim.

Hassan Bey Abdel-Moneim was the big dog, my great-great-grandfather or the OG (Original Gangsta). He moved from Egypt to Sudan in the 1800s and became a wealthy businessman. He had nine children – six daughters and three sons. The women married into other wealthy Sudanese families, which is how I am related to almost all the big names in Khartoum, and the three boys married a number of women and had a multitude of offspring. Polygamy was the norm at the time, which resulted in us having an enormous and diverse family tree. The wealthiest brother was Ahmed, who had a total of twenty-four children – eighteen daughters and six sons. Ahmed and his family descendants are my business-focused uncles and aunts. Super sharp, always on point. The second brother, Mohammed, had the fewest children; with six sons and daughters in total, they could fit the family into a minivan.

My great-grandfather, Abdel-Magied, fathered a modest eighteen children. He was particularly focused on education, so my line of the family spent their inheritance on educating their sons and daughters to the best of their ability. The strength and value of education was heavily emphasised throughout the

Abdel-Magied line and resonates strongly with both my father and my mother. This inherited focus shapes the way my brother and I view the world.

The Abdel-Moneim family was one of the most influential in the development of the capital. Today, the families with influence are different and much of the Abdel-Moneim asset base has been sold off, but the old-money pride and correlating conservative values still remain.

My mother's family was from a line of rural villagers who moved to the capital city for a better life. The standing of the family is incredibly important in Sudan; individuals don't just get married, families do. When it came to my parents being together, the fact that they had equivalent levels of education reduced the difference in social stature significantly. The relationship was made easier again because my father was a long-time friend of my mother's older brother and so the families were already well acquainted.

My mum is a lot like me (or rather vice versa). When I see her running a community forum or organising a conference, I sometimes wonder what she would have achieved if she'd been given the same opportunities as her children. My parents sacrificed their place in their community, the support of their family and their professional careers to secure a better future for my brother and me. Even though my parents were still quite young when they moved to Brisbane, not having grown up in Australia was always going to be a barrier to them realising their full potential here. The lack of shared memory, the absence of school and university networks, the slight xenophobia that characterised the 1980s and 1990s in Queensland all meant that my mum was at a disadvantage, but she accepted that so the next generation would have it better. She did everything in her power to make sure we would – not only my brother and me, but an entire generation of young Muslims in Australia and around the world.

Was there then extra pressure to 'succeed', given my parents had sacrificed everything for my future? No more than for any other migrant kid. There is a level of existential responsibility, debt even, which sits in the mind of migrant children that means sometimes our decisions are made, whether consciously or unconsciously, out of respect to our parents and the sacrifice they made. It is not something that can easily be explained in cold, rational terms. Understanding that your parents thought your future was more important than theirs can be a burden, or a boon, depending on numerous variables: the way your parents moved (refugee arrivals can have a different outlook to skilled arrivals, for example), the way you were raised (whether or not your parents expect you to live in exactly the same way they did, or adapt), their expectations and ideas of success, and so on. There's no doubt, though, that the knowledge of the sacrifice your parents have made weighs heavy on your consciousness. To know that but for one decision made by our parents, our lives could have been entirely different – that tugs on a person's soul, either anchoring you to reality, or drowning you.

For me, my parents' sacrifice grounds me to the reality that the world isn't fair and we must all work to change that, particularly if we've been able to somehow 'succeed' despite the lottery of birth. Looking at it this way, I see my parents' sacrifice as a blessing – an opportunity that must be capitalised on, otherwise the sacrifice is wasted. I see their move as incredibly selfless and generous, and wonder whether I would ever have had that courage. It is inspiring. Constantly and unchangingly inspiring.

My father has a brilliant mind. On a good day, he'll pull out his PhD from Imperial College with pride and flick to a page towards the back. 'You see this?' he says, pointing to an equation that covers the entire page. 'I made this equation up! Look at what your dad did.'

Dad hasn't worked as an engineer since leaving Sudan, mainly because the market in Australia was tough. He joined a group for unemployed engineers and some of the people he met there are still family friends. When he couldn't find work in engineering, he set about searching for another way to support his family and began studying IT. I never questioned his reasoning for leaving engineering behind, but I can only imagine the bittersweet pleasure he must get from having both his children work in the field of his beloved passion. I am not sure if we were directly influenced, but somehow both my brother and I ended up studying engineering. I majored in mechanical engineering with a focus on structures in motorsport – designing a racing car chassis – and my brother also studied mechanical engineering, with a second major in aerospace. My brother has a different personality to mine, and even though we studied the same course at the same university, people often don't realise we are siblings. Yasseen doesn't tell people we're related if they don't ask, and in some ways I understand that. His reasoning is 'that it just never comes up'.

We've never really talked about why he doesn't mention that we are from the same family, largely because he doesn't like these kinds of conversations, but I imagine Yasseen wants the space to create his own identity outside what others think of me, and he is succeeding at doing that. My identity at university was built around advocacy and motorsport; his is in the field of aerospace, mechatronics and robotics, where I'm sure he'll be outstanding.

I probably don't tell him enough, but truth is, I'm proud of my little bro.

I eventually moved from structural and design mechanical engineering to drilling engineering – more linked to the oil and gas industry, but with some of the same core concepts. Drilling engineering is focused on the design and delivery of drilling wells in a manner that is as safe, economical and environmentally friendly as possible. Although both of our fields are from the same world that my dad specialised in, the concepts and analytical tools Yaseen and I use became different after the first year of university. My father had always been someone I could ask for help when solving a problem in physics or maths at school, so I distinctly remember the moment at the end of the first year of university when my father looked at a question on dynamics I was doing and shook his head. 'I didn't study these concepts. *Khalas*, you are on your own now. Baba can't help you with these.'

He may not have been able to give advice, but he did want to learn and so would often ask me to explain a concept back to him, not only helping me to understand but sharing that love he has for the logic of the discipline. My dad still loves getting the Institute of Electrical Engineers magazines and passing on articles of interest to my brother and me, hoping for a technical discussion. He gets great joy out of learning about the technology behind drilling then surprising me with oddly detailed questions about my job. 'See, Yassmina!' he might say after a particularly gnarly question on the use of magnetic interference in intercepting another well, deep underground. 'Your dad knows what's going on, ah?'

Although I've always been aware that my father was a significant figure during my upbringing, his personality has shaped me in ways I'm only just beginning to understand. Baba has a presence larger than his physical stature; as an academic in Sudan he was respected in the community and built his identity around being a learned person with authority. He expects to be listened to and his opinion deferred to and it's difficult to change his mind once he sets it. An engineer through and through, Dad prides himself on being objective and logical, sometimes painfully so, which is one of the main reasons I had to learn to articulate my point of view growing up: my household trained me from a young age in the art of debating.

★ ★ ★

In late 1992, my family arrived in the big country town that was Brisbane then with $2000 and a couple of suitcases. University lecturers were denied exit visas under the new government, so my mum and dad had no option but to leave Sudan via Egypt under the pretence of a weekend away with the family up north, packing only bare essentials and holiday clothes. My parents hadn't announced their departure to the extended family and they were initially criticised by some in my father's family for running away from home. 'Sudan isn't too bad yet,' they said, 'so why would you leave?' It was a time when many people were unsure about whether to stay or leave because nobody knew what life under the new government would be like. One person from almost every family with the means left Sudan during this period, which eventually led to the incredible Sudanese diaspora around the world that I so strongly identify with. We stayed in Egypt for a few months with my father's extended family while we finished up the paperwork for his skilled migrant visa and then snuck away on an EgyptAir flight to Brisbane, where we were met by Ian Hamilton and his family. He'd assured us that the weather was fine: that although it was humid, our landing was going to be much better than my aunt's experience in Norway.

I was a shocking passenger on the flight to Australia. It's a twenty-four-hour journey and I was not a quiet, calm or obedient child. My mother says I cried almost the entire flight. As she has told many friends, the only time I stopped crying was when I realised my bassinette was right underneath the screen the film was being shown on, and that if I stuck a limb up, I could create shadows. Just another way to be a right nuisance, really. I am not sure my family thinks much has changed since then!

We stayed with the Hamilton family for a few months while we found our feet and my parents adjusted to a new world and an unfamiliar system. The family shared their old Queenslander with us, a fitting welcome into the nation and state. The house sat right at the back of a large plot, seventy metres or so from the front gate down a concrete pathway, cracked by the heat, leading to the front veranda. I remember the door opening into a family lounge area, wooden floors worn from the pattering of so many feet, with the bedrooms and kitchen off the main space. It was homely and the family embraced us, sharing their lives.

'We met your parents at the old Brisbane international airport in mid-1992,' recalled Ian. 'A day or two after you arrived, Faiza and Midhat weren't feeling well and it turned out to be chickenpox.'

What a start to the journey of a lifetime.

We had caught it on the plane over from Sudan. Apparently my parents offered to move out to protect the host Australian family, but the contagious period had come and gone. My parents and I got sick, and it was the first of many bonding experiences! The Hamiltons are still family friends, although the children are now scattered around the world. When we do get the rare opportunity to meet up as a group, they fondly share stories of our arrival and gradual adjustment, and how the first word they learnt in Arabic was '*La'a!*', meaning 'no', something my parents were constantly yelling at me as I tried to stretch the boundaries as a toddler.

It seems I've been predisposed from the get-go to seek forgiveness rather than permission (if I end up seeking anything at all). As a child I always did what I wanted, regardless of whether that was approved of or not. I pushed the boundaries as far as I could, discovering my limits by gauging the reactions of those around me. Rightly or wrongly, this is an attitude I've carried with me throughout my life, and it has led to both good and bad outcomes. Pushing boundaries in the social space is a great way to break stereotypes, create new narratives and, possibly, change the system completely. Pushing the boundaries when it comes to safety in a workshop or speeding on a car or bike is less intelligent, but I've always been one to learn the hard way.

Brisbane was a monocultural town in the early 1990s. Baba claims we were one of the first Sudanese families in the entire district, and we were most definitely the first in our neighbourhood. I don't quite remember what it was like, but I have no doubt it was a memorable transition for my parents. Being so visibly different, both as Africans and Muslims, meant that we were quite the novelty and there was no hiding from our difference, for better or for worse.

We were constantly reminded of our 'uniqueness', mostly in small ways – people staring, or not knowing how to refer to my mother's hijab. There were also the little, humorous cultural differences, often manifesting themselves in the way we used the English language. A good example that gets told around the dinner table whenever we meet up with Ian's family is the time they invited Mum and Dad to a get-together with some friends who asked them to bring a plate.

'We thought they just must not have enough crockery for everybody!' my mother laughs when retelling the story.

'*Aywa wallai*,' my dad says, agreeing with my mother in Arabic.

'So we took a few plates, and knives and forks as well. They must have been struggling, we thought; they'd need more than just the plates if they didn't have enough for all the people they invited and were asking us to bring our own! We can be generous and take more cutlery! When we got to their house and gave them the empty plates, they were just as confused as us!'

There was mostly novelty in the interactions my parents had with the locals, although occasionally there would be the exception. People often thought my parents were either Aborigines or Malaysians, because Sudanese people hadn't quite entered the consciousness of your regular Queenslander.

At times, my super chubby two-year-old figure, overly gregarious personality and voluminous afro acted as an icebreaker. I was that child who wandered over to random families' picnics at Southbank and sat down on their mats, trying to make new friends. My innate friendliness, combined with the naivety of my youth, plus the novelty of being African-Arab meant I was always seen *and* heard as a child. We spent a lot of time in parks as a family, partly because green, open and public spaces were so special and rare in Sudan that it was a luxury for my parents, and partly because social activities in Australia were built around alcohol. As practising Muslims, my parents don't consume alcohol, so they weren't going to spend their downtime in pubs, bars or clubs and this restricted their socialising options. We were also on government support to start with while my father looked for work, and so parks were cheap entertainment. It became tradition to spend weekends in the 'Aussie' way, having a barbie in the park. My father loved the concept of free barbecues so much that years later, when my mother bought a barbecue for him as a gift, he still preferred to use the one in the park down the road. Why? Because it was free, he said, and easy to clean and use! My mother's exasperation was lost on his engineer's logic and I think we've used the purchased barbie a total of three times.

I once asked Ian whether he felt any cultural shock when writing the letters to Mum or when my parents came to Australia. His response confirmed the power of personal connection; by corresponding with someone so far away, he said, Sudan was no longer just a country on a map but a beautiful land full of actual people, living their lives, just like him.

The way Ian speaks about the change in his perspective reinforces a notion that is relatively undisputed – that human connection can have an enormous impact on humanising any seemingly foreign or remote community or group of people. The focus these days is on advertising and campaigning; however, they are only part of the solution. To fundamentally make a foreign people seem familiar, some level of human connection is required.

'It was probably more of a shock for your parents,' Ian reflected. 'One meal time Midhat [my father] looked at the table and said, "But where's the bread?" We hadn't realised bread was an essential element in the Sudanese culture, whereas it was optional for us.'

I could just imagine my father's confusion; I would never see him start a meal until there was bread on the table.

It is humbling to think that this Australian family opened up their lives to us, a group of strangers from the other side of the world. Being welcomed in this 'true blue' manner shaped the way we thought about our new country and set us up for success. Our first interactions with Australians were positive and welcoming, but I can only imagine how difficult it would have been to feel like we belonged if when we arrived, scared and alone, our neighbours were cold and distant.

So why did this family open their doors to us? Part of the reason came from the fact that they were a religious family; they had a generosity of spirit and valued the community. I also think part of it could be that intangible 'Australianness' that more often than not treats others with kindness, empathy and respect. That was the Australia my father glimpsed on his travels. Because of his experiences during his time in the UK and the institutional and underlying racism he witnessed at Imperial College, my father still believes that, no matter what, Muslims and people of colour, particularly of African descent, will never be seen as equal in England. 'Australia is different,' he tells me any time the UK comes up in conversation. 'That's why we picked Australia. There is a meritocracy here!'

Now, I feel like there may be caveats that need to be applied to that statement, but the reality is our initial experience included a support network that made us feel like we belonged. We moved out of the Hamilton house into a place just down the road that they helped us find, and became close friends with our new neighbours, Maggie and Bruce. Regardless of attitudes on the street, we had a support network in the mainstream community and that made us feel like part of the fold. This may not seem significant, but remember that Queensland was just emerging from the enlightened Bjelke-Petersen era!

Play it forward twenty or so years, and I cannot say with confidence that we extend that same hand of kindness to the migrants, refugees and asylum seekers that come to Australia today. Some have forgotten the essence of who we are and have become fearful and entitled, spurred on by divisive language that does not actually reflect our real selves. There are some programs that do welcome families but help from a service provider is not quite the same as being invited into a circle of friends, into a family home. There is very little that is more powerful than a simple act of kindness: a smile or a shared meal. It doesn't take much to make someone feel welcome, so why does it seem as if we have forgotten how to do that?

For my mother, the first few years in Australia were desperately lonely. She will occasionally share shards of memory.

'I cried every night for two years,' she once told a friend. I was listening in on the conversation, hidden around the corner in the kitchen after I had served tea. My mother's voice wafted over from the lounge room, as she retold an experience she would never have burdened me with. Her voice quietened and I had to strain to hear the last line: 'But I had nowhere else to go.' There was no communication with home, bar a two-minute call from the payphone down the road once a week. The connections she made in the neighbourhood were therefore her sole source of energy. Knowing Ian's family, as well as our neighbours, was vital. Not only did Mum lose her social network and family in the migration process, but she was cooped up looking after a baby when she had just started hitting her architectural prime in Sudan, so her sense of worth would have taken a significant hit. For some time Mama didn't want to be in Australia. What could she do, though? They'd bought a one-way ticket and escaped the regime. They couldn't go back.

My parents went from being well-respected professionals to being unemployed and on welfare. My father is always quick to point out that we came off Centrelink as quickly as we could, but in reality it wasn't that straightforward. They had no jobs, so Mum stayed home and looked after me while Dad set about finding a way to put food on the table. Mama had been working as an architect in Sudan, in a nice job in the city of Khartoum. In Brisbane her only option was housewife duties. Her tertiary qualifications were not recognised in Australia, a common situation affecting many migrants and refugees and one that wastes so much potential. It saddens me when I see my mother watch an architecture show on TV or hear her remark on a beautiful building design and realise she misses her calling, a calling she was forced to give up for my brother and me.

What the photos from this time don't depict is the struggle of settling in. We lived a simple life, starting out on bare mattresses. Coming in as skilled migrants meant that we weren't part of the humanitarian refugee system and did not have the formal institutional support services a typical refugee settlement program supplied, programs that would include helping my parents secure employment, set up bank accounts, register for Medicare and so on. My parents were left to fend for themselves.

Those first two years were tough. It doesn't appear that we were connected to the Muslim community during that period, although there was one. The Muslims in Brisbane at the time were largely Pakistani, with some Egyptian and Lebanese, all spread around this sprawling city. We really only started becoming engaged in civic life once I began school and my family entered an entirely new subculture in Brisbane, the local Muslim community. This was a community we would be part of for years to come, a community that understood the migrant struggle.

My mother only opened up about our transition period once, giving me an insight into how our mindset had been formed.

'What was it like, Mama? How did you leave everything?'

'Ah, Yassmina . . . Understand that we were the ones who chose to come here. We weren't forced by circumstance but came with an optimistic framework and mindset.'

'*Ya3ni* [the Arabic word for 'like'], what does that mean?'

Mum let out a breath that teetered on the precipice of a sigh. 'Yassmina, some people are driven by fear. Others are driven by trust. We were always driven by trust. We believed we had the capacity to deal with anything that came our way. We trusted in ourselves, in the world around us. We trusted in the power of education. We trusted that if we worked hard, we would be rewarded and we would be able to achieve what we wanted to achieve, *Inshallah*.'

I wondered if that was my mother's way of saying they had trust in Allah, trust that He would always put them in the right place at the right time. It's this belief in our own abilities, through the strength of Allah, that underpins all that my family does. This same attitude is likely the reason my instinct is to throw myself headfirst at any challenge, figuring it out along the way – I trust that I will be able to, *Inshallah*. The truism that 'everything happens for a reason' gives an avenue to find meaning in even the most difficult experience.

Believing that you have the capacity to handle anything that comes your way is incredibly empowering. Ideally, if you have the underlying confidence that you can do anything, you just have to figure out how, so having this trust helps you move beyond self-doubt to a place of self-reflection and analysis.

My mother was not doling out random advice: trusting in her own capacity was how she had dealt with starting with nothing and creating a new life. 'When we arrived we knew *only* Ian and his wife. We had $2000, two suitcases and a belief. We had to trust that it would work out, *Inshallah*. And we also believed the West had something good to offer.

'Was I discriminated against? Yes.'

I shook my head in disbelief.

'Was it frustrating? Of course!'

'Mama! Does it still happen today?'

'Of course, Yassmina, of course. Your father and I are too different and come from somewhere too foreign to ever have "made it", or progressed to high levels in society. But you either fight it and exhaust yourself, or move on to something else. You have to pick your battles! I also never believed I was lesser. I was open-minded and genuine, and in Australia, people value those who are genuine.'

It was one of the first times we had talked about discrimination limiting us. We spent so much time as a family working on behalf of others, empowering them to navigate the systems and structural inequities in the world, that we didn't often turn the mirror back on ourselves. My parents did everything the 'right' way. They followed the rules, they were smart and worked hard and spoke the language, and yet they still felt the effects of discrimination. It didn't fit with my viewpoint of the world at the time, but it gave me an insight into the reality of unconscious bias and structural inequality – phenomena that are much more insidious and difficult to call out.

'Your father and I didn't have time for excuses. We wouldn't say "I didn't get that job because I was Muslim, or because I was black, or because I was different". We couldn't afford to do that, and there is no value that comes out of it! We would look at a situation and reflect and think, *Okay, what can I do better next time?* Deep down, it is about choosing to not have a victim mentality. We are *not* victims. You can't let that get you down. It just makes you more resilient.'

That sounded more like it. This pragmatic way to approach the problem felt more comfortable; it sat well with my logical, engineering-influenced approach to life.

'Just remember, we can't blame others, and we can't follow what others are doing if we want to make change. Remain respectful! Make your own choices. Pursue things *hard*. Remember to always have integrity.'

Words can never express how grateful I am to have role models like my mother and father. People search high and low for mentors to help shape their future, guide them down the right path and provide them with the advice that will enable them to realise their potential, but I never had to look further than across the dinner table. I was born into a family where my two parents epitomised all that I would learn to value in life, and then some. *Alhamdulillah* one thousand times over does not cut it, and I live in their eternal debt.

Chapter 2:

Early Days

Almost two years after we arrived it seemed that Brisbane was not ready for this jelly, so my family moved further north, travelling to Singapore for my father to take up a position teaching electrical engineering at a polytechnic. Despite Baba completing a diploma in IT, he hadn't had much luck finding meaningful work in Australia. It was in Singapore that the first moments I can just remember took place.

I went to a Chinese kindergarten, proudly wearing the green-bibbed and white-bodied uniform. In the class photo my afro piglets and bright, shiny brown face stand out among the sea of my Asian classmates' faces. Apparently, I even spoke Mandarin, because that's what most of my friends spoke.

We lived in an apartment building with many other expatriate families, so all my friends lived in the same area and my parents' social life bloomed. We would go out on the weekends with our friends and visit parks and markets, try new foods and watch my mother play badminton. The community was diverse, and I had Arab, Chinese-Singaporean and Caribbean children among my besties. These expat families eventually became our extended family, as my parents craved the large support network they were accustomed to in Sudan and missed in Australia.

My little brother joined the family during this time and I swung wildly between loving having a playmate and hating the fact that he got all the attention. He was, and remains, adorable and well behaved, a blessing for my mother. We moved back to Australia shortly after he was born. My father's contract was finished, and there was a much higher chance of becoming full citizens in Australia than in Singapore. We arrived back in Brisbane ready to jump right into life: my father hoping to get a job, our family to get citizenship, me to start my schooling, and us all to continue building a life in the lucky country.

Our first home when we got back to Brisbane was a modest two-bedroom house on the southside, not too far from our friends and previous neighbours. It was brown brick, small and suburban. I would wait out the front for the Islamic College of Brisbane's bus to pull into the driveway every morning around 7.30 am, the plain twenty-one seater driven by a local uncle – given we use 'uncle' as a blanket term to refer to an adult male in our communities. The photo taken on my first day of school shows me standing tall, shoulders thrown back, toothy grin and black shoes gleaming. The small white hijab that was part of the school uniform frames my face, and the checked long-sleeved tunic and green pants blend into the green of the front yard. I couldn't wait to go to school; learning was all I wanted to do. Even at that stage, I felt there was so much to find out about the world!

My childhood was what I would consider relatively conventional, in the Sudanese sense, as my parents did their best to bring me up with both Islamic and Sudanese values despite the completely different circumstances of being in Australia. Conventional for us meant broad African/Arab values: family and faith were our first priorities, closely followed by education and then play, but even then, play usually had a purpose. It felt normal, but we all think our way of experiencing the world is normal.

The role of faith in my life when I was growing up was never at odds with my environment; as a young child it was found in playing with my mother's scarves, or standing next to my father, copying his movements while he prayed, learning the dos and don'ts of *Salah*, Muslim prayer. Muslims pray five times a day: once at dawn (*Fajr*), around noon (*Dhuhr*), in the afternoon (*Asr*), after sunset (*Maghrib*) and at night (*Isha*). Praying doesn't take long, and essentially the idea is to have regular 'time out' points during the day, to recentre yourself and provide a moment for reflection, meditation and connection to Allah. The method of praying is also quite physically active, with specific structured movements allocated for each time slot that every child has to learn.

One time when I was little, I was praying next to my father and right after we began I let off a cheeky little gas. We continued to pray, my father not making any comment. As the prayers ended, we closed off the prayer with the usual *Salaam*. While sitting on our knees, we turn our head to our right shoulder and say '*Al Salaamu Alaykum wa Rahmatullahi wa Barakatuhu*', which means 'May the Peace and Blessings of Allah be Upon You', and then we turn to our left shoulder and say the same. On each shoulder, Muslims believe, there is an angel recording every deed. The angel on your right shoulder records your good deeds and the angel on your left shoulder records your bad deeds. Together they are called *Kiraman Katibin*, or the 'honourable scribes'. The way these scribes work gives some insight into the underlying mercy of Islam. Good deeds, thoughts and even intentions are recorded instantly by the angel on the right – even a good intention is recorded. The angel on the left, however, waits a day before recording a 'bad' deed, and does not record bad intentions. If the individual seeks forgiveness within the day, the deed may not be recorded at all. There are also various times in a day and in the Islamic calendar year during which bad deeds can be removed from the ledger.

After nodding to the *Kiraman Katibin*, my father looked at me. 'Yassmina, what did you do at the beginning of the prayer?' he asked gently.

I looked down, not sure if I was about to get in some sort of trouble. 'You mean the *purrut purrut*?' I said.

My father nodded. 'If you do *purrut purrut*, should you keep praying or stop?'

I searched my mind, unsure of the correct answer. *It's a 50-50 chance*, I thought, taking a punt. 'Keep praying?' I answered, hope in my voice.

My father shook his head. '*La'a*, Yassmina. If you do this, you should say *Al-Salaams*,' he nodded to his right and left shoulder, 'then go do *Wudhu* again and start to pray from the beginning. *Purrut purrut* breaks *Wudhu*, okay?'

I nodded, taking it all in. *Wudhu* is the ablution or the washing process that Muslims do before prayer to ensure that we pray cleanly. It's pretty straightforward, but it's described in intimate detail in the Qur'an and *Sunnah*. So much of Islam is open to interpretation but things like how to pray and how to do *Wudhu* are not, which means there's relative consistency in these processes around the world. *Wudhu* involves washing your hands, nose, mouth, face, and arms up to your elbows, wiping your hair, neck and ears and then washing your feet. Each wash is to be done thrice. There is also a number of things that break your *Wudhu*, like going to the toilet, bleeding, sleeping or, as I learnt, passing wind.

The way my father gently led me to find the right way in this story is a hallmark of the educative style he used when I was growing up. Baba would never answer my questions directly, but would counter them with his own, forcing me to think. He only really got involved in my formal education during the later years, once my mother began to work and I had reached high school. In my younger years, it was always my mother who helped me with my studies.

My mother was the reason I was ready to go to school at the age of four: her expectations were always high. I remember countless weekends sitting at the dinner table in our apartment in Singapore, books strewn across the table, Mama painstakingly teaching me the building blocks of a primary education: reading, writing, comprehension, adding, subtracting, and even multiplication and division.

She taught me so well that back in Australia the local kindergarten turned me away. A few days after I started, the supervisor approached my mother while she was dropping me off in the morning to say they thought it would be better to enrol me in a school nearby.

By that point, I could read, write, multiply and divide and had developed into quite the show pony, so I imagine having me flaunt my knowledge while the others were trying to learn the alphabet was quite frustrating for the teachers. Their suggestion was duly taken up by my parents who went about finding a school that would take me. Public primary schools at the time turned me away due to my youth, and so the only option that worked was to send me to the newly formed local Islamic school, the Islamic College of Brisbane (ICB).

Being younger did not seem to make a difference to how others saw me, perhaps because I was always tall and so seemed older. I wore my age as a matter of pride, as if to say *See what younger people can do? I'm beating you at your own game, classmates, and I'm not even your age!* This is a sentiment that has been carried through my life, a belief in the power of young people and our ability to change things up, make things happen, defy expectations.

My youthful attitude could have been taken for either arrogance or confidence. Which label it was given may have had something to do with 'gendered labels' and the reality that certain behaviours are celebrated in young boys and dissuaded in young girls. The example that is often used when talking about gendered descriptions for young children is the use of different terms when referring to children who display authority over their peers: in young girls, this is referred to as bossy and in young boys it is referred to as leadership. I was often labelled with terms like bossy, but never took it to heart, accepting that it was probably true. But not every young girl has a positive experience with that description and it frames their perspective about certain behaviours from an early age.

When I began at the ICB, it only went up to grade three. But it grew each year as the students progressed, so we were one of the first few classes to go through the school. As a result, the entire school community – teachers, parents, students – were all excited to be a part of this new initiative, part of making history. My classmates were Somali, Pakistani, Bosnian, Lebanese, Jordanian, Indian, Fijian, Algerian and Afghani, and we were all Australian. It was a multi-everything environment, but that was our norm. Everyone was working together to build a future for their children in Australia that would also fit in with their Islamic values. They were creating a safe haven for their children and shaping that world.

Hopeful – but also filled with the drama of a Bollywood film or an Egyptian TV soap. Our religion brought us all together, but we were from diverse cultural backgrounds, with varied levels of education and societal privilege, which caused friction when parents wanted different outcomes for their children or dealt with conflict in disparate ways.

Many of the families had come to Australia as refugees and had a different mentality to those who'd come as skilled migrants and those who'd lived in Australia for generations, of which there were a few. For most of us kids it was simple. We were born somewhere else, or brought up in a family that hailed from another land, but, ultimately, we were Aussie. Different kinds of Aussie, but Aussie all the same. Yet, if pressed on 'where I was from', I would probably have said I was Sudanese. The concept of being 'Australian' hadn't entered my vernacular yet, and I was not expected to show allegiance to Australia above all else, as we are expected to do today. As young kids going to an Islamic school, we may have been part of different cultural communities, but at that age and at that time our identities were uncomplicated. It probably helped that there was no one to invalidate our ideas of identity: no one said 'you can't be Australian', and so we just didn't think about it.

For some kids though, their attitudes were inherited from their parents who did not yet feel 'Australian' and so their country of origin was the nationality they identified with the most. For those kids, being Australian was seen as being 'Western' and 'copping out'. This was mainly in response to the foreign policy of various Western nations at the time, particularly the USA. It was a sentiment that would start to show itself more as the years went on, but not one that interrupted my space in a conscious manner – not until the events of 2001.

The ICB was a true community school, from the way it was run to the demountable buildings that housed our classrooms. The premises were hidden away in the Karawatha Forest, down a long single-lane carriageway, unlit and looming: the forest always felt like it was bearing down upon us as we drove through.

I met the school principal when we visited the first time, a genuine, mild-mannered Fijian migrant who said they'd be happy to take me on for a one-week probation and, if I could keep up with the class, they'd allow me to attend. I was not aware of this condition, but walking into the grade one classroom a few days later, I was ready to show my chops.

The teacher called me up to the front of the class to introduce myself and asked me to write my name on the board, if I could.

'Yassmin,' I printed carefully with the chalk, then turned to hand it back to the kind Pakistani woman.

'Yassmin, how many numbers can you count for us?'

'Up to whatever you want, Miss!'

I would always remain an overenthusiastic student. Back in those first few years of school, I had a habit that would drive teachers up the wall: when I had my hand up for a question, if I wasn't seen immediately, I began to click my two fingers while my hand waved in the air. *Click, click, click.* When my right arm tired, I'd prop it up with the left, supporting it at the elbow joint so I could keep my right hand up in the air while I fidgeted and waited to be picked. At the same time I'd be holding my lips tightly together to keep myself contained, thinking if I let them open, my question would burst out, entirely beyond my control. It took being admonished by the principal himself to dissuade me of that particular habit.

I questioned everything, all the time. On reflection, intense curiosity has been one of the few constants in my life. I always wanted explanations for why things were the way they were and asked my parents 'why' incessantly. They entertained my curiosity; if they were ever unable to give me an answer they would help me find it. I devoured the 'Tell Me Why' books, rereading sections over and over and over, absorbing the faux-watercolour illustrations of tapeworms and the moon, biology and physics sitting side-by-side in thick volumes of wonderful knowledge. I would sit cross-legged on the floor after school and on weekends, flicking through pages of questions. My favourite was a section on strange diseases, which meant I learnt about typhoid and rabies, parasites and yellow fever at an early age.

Who knows why I wanted to learn so much. Perhaps it was simply a desire to understand and make sense of the world around me. Yet it was childlike and impulsive; I didn't stop to think before I asked a question or pressed a button, did a makeshift science experiment, or climbed a tree to see what was up there. Curious was my constant state of mind and that meant I was never, ever bored. As my mother would say, I was always on to the next thing.

School was the hub of the growing Muslim community in Brisbane and so it hosted some major events, from the yearly school fete to the Eid prayers that Muslims partake in twice a year, the equivalent of Christmas. Eid was always a fantastic day at the ICB. There was never enough parking so the streets leading up to the school would be lined with cars. Ours would be among them, squeezed in haphazardly between a bush and an adjacent car's side mirror, just a little too close for comfort. Getting out of the family Corolla or Camry, we'd join the masses of brightly dressed Muslims walking along the road towards the school, white *Jalabeeyas* (the long white tunics that Arab men traditionally wear) gleaming in the early morning sun, various cultures reflected in the national dresses worn by everyone around us. You could hear the *Takbeer* from hundreds of metres away, almost like a chant from a football field: '*Allahu Akbar, Allahu Akbar, La ilaha il Allah, Allahu Akbar. Allahu Akbar walillahi alhamd . . .*'

It was the only time we heard this sonorous chant in Australia – 'God is great, there is no God but God' on repeat – as it's usually only done on Eid day. Joining the crowd as we walked closer to the prayer area was always a reminder that we were part of something bigger. We would pray in the oval area out the front of the classrooms where, on a typical day, boys and girls would be running up and down with a soccer ball, kicking up dust and claiming fouls. Large tarpaulin sheets were laid down to protect those praying from the dust and grass, but almost everyone brought a *Salah* mat with them to put on top of the tarp to provide a clean, soft surface for the reverence. We would stand in lines for the prayer, shoulder to shoulder, each pair of shoes placed next to their owner so as not to be intrusive.

'*Eid Mubarak!*' we would say to one another in excitement after the conclusion of the sermon. Eid was always a day when we saw friends, connected with families, and essentially came together in the most festive atmosphere possible, and it all happened in the school grounds.

Most of my memories from school are mundane. My best buddy changed a number of times early on but I settled on Hafsa as the years progressed. No matter where our classroom was, all the girls usually looped around the grade one block because it had shiny windows in which we could check our reflection. Some girls cared more about this than others.

After walking around the grade one block, we would swing by the admin block and down the main path to the entrance of the school. It was here, nestled next to the front gate, that the cop was stationed in the years post 9/11. Walking past that cop would become the norm for us.

ICB was just like any other school, aside from the Arabic and Islamic classes three times a week; these were a large part of the reason my parents chose to send me there, as well as the collective *Dhuhr* prayer before lunch. The small scale of the school was ideal for newcomers to Australia. Not only did it create a vibrant community with Islamic values, but studying Arabic and Islam there allowed me to learn about my religion in a safe space. These were taught as independent subjects, the same way other schools taught religion or French. Studying the language and faith of my family has made a huge difference to the way I connect with my Sudanese roots and moored me in my heritage. Speaking a language is an enormous part of being able to participate in a culture and I am grateful I can visit my family in Sudan and be part of the fabric. Many of my cousins who grew up outside Arab-speaking countries and don't speak the language find it difficult to slot back into that world and are made to feel even stranger than they already do due to their cultural differences. I also have friends in various diasporas in Australia whose parents consciously decided they didn't want their children to grow up speaking their native tongue so that they wouldn't have an accent that was 'unAustralian', and very many of them lament their inability to connect with their roots now that they're older. It can be disenfranchising to not be able to connect with your history.

My father made it a priority to return to Sudan to visit the family. Our first trip back was due to my maternal father's passing, while my mother was pregnant with my brother in 1994. Every two years after that, we would pack our bags and take that twenty-four-hour trip over to Khartoum during the Australian summer. It wasn't until I was much older that I realised the privilege those regular trips were – that not every family is able to do the same. I can only imagine how hard it must have been to scratch together a sum of almost $10,000 every couple of years on a single income. But I know how important it was to my father that we made this biennial pilgrimage. Not only did it mean that we always had an appreciation for where we came from, but we also gained some understanding of how lucky we were to be living in Australia.

Our childhood trips to Sudan feel like they occurred in a different era. They remind me of how exhilarating the airport used to be. Airports were places that signalled adventure. We'd usually visit a new country each time as well – a side trip to Qatar, Egypt or the UAE, depending on the timing and cost.

The plane trips alone were exciting. This was before the time of individual screens and on-demand entertainment, so we would usually be seated in the bulkheads or at the exit rows, allowing my brother and me some room to play with toys or colouring books on the floor. Occasionally we'd meet other children on the flight and run up and down the aisles, playing tag. When I got a bit older and braver, I gave in to my curiosity and asked the flight attendants if I could see the cockpit. It must have been 1997 when I first had the opportunity to walk to the front of the plane and meet the pilot and first officer. I got their autographs and was in awe of the hundreds of buttons that gleamed, blinked and glowed from every corner of the cabin.

When compared with my first memories, it is a shame to realise how the airport these days is a source of dread for so many Muslims, and, for me, is now associated with work more than anything else. Alas, the romanticism of an awaiting adventure has been forgotten.

Our holidays in Sudan were an exercise in learning the family tree, practising the language and finding out more about our heritage. We would spend the first week or so visiting both sides of the extended family, the week in the middle on an adventure visiting a regional area in the Sudanese 'outback', and then a final stint visiting the extended families again, bidding farewell.

Learning Arabic also let me engage more fully with Islam: being able to read the Qur'an in Arabic, no matter how slowly and haltingly, is unlike any other experience of it. It is almost indescribably important for me to be able to read the Qur'an myself, to have an appreciation for the language and the message. My only lament is that I still can't fully appreciate the nuance of the Arabic language. It is said that poetry in Arabic is unlike that in any other language due to its beauty and complexity; Arabs claim that was the reason the Qur'an was released in their language. With that complexity come barriers to comprehension, however, and although I can read the Qur'an *Alhamdulillah*, it is more difficult for me to understand and interpret it, as the language used is to spoken Arabic what Shakespearean English is to Cockney. I continue to read the Qur'an though in an effort to unpeel its nuances, each reading allowing more insight into the beautifully complex scripture.

Spending seven years at ICB, in a safe world where my home

environment reflected what I saw at school, was vital for my confidence in my identity. Sure, the school was a bubble, but growing up in a bubble of your parents' choice is not unusual, and this one meant that by the time I left for high school and was launched into a different and far more challenging world, I had a solid foundation in my faith, my language and a belief that my culture was worth something. It made my parents confident that I had inherited and believed in the value system they hold dear. Being around people who shared our beliefs was important for my parents, as they felt a value system steeped in faith was one of the most essential things they could pass on to my brother and me. With the right value system, they could trust we would make the 'right' decisions, *Inshallah*; their confidence in the foundation they provided was also what allowed them to give me more freedom as I grew up as they trusted in my ability to guide myself in accordance with Islamic values.

My parents were active in the school community, working with the Parents' and Citizens' Committee (P&CC) for a number of years, driving fundraising events and fetes, and encouraging teachers to enrol us in tests and competitions to raise our standards. The school community provided a comfortable social network for me and my parents.

Hafsa was my late-primary-school soulmate, my school PIC. We both loved reading, had a disdain for what we saw as superficial interests such as make-up, liked sports (Hafsa was into cricket, I liked soccer) and were both academic. We also had a healthy interest in the boys in our classes, but Hafsa was always more discerning than me. She was also quieter, and often acted as my conscience. I was loud, impulsive, brash and argumentative if pressed, which at school was often. Although I loved learning, I could be a nuisance. Hafsa was more introverted and avoided confrontation, often patiently listening to my rants and offering wisdom beyond her years. She was the yin to my yang, her influence toning me down and keeping me real.

Our friendship was cemented in grade five, that vicious year when girls make sport of being as cruel as they can to one another. There was a core group of five or so girls at our school who made up the 'in crowd'. One girl would always be on the outside, currying favour to get back in the good graces of the group. Every week or two it would be a different girl's turn to be in the doghouse, and the rest of us would devise terrible ways to make her prove her loyalty.

One week when I was on the outer, the girls had instructed Hafsa to make me do something particularly heinous – putting my hand into the toilet bowl to retrieve something – and this time, Hafsa wasn't prepared to be the bully: 'No! I'm not going to make her do that!' With that line she chose me over the girls, and we became Best Friends Forever. We were the kind of BFFs who would buy things for each other and fill in little notebooks about our lives. Our mothers often volunteered together as well, which meant plenty of extra time for us to spend hanging out at Hafsa's house, near the Kuraby mosque. This was our second regular mosque, which my family began attending once we moved closer to the ICB. Most of my memories of the mosque are about Ramadan, although we went through periods of our lives where we would go once a week for Islamic class, or simply to pray *Isha* with the congregation. The mosque is like the Muslim watering hole, where we would meet our friends and catch up with people's news.

My mother and Hafsa's mother were both active in the Islamic Women's Association of Queensland, along with a couple of other ladies who became family friends, like Aunt Galila, a stalwart of the community. Mama and Hafsa's mother were well educated and articulate and they quickly became close friends through their work, which was perfect for me as it meant more time with Hafsa!

Aunty, as I called Hafsa's mum, had a lovely melodic voice and always wore the *Salwar Kameez*, a loose-fitting tunic and pants ensemble, often with a matching scarf, which is the traditional clothing of Pakistani women.

Her family was Pukhtun, from Peshawar, meaning they originated from a state in Pakistan to the north of the country, said to be very beautiful. Pukhtun culture is quite strict so her family was bound by social norms I didn't always understand, mostly to do with how she spent her time and with whom. She wasn't allowed to hang out with me unless our parents vetted the event well beforehand. Their house was the coolest, though, because her father had a green thumb and they had a large garden that produced a lot of fruits and vegetables Hafsa was very proud of — tomatoes, cucumbers, and even watermelon! The grass was lusciously verdant, and her father had built an impressive retaining wall that circumnavigated the entire backyard.

Not only that, but they had guinea pigs! Hafsa's guinea pigs inspired my brother and me and, using Hafsa's example, we eventually convinced our parents that they were clean animals and that we should get some of our own.

Hafsa and I were nerds; there was no two ways about it. Even though I wasn't sure what that really meant, I wore the label with pride. Our nerd status was cemented in grade five when we picked up knitting and crocheting as our favourite pastimes. I've stopped knitting regularly, but it's something I'll occasionally take up for its soothing, rhythmic repetition. I don't quite know why we decided to start but it became a lightning rod for ridicule, although that never bothered me. My mum and dad would often say, 'Don't worry about what the other people do; we're not like everyone else', and by introducing that concept early they inculcated a belief that social norms shouldn't have power over your individual choices. 'We're not like everyone else' didn't come from a place of superiority; it was often used when they weren't allowing me to do something all the other kids were doing – a sleepover, school camp and so on. It was about making a conscious choice about what we want to do and not being controlled and directed by peer pressure.

The first time I owned being a nerd was after being teased by a group of the boys. I was a blustering mess in my defence. My bestie had capitulated and retreated into the classroom and I had followed her. As I walked away I heard their words biting behind us, so – pushed to my limits – I went back out to the door and yelled at them: '*So what if we're nerds!* I like being a nerd!'

Guffaws ensued, but it was never brought up again.

Part of being a nerd was being keen to learn things that were slightly uncool at school, like trigonometry, financial literacy and public speaking. Funnily enough, my nerdier skills became incredibly useful only after I graduated.

Mama would always tell me that Allah gives us all individual gifts, and one day we will be asked what good we did with those gifts. I love sharing stories on a stage, and I have found that people want to listen. Is it not then my responsibility to use that for good?

I didn't do very much formal public speaking until grade seven, when I was entered into an interschool speaking competition. For some strange reason, I chose to talk about obesity. I scratched my speech in the back of a notebook, practising it with my mother and English teacher, who had nominated me for the competition.

It came and went without fanfare. I stood in front of the class, shaking with nerves and anticipation. I talked too quickly, my hand movements were jerky and I didn't make it past the first cut. But the judge came up to my mother and me after the competition to give us some feedback, which she hadn't done for anyone else. She was an Anglo woman in her twenties with straight dark brown hair cut in a bob. As she leaned over the desk to talk to me, her hair swished down perfectly, framing her face in a way I knew my hair never could. 'You seemed a little nervous,' she said. 'But you know what? You have something special. When you speak, people listen. You have the ability to make people listen. You can use that!' She looked at my mother and me with this kind of earnest hope, and in that moment I believed her. My mother thanked her and she went on her way, never knowing her words would always be remembered by this eleven-year-old Muslim girl with hopes of changing the world.

My next chance to speak in public came a few weeks later, when I was selected to give the speech at the grade seven graduation ceremony. My parents filmed it and it's hilarious; the kind of video we pull out whenever we want a laugh. In the clip I'm standing behind an enormous lectern, so all that's visible is the top half of my face. I had taken the judge's advice and gone for confidence, but it hadn't manifested in a way that made any sense: I had decided to punctuate every possible moment with a facial expression and a movement of my eyebrows. So throughout the speech, all that is visible over the lectern is the top of a hijab, brown eyes and a couple of thick black eyebrows going up, down, left, right and every which way, in an attempt to make my speech more engaging.

It made for classic Abdel-Magied family home entertainment, and for years to come, whenever I made a big speech Dad would pull the video out and remind me where I came from. At some stage my father decided that if I wanted to play a role in society, I was going to have to improve my game, and so when I moved to high school I enrolled in the debating club, my training ground for the next five years.

But even though speaking has become a big part of my life, reading has always been my ticket to ride. It was my love of reading that helped label me with the flattering title of 'nerd', and it has been a permanent and prominent facet of my life ever since the night my father introduced me to Enid Blyton.

'Ah, *Khalas*, Yassmina! You're a big girl now! Isn't it time you read big books, novels?'

I was seven, in grade three, and my dad walked into the bedroom; I was sitting on the edge of the wooden bed, legs swinging off the side, flipping through the pages of some picture books I'd just borrowed from the library.

Dad sat down next to me, placing his lunch-box-turned-briefcase on the floor beside his feet. It was one of those A4 plastic zip-up lunch boxes, but he would also use it to carry the morning paper and, on rare occasions, any extra work he brought home. As a result, it was always bulging.

My father respected the divide between family life and work life, and it wasn't until I started working that I understood this wasn't true of everyone. Occasionally, Dad would take a training course that meant he was late home once a week, but throughout my childhood, both my parents were almost always there. It was about priorities for my father, and he's often said, 'Islam first, then family, then career. That is how I make my decisions.' He says it without resentment. For my father, it is a simple fact of life that when he moved to Australia he put his family before his career: 'I could have become anything but I chose to sacrifice it all for family and I would never change that.' That was his chosen reality and, as such, all of his decisions since have been made according to these priorities.

I do wonder whether or not I will mirror my father's family time ethics; whether I will be selfless enough to sacrifice for family or whether I will choose to make my career and my work a foundational pillar of my life. It is one of the aspects of the difficulties faced in 'Eastern v Western' thinking: family does not carry the same value in Australia as in Sudan, and so giving up career opportunities for family is often not valued as highly as sacrificing family for career. For all that we talk about work-life balance, it is never to balance life with work, it is always to balance work with life.

Back at the house, Baba said, 'Next time you go to the library, ask the librarian for books by an author named Enid. Enid, okay? Enid's books are quite good.'

My father had read Enid Blyton's books himself as a child. Having gone to a school in Sudan that was run by one of the churches, his early education was quite influenced by the British and their tastes in literature.

Oh, what a world! I couldn't get enough of the Secret Seven and the Famous Five; I devoured the adventures hungrily, constantly wanting more. The Famous Five held an edge over the Secret Seven for me, but that was possibly because of George, the first strong female character I felt a true connection with – she was the kind of girl I wanted to be.

George was short for Georgina, and she had a short haircut and an attitude that took no prisoners. I was drawn to the fact that she was just as tough as the boys, if not tougher. She went out of her way to prove herself, constantly trying to do what people said she couldn't, being a little rude at times, but always being a boss. 'The best son anyone could ask for,' someone once said of George. I found myself relating to a 'masculine' personality in a female role. Whether this is problematic or not I am unsure; it is interesting to see that it is a theme that repeats itself in a variety of situations. I was, and to some extent continue to be, drawn to the concept of being strong, independent and adventurous, and often lived those adventures through characters who were making things happen, who were defying the norm, and doing what they wanted.

As children, we tend not to pay attention to the nuances that adults understand as problematic. However, we do absorb the behaviours around us and implicitly understand what is considered right and wrong, what is 'okay'. That is why it's so important to ensure that young girls aren't only given gendered toys like dolls to play with, and aren't only congratulated on their looks. When we are growing up, these behaviours influence our self-worth and what we understand as valuable, so I make a point of always purchasing microscopes or Lego for young nieces, or the daughters of my friends, just in case there is a budding engineer or scientist among them.

My mother's experience of Enid Blyton's book is entirely different again, because she read the Egyptian version modelled on Blyton's books, which are set in Al-Makhadi, the affluent part of Egypt's capital. 'Al-Mughamirun Al-khamsa', or 'The Five Adventurers', was a series penned by Mahmoud Salem in the 1940s to 1960s.

One of the main differences, though, is the characters and their stereotypes. Takhtakh (full name Towfeeq khaleel Towfeeq kharbotali) was the leader of the group, and is characterised as being 'chubby with superior intellect', a marked difference to the tall and handsome Julian, the leader of the Famous Five. Anne's character was re-imagined as Loza, and she was also extremely intelligent and often solved difficult puzzles, although she wasn't beset by the same confidence issues as her English counterpart. There was no Egyptian tomboy, however; George's character became Nousa and is a more typical female character, although she's also smart and collected all the information that the team needed and used. Dick was known as 3atef and the dog went from being Tim to being Zenger. If I had grown up in Sudan reading stories with these characters, my world view may have been shaped differently. I would not have had the same character role model in George and may not have realised that it was okay for a girl to possess adventurous, perhaps even masculine, qualities.

It is possible to read anything into the reinterpretations but I find it fascinating that the female characters in the Egyptian version were not made fun of because of their femininity, or thought of as lesser for having female traits. On the contrary, women were seen as strong, although their strength was limited to certain spheres. This is an interesting nuance and one that sits underneath the conversations that culturally and linguistically diverse communities have about the power and strength of women. Having been exposed to more than one manifestation of the strength of women from an early age meant I believed that women had a place in society and were powerful in their own right. What that looked like, however, differed between communities and that was something I was just beginning to discover.

Chapter 3:

The Day It All Changed

'Okay, so do you know what a paradigm shift is?' I asked. The young Pakistani boy looked up at me with a blank face. It was 2009 and I was a poor second-year university student trying to make a little cash on the side tutoring students in the community. I would take over the dining-room-turned-study at my parents' place, searching for ways to illustrate the terms required for grade ten critical-literacy studies.

'It's kind of like . . .' I struggled to find a way to explain. 'Ah! Do you remember September 11?'

His eyes flickered from side to side as he seemingly searched his memory before finally shaking his head.

'Yeah, okay that — wait. What? You don't remember? The planes that flew into the building? That changed everything . . . ?'

'Ah, yeah, I don't remember it but I think my mum told me something about that. I was pretty young when it happened I think . . .'

My mind was blown.

The events on the morning of September 11 shaped my early

history more so than for most, because, as a Muslim, my world was permanently altered and intimately affected. The tragedy was used as the justification for many a breach of justice in the name of the 'War on Terror'. Yet I had the privilege of knowing a world *before* 9/11 – a freedom that Muslims growing up today might not have. Realising this was a paradigm shift in itself.

Everybody remembers where they were when they heard the news. I was ten years old and although turning double digits had felt like a pretty big deal, I was still a child, one that was going to have to grow up quickly to deal with the dark whirlpool that society was about to become.

The morning started as normal; I ate yoghurt for breakfast as Wednesday was yoghurt day in our family.

My father had a strict breakfast schedule for us, although my mother was exempt due to her preference for only having tea, white with no sugar, in the mornings. But for the rest of us, Mondays and Thursdays were for toast (peanut butter, marmalade or honey), Tuesdays we had cereals (Weet-Bix or Cornflakes), Wednesday was yoghurt (natural) and Friday was our free choice of either toast, cereal or yoghurt.

I usually ate cereal on Fridays; I could down nine Weetbix with my eyes closed, three bowls of three Weetbix, for the perfect milk to wheat ratio. I would sprinkle raw sugar on top, savouring the crunch, the release of sweetness. Wednesday was always a struggle, as I really couldn't stand the taste, smell or texture of natural yoghurt. Greek yoghurt with lots of honey was the compromise. I never questioned my father on his strict breakfast schedule until I had moved out and was no longer beholden to the plan. 'Oh, that was to balance your diet. That way, you wouldn't fall into bad habits and would have a healthy eating plan without even thinking about it.' Pretty good, huh?

The usual morning bustle of uniforms and lunches ensured I didn't guess that anything was up on that particular Wednesday until my mother made an offhand comment on her way out the door: 'If anything bad happens at school today, let me know. Call me at work.'

'Why would anything bad happen at school?'

'Haven't you heard yet, Yassmina? America has been attacked. Read the paper.'

I still distinctively remember my ten-year-old fingers fumbling with the newspaper, the black ink smearing the tips of my fingers.

As I unfolded the pages I stared at the now infamous imagery of smoke billowing out of the two towers. Whoa . . .

I rode the bus to the ICB that morning without incident but the playground was abuzz. Only one girl had yet to hear about it, and I duly informed her with aplomb.

A few days later, my best friend was the first to mention *that* name.

'They think Osama did it.'

'Who is Osama?'

'Osama bin Laden. He is in Pakistan or Afghanistan or something, my mum said.'

'That's weird. Why would he do something like that if he was Muslim?'

With hindsight our innocence is startling. Little did we know what that name would begin to mean, what that broader discussion would portend. It was the first of many conversations we would have over the next few years, asking why someone, if they were really Muslim, would do such a thing?

It would not be audacious to say that every Muslim living in the Anglosphere has a pre- and post-9/11 life. In Brisbane, we were thrust from being a relatively obscure religious minority to the visible embodiment of 'the enemy'. My understanding of the situation at the time was only rudimentary, but it would have been impossible not to notice that some things had changed. At least I have a recollection of what it was like beforehand. My brother, who was seven years old at the time, says that he doesn't really remember much. 'All I can remember from back then was an urge to always be playing soccer,' he's told me.

It's likely that because I was in an Islamic environment I did not feel the changes abruptly, unlike friends who have shared their experiences of being in non-Muslim environments at the time and who were less shielded from the vitriol. The process for me was like being the proverbial boiled frog: the frog doesn't realise the water is getting hotter and hotter until it looks around and realises the water around it is bubbling . . .

It started with the small things.

My parents used to send my brother and me to vacation care during the school holidays, where we would spend our days playing backyard cricket and Nintendo and doing crafts. The care centre, which was associated with Griffith University, was nestled in among the bushland, right next to the gym where, years later, I would return to begin a short-lived boxing career. The front gate led straight onto a large astroturfed front yard with an enormous eucalyptus tree in the middle, and we would usually interrupt a slightly skewed cricket game happening around the tree as we walked in. On the left-hand side of the lawn was a playground with wood chips, swings and the usual climbing paraphernalia, and on the right-hand side was the centre itself.

My time at vacation care was full of fun and lots of learning. I remember the first time I met another African-born child, even though I didn't believe it at the time. He was a new kid I had a crush on – I liked his light brown hair and his easy smile; he laughed at my jokes and I thought he was funny. We liked the same sports, and he was as white as a lily and cute as a button.

In the afternoon, while we were waiting for our parents to pick us up, I asked where he was from. I told him that I was African, because I was born in Sudan.

'Oh,' he said, 'I'm from Africa too!'

I burst out laughing. 'How can *you* be from Africa? You're white!' I thought it was absolutely hilarious that this kid thought he was from my brown continent.

'No, seriously! I'm from South Africa! I was born there; we only just came to Australia.'

'No, I don't believe you – you can't be African . . .'

We continued arguing until his parents arrived and I bid him farewell. When my mother came to pick up my brother and me, I decided to share this ludicrous story: 'Mama, there was this white boy who thought he was from Africa! How funny is that?'

'Why is that funny, Yassmina?'

'There's no such thing as a white African! All the Africans are black!'

'Yassmina, there are some people who are from Africa who are white. White people came to Africa a long time ago and they have lived there for a long time, too.'

I was astounded and couldn't understand how an identity that I had associated with a colour for so long could suddenly change. All the people I had met who considered themselves African were brown or black, and now a white person was African? What did this mean? Could anyone be anything?

This may have been my very first paradigm shift about identity, at the ripe age of nine.

I never saw that white African lad again.

Crushed crushes aside, the centre was a fun and carefree environment; the supervisors were mostly university students and they kept us occupied. My memory of them is that they were all Anglo, and so some things got lost in translation.

One summer, when I was eight, the Brisbane humidity turned itself up and I began to complain about the heat. The supervisor, a leggy brunette, frowned at me. 'Then why are you wearing such long pants? You need to wear shorts when it's this hot!'

I looked at her legs, which were thin and tanned, and although I was still too young to internalise many of society's beauty standards, even I knew that was how legs were supposed to look, and that mine didn't look like that. Mine had black hair on them for one, and my knees were dark because of my brown skin. Her knees were so white and clean!

'I don't think I want to wear shorts.' I looked up at her, puzzled. Why was she even suggesting this and why did it matter to her?

'Next week you're going to have to. You can't walk around in the heat with your legs all covered up! It's crazy.'

I remember being a little uneasy at the time. She possibly didn't realise what she was asking of me – even at a young age I was encouraged by my family to dress conservatively, whether because we were Sudanese or Muslim I couldn't tell for certain. But I did know that I didn't own any shorts.

In the car heading home I informed my mother. 'The vacation care says I need to wear shorts.'

'You need to do what?'

'They said I need to wear shorts, because of the heat.'

My mother looked at me over her glasses, one eyebrow up, both hands on the steering wheel.

'*Tayib* [okay].' She pursed her lips, obviously unimpressed. 'Let's go buy some shorts, *Baga* [then].'

We found a pair of white shorts in Big W that seemed to fit. They finished comfortably enough around my knees when I was standing, but when I sat down they disturbingly came halfway up my thighs. I didn't look like any of the girls in the ads, I thought, looking at myself in the mirror. I just felt disappointed and unsure. Although my shorts were greeted with approval that next week, I returned to my long pants after a few days, feeling exposed and hairy next to my white friends with legs like the girls on TV.

A little while after 9/11, and after I started wearing the hijab at vacation care, the carer and the older lady who worked in the office started asking me about Islam. 'Why do you wear that on your head? What does it mean to be Muslim? Why do you pray?'

I answered their questions the best way I knew how to, and then consulted with my parents around the dinner table when I got home. I first showed my parents the Paddle Pop stick box that I had made, having painstakingly arranged the sticks in a structurally sound manner then doused it in superglue just in case my design was faulty. Once they *oohed* and *aahed* over my creation, I proceeded to proudly share the story of my little stint educating people about Islam.

'The lady, she asked me about the hijab, and about praying, and then when I went to pray *Dhuhr* in the library the other kids wanted to know what I was doing so I explained, and then for *Asr* I went outside and prayed in the backyard and let them all watch so they know we're not scary at all!' I said in one big long breath, then looked at the faces of my parents.

'*Wallahi kwayis*, Yassmina!' my dad said, indicating his approval.

He got out of the chair and walked to his desk, picking out an A5 blue booklet with 'ISLAM' written on the front. It was also decorated with a minaret and hands cupped together side-by-side in prayer, all traditional Islamic motifs.

'Give this booklet to her,' he said to me in Arabic. 'If she has any more questions about Islam, she can come to us.'

At the time, I thought, *Cool! She might want to become Muslim! How exciting would that be, another Muslim person in my life?* What I hadn't figured out yet was that she wasn't curious because she thought the religion was amazing, but because she associated it with the oppression of women – I was a child who didn't want to wear shorts, her natural garb! Every word I said would be repeated by these supervisors as gospel – often because they had no other source of information aside from the news reports, and they could be biased, shallow and inflammatory. It was most likely they were taking the word of a ten-year-old as the truth about this diverse, widespread religion. Without realising it, I had become an unsuspecting ambassador for my faith, being asked to speak for Islam whether I wanted to or not.

The supervisors never did ask my parents about Islam, and I suspect it was because my parents fit their stereotype of Muslims more than I did. I think my parents saw these interactions as opportunities to provide positive interactions with the wider public about Islam. As long as I was not being attacked or hurt, they encouraged me to approach every situation with the mindset that it was a chance to educate people, to broaden their horizons and to share what our religion truly was about. A chance to show that we were not so different, really.

Like the gradually heating water in the pot, the other small changes in society's perception of us are more difficult to remember as discrete events. At some stage I started hearing stories about my friends getting their hijabs ripped off in the supermarket; once in a while someone would yell 'towelhead!' at me from a passing car. Getting stared at while we were out shopping became pretty normal, but I told myself it was because I was so good-looking that people couldn't turn away. It was my secret self-empowering Beyoncé talk: 'They're looking at you because they wish they were you, Yassmina!' I would tell myself, and it worked.

The attention was kind of exciting at the time. It almost felt like we were in a film or in one of my books. It did not seem serious; it just felt like an adventure. We would compare notes at school and see who got the worst hate that week.

'Did you hear the bus got glass bottles thrown at it yesterday?' someone said to me at assembly, as we stood in lines facing the principal while a young boy read a verse from the Qur'an in prayer out the front.

I subtly turned my head, not wanting to get in trouble for talking during assembly but keen to hear more. I was almost disappointed that it wasn't my bus – what would that have felt like?

'Oh, whoa, really? That's crazy! Are they okay?' I whispered. My classmate shrugged and we shook our heads in collective but naive disbelief. How much outrage can you truly have as a ten-year-old?

Hoons drove into the car park of our school a few weeks after that event and caused a ruckus, yelling racist garbage. My memory of this is vague, but it was shortly after that incident that a police officer was stationed at the front of our school to give us some protection, although perhaps this was more a symbolic move to show the police cared, because what would a single cop be able to do against a racist rabble?

The police officer became a source of endless curiosity, and we would spend hours after school sitting across the footpath from his or her spot at the wire front gate, cross-legged and attentive, asking this foreign creature about their world. We were not in the least afraid of this police officer. We would ask about relationships, what it was like to do the job, and if he or she had ever seen any grizzly fights. We would ask to see the gun, the torch, the baton. We did not fear their presence, but were fascinated by this instrument of authority, this white person in our world.

But as time went by even we ten-year-olds began to believe the police weren't on our side. We started to hear stories about cops stopping people because of their beards and their hijabs. It was often rumour, someone's mother, an aunty, or a friend. As the months went on and the talk in the media began to turn to the invasion of Afghanistan, the mood went from being exciting and adventurous to confusing and frightening. What had been certain was called into question. Was the police officer out the front of the school really there to help? My mother considered not going to work for a few weeks, and we were constantly attending strange 'community forums' with other families. Our parents would discuss issues like police–community liaison strategies, the language of the media, protection of school children . . . and I would play with the other kids, thinking it awesome there was another opportunity for us to hang out.

It still didn't feel connected to ME. It felt like everyone had just got it wrong. Yeah, we were being blamed for something, but surely these people actually realised we were just like them? It didn't occur to me that others might truly hate my family and me because of what had happened. It all still felt like a game.

Mrs Deen, my teacher at the time, was cognisant that we lived in a changing world and her way of encouraging us to talk about current issues was to have 'News Time' in class. Everyone brought in a piece of news each morning, and just before we were released from class at the end of the day, we would stand behind our tables and share our piece. It was always a mixed bag because our parents, from all around the world, watched different sources of news. Pakistani classmates had news from Pakistan, with Kashmir a common theme. One of my classmates was from Chechnya and he would bring updates from the Chechen conflict. At the time, I didn't realise I was hearing about the second Chechen war, but we got a blow-by-blow account of everything that had happened. My classmate always got so upset and I didn't understand why. I didn't see that it was *his* family he was talking about, and they were always in real danger. I wish I had paid more attention, but at the time it just seemed like yet another war and all of our countries were involved in some sort of conflict. I remember thinking, *Oh, you have news about Chechnya* again? When the USA and the UK invaded Afghanistan, it was simply another item in 'News Time'. It wasn't until I left the warm cocoon of the ICB environment that the realities of being Muslim in Australia really started to make themselves felt.

It makes me sad that there is an entire generation of young Muslims who don't know what it was like before we became the face of the amorphous 'enemy' in the country we grew up in. The anonymity of an Anglo-Australian and the privilege to choose the way the world perceives them and reacts to them is a freedom some young Muslims will never know.

The issues that Muslims face in Australia have regularly been compared to the issues other waves of migrants have experienced in the past. Time and time again people have said, 'The Chinese went through this, the Vietnamese, the Greeks and the Italians all did their time, so it is just the same for Muslims. Give it time and it will be fine.' Yes, Australia has had waves of migrants go through teething pains before becoming part of the cultural landscape. However, I do think that our current situation is a little different.

Today, the enemy is not a single race far away, at a border that could be clearly defined, whether it was, for example, Nazi Germany or the Ottoman Empire. Now the enemy has been characterised as an ideology, a belief system; the enemy is 'Islam'. Why? The actions of an individual from a marginalised group are often seen as the representation of the entire group rather than attributable to the individual. In our case, partly due to history, partly due to ignorance, rather than prosecute individual Muslim perpetrators, the entire 'group', Islam, became the enemy after 9/11.

There are people in all religious groups who use their faith and a divine decree to justify their violence or vitriol. There is not enough engagement, interaction or even basic knowledge about Islam for the general public to separate violent extremism in the name of political Islam from the peaceful and practical religion that millions of Muslims practise around the world and in Australia.

It should also be noted that the 'Islamic community', or the '*Ummah*' as some Muslims like to call it, is incredibly diverse – as my own little school showed.

Ah, the intricacies of the Muslim communities. This is another topic that is difficult to talk about, hard for fear of 'airing the dirty laundry'. It is hard for someone within a marginalised group to talk about issues within that group in a public forum as it makes more sense to have one voice and a united front. Airing the dirty laundry can add fuel to the fire and legitimise the hateful voices that are bleating with ignorance. However, to lump 'all the Muslims' together when talking about 'Muslim issues' is hugely problematic because within the *Ummah* there are innumerable different cultures, ethnicities, tribal groups and nationalities. Each group brings with it their history and cultural norms and these norms are often then conflated with Islam. Muslim communities generally split along largely cultural and national lines, so on top of dealing with outside pressure, internal fissions must be navigated.

How does this play out? At the basic level, each cultural group has its own mosque. It is not a formal position but an unwritten rule: people would go to the mosques where they felt comfortable and where the practices largely mirrored those of their countries of origin, similar to a German going to a German bar, an Irishman to an Irish pub.

So the next time you see someone representing 'the Muslims', remember, they don't represent 'all the Muslims', if I can be glib. They represent themselves, and if they are elected to lead a group then they represent that particular group. The experiences of Muslims are diverse and those of a Lebanese woman in Western Sydney are not the same as those of a Sudanese in Darwin and definitely not the same as those of a Fijian Indian in Mount Isa. Each group has its own battles, perspectives and solutions. Given that Sharia means there are technically many interpretations of the same source material, to expect a single answer from Muslims to *any* question is perhaps hoping for a little too much.

This may not be the easy answer, but it is closer to the truth than saying, 'On behalf of all the Muslims . . .'

Something that makes the situation facing Muslim migrants different from that of other migrant groups is the perception held by some Muslims (regardless of cultural background) and non-Muslims that Eastern and Western values are incongruent. The dissent is no longer a case of *We don't like their food and the fact they like living in extended families and speak a different language*, like with the previous waves of migrants. This is about values: *Their values are not like ours. They don't respect their women. They don't like freedom. They like violence and killing. They are choosing this, so they shouldn't come here or won't belong here until they choose to be Australian, and that means taking on Australian values.* On the other side of the fence, some Muslims will have equally low opinions of their Western counterparts: *They don't care about family or each other. They invaded our lands. They have no respect, for their women, for history, for anything that isn't Western. They are hypocrites, saying we are violent but doing the same in our countries just under false pretences of civilisation. It's like the Crusades all over again.*

Of course, this is flawed logic, from both sides, based on ignorance. In Islam's case, it doesn't help that people seem to think Muslims are making a bad choice in signing up to a belief system they see as backward. 'Why would you believe in a religion that's oppressive to women?' I've been asked, multiple times. The implication is that I'm actively choosing to follow the wrong path, and that is problematic on so many levels, not least because often that opinion is based on incorrect information. Take the concept of Sharia law, a term that is thrown around in the news and in the media willy-nilly, scaring people into believing Muslims want to start chopping off people's hands for nicking a banana and stoning anyone who may have even thought about extramarital relations. Oh, drop 'Sharia law' into any conversation and watch the sparks fly!

Gaining an understanding of these sorts of concepts is one of the best ways to overcome the perception that Islamic and

Western values are incongruent because it is an argument that is fundamentally incorrect.

As previously mentioned, Sharia is like common law with an unchanging core based on the Islamic objectives of the protection of life, offspring, mind, property and religion. The main sources of Sharia law are the Islamic holy book, the Qur'an, and the Prophet Muhammed's (Peace Be Upon Him)[1] sayings and actions. These are known as the *Sunnah*, and are where Muslims get their understanding of how to live a good life.

The practical detail for Islamic law comes from interpretation of the Qur'an and *Sunnah*. All that detail fits under something called jurisprudence, or *Usul al-fiqh*. *Usul al-fiqh* covers quite a lot, but it essentially means interpreting the broad rules set out in Islam's two main legal sources into law that is relevant to the current time and place. There are a fair few ways sources can be interpreted but in Islam there are two main methods: consensus and analogy. Consensus is when the 'learned community' agrees on something, usually something that has already happened. For example, the standard number of extra prayers Muslims pray each year during Ramadan (the month of fasting) was a result of consensus.

Analogies are rules extrapolated on methods and processes detailed by Islamic schools of thought, based on what is already known – don't drink beer because wine is prohibited, for example.

The laws themselves are broadly split into two types – laws relating to an individual's relationship with God (*Ibadat*) and the laws that govern society (*Muamalat*) – and can be further categorised into four fields: rituals, sales, marriage and injuries.

---

1 Note that Muslims will always say 'Peace Be Upon Him', PBuH, or SAW, the Arabic acronym, after the name of the Prophet Muhammed SAW, to show respect.

The laws cover almost everything to do with how Muslims live their day-to-day lives. Prayer, fasting, food and drink, sales, loans, cultivating wasteland and even shares are covered. There are laws that relate to marriage, familial support and custody rights, and very specific rulings about the laws of war and peace, homicide and so on.

The rules about individual actions, *Ibadat*, are pretty uncontroversial, and by following these rules Muslims in Australia practise Sharia law without infringing on the rights of others. Praying five times a day, how to do *Wudhu* before prayer, is all covered in *Ibadat*.

The rules that govern society are generally what come to mind when Sharia is referred to in the media. One of the main rules of this part of Sharia law is that Muslims must follow the laws of the land they are in, regardless of who is governing. So by following the law of Australia, for example, Muslims are following Sharia law. Muslims aren't seeking to 'impose' Sharia in Australia – they're living and practising it already, despite inflammatory and inaccurate depictions to the contrary.

The application of Sharia law has changed over time, and that's where this discussion gets tricky – when we need to bring in colonisation. It's strange to talk about colonisation so often, when it feels as if it was an age ago, but the colonisation process changed everything, including, in some ways, Sharia. It started with the British East India Company (EIC) and the Dutch entering India and Indonesia in the late sixteenth and seventeenth centuries; these movements eventually led to some pretty drastic changes in how Sharia was practised and understood.

Colonisers brought with them particular ideas, including the 'nation-state' and the codifying (translating and writing down) of laws. Because colonisers saw Islam as distinctly different and therefore a threat to the system and civilisation that they understood, they began remodelling the legal system.

One of the main things about Sharia is that it was meant to be fluid and able to change for every time and context. If things were working as they technically should, you would have multiple interpretations of the same source material *at the same time*! When the English and Dutch arrived, they started to translate, write down and convert Sharia – as they understood it – into written law. This may have seemed harmless, but in doing so they turned Sharia's awesome fluidity into rigid laws that couldn't be changed even if the times had. They took away the interpretative element of Sharia that it depended on and Islamic law became unable to do what it needed to do to function. That ain't right.

What's even more galling is that the colonisation process actually wound back progressive aspects of Islamic law to conservative Western standards. Sharia and Islamic law had given women rights and privileges that were advanced and equalising and that didn't yet exist in the Western context. When the laws were translated, those nuances were removed and the patriarchal colonial culture prevailed, writing the rights women had enjoyed under Sharia out of the system entirely.

What does that mean? Well, things like the idea that 'Sharia law' says the man is the head of the family to be obeyed without question was actually drawn from biblical sources and added after colonisation, completely changing the original intent of the Islamic ruling. 'For a husband is the head of the wife.' (Ephesians 5:23)

Another great example is that certain colonial governors believed Islamic law allowed criminals to escape punishment too easily, complaining that Sharia was 'founded on the most lenient principles and on an abhorrence of bloodshed'. Given Islamic law's current reputation, this is kind of ironic.

Sharia law may sound foreign, especially if you don't know much about it, but it doesn't need to be feared. At its essence, it's about finding a way to live a good life, and by practising as Muslims (praying, fasting, eating good kebabs), millions of people around the world are following Islamic law without coming into conflict with the law of the land. Muslims are well accommodated in the current legal system and there is no reason why this should change. Fear-mongering about Sharia law and portraying it as a 'threat' to Australian society serves only to bolster the damaging and dangerous 'us and them' narrative, ultimately helping no one but terrorists.

There is a verse in the Qur'an that sums it up for me:

True piety does not consist in turning your faces towards the east or the west – but truly pious is one who believes in God, and the Last Day; and the angels, and revelation, and the prophets; and spends their substance – however much they may cherish it – upon near of kin, and the orphans, and the needy, and the wayfarer, and the beggars, and for the freeing of human beings from bondage; and is constant in prayer, and renders the purifying dues; and [truly pious are] they who keep their promises whenever they promise, and are patient in misfortune and hardship and in time of peril: it is they that have proved themselves true, and it is they, they who are conscious of God. (Qur'an 2:177)

It might be difficult to decipher if you are not used to reading religious texts. I am not a scholar, just a Muslim woman making her way in the world, but to me this verse means that God looks at more than simply how much you pray or what you tell other people to do. It is about being the best person possible: patient, kind, helping others. To me, Islam is not just about what you wear, how you walk, what your job is. It's about character. It's about being someone who works to make the world a better place. It is also not necessarily about following a specific hierarchy, because that structure does not exist in the Islamic context. There is no one spokesperson, there is no one correct answer for most of the questions – the plurality of the religion is part of its beauty and why it remains relevant no matter the time or place. That said, it does make it difficult to have a single, united message and story when we are not a single community. So the misconceptions continue, and even as children we became aware of the contention our faith was causing, although we couldn't understand why.

In 2002, our local mosque was burnt down and abuse scrawled on the fence in spray paint.

When I tell people this they tend to be appalled. It's a shocking act of vandalism. But at the time my classmates and I accepted it as our reality, too young to understand how life should be, or was, for other kids – for non-Muslim kids. We just realised that bad things were happening and people were blaming us for it. That became the narrative of our childhood. Bad things happen overseas, we get the repercussions. I remember hearing about the mosque and thinking *Gosh, it really* is *like being in a movie*. It did seem odd to me that someone would go to the trouble of burning down the place in which we prayed. What did we have to do with anything that was happening overseas?

We started going to another mosque while ours got rebuilt. My father spent weekends helping reconstruct the new mosque with others from the community. Officially, they called them working bees, but Dad always called them his busy bee days – he saw these phrases as the same thing, an illustration of how some nuances get lost in translation. The man who burnt down the mosque was prosecuted, but as we drove past the shell of the building on our way to school, it was a regular reminder that some people didn't think we belonged. Nothing was to be gained from getting angry, so we simply accepted the reality and moved on – or that was what our parents told us, anyway. Perhaps my parents had a different experience and understood the community anger. Perhaps, but they hid it well.

Even in hindsight, I'm neither shocked nor disturbed by events of hatred that were aimed towards my communities, which might seem strange. Different people chose to deal with the general onslaught of hatred after 9/11 in different ways. Often people got angry. As I grew older and had to negotiate this hatred, I mostly chose to only barely acknowledge it and then to look at ways to move beyond the act itself. You could call this a survival mechanism; if I were to think about the injustice too hard I would wallow in pity and all-consuming anger. These are legitimate feelings when someone attacks your faith and your community, but they aren't useful ones for me. It probably also helped that my parents didn't entertain an 'us and them' rhetoric in our house. To the contrary, there was always discussion of what we needed to do to bring people together, to calm people down. What vigil were we going to attend? What was happening in the conflict zone? When was the next town hall meeting and how could we help? I was brought up by parents who wanted to do everything possible to keep the community intact. After all, we had left our country and community to create a new one here, and we weren't going to let it be slowly taken apart. That perspective is probably an enormous reason I have the outlook I do. At the end of the day, the mosque burning down was a dislocating experience, but we were migrants. We were used to adapting to whatever was thrown our way.

Chapter 4:

Hijab

I decided to wear the hijab on 10 November 2001, the day of an Australian Federal election. I chose an auspicious date for this turning point in my life, the day I started to dress like a 'Muslim woman', just in case I forgot. It would be a date I could look up in the history books, an old memory trick I picked up from a book from my father's shelf in Sudan.

I hadn't given the decision very much thought. I consulted with my friends at school, some who wore the hijab 'full-time' and some who did not, and then decided. My mother had worn the hijab for as long as I could remember, but we had never discussed it specifically. I had always assumed that at some point, when I became a woman, I would wear it just like my mum did. In some ways I made a powerful decision on a whim. This was a whim I felt was right at the time, and one that would shape my future beyond anything I could have anticipated.

In Islam, we are not judged on our actions until we reach adulthood, which is when we hit puberty. For women, that moment is straightforward: it comes with the arrival of your period – this is a generally accepted norm. For some Muslim women, they will start to wear the hijab 'full-time' once this happens, and some women will opt not to; there are cultural and personal reasons for these decisions.

I thought I had reached that stage of adulthood, even though I would only really get my period two years later. I decided that I had matured enough and it was time for me to step up to being an adult. I had no patience to wait for the 'usual' time it took for something to happen – I had decided that at the age of ten I was now an adult, and that was that!

My decision had nothing to do with the events of September 11; it was about doing what I was taught an adult Muslim woman was supposed to do. I didn't connect wearing the hijab with 9/11 at all, because at the time it still seemed like an event that was so far removed from my reality. I can understand why people would think they are related (I have often been asked if I wore it in protest), but even in hindsight I think my motivations were more religiously focused than political. My identity was simply uncomplicated as a young Muslim. I knew the 'right' thing to do by Islam was to start wearing the scarf when I was of age because I knew that Muslim women wore the hijab. So, once I became a woman, I would too. It was the equivalent of wanting to wear your mother's lipstick, a stepping stone up into the world of womanhood.

Wearing the hijab wasn't the radical change it could have been either; after all, I went to a Muslim primary school where the hijab was part of the uniform. We wore it most of the day every day, anyway.

It may have been uncomplicated as a child, but as I got older I discovered all the different dimensions that came with that choice. My Muslim identity became clearly visible and therefore

I was expected to speak about it constantly. It also meant being held to a higher religious standard because the hijab becomes a barometer of your religiosity, going through regular teenage angst about your body with the added dimension of the hijab, and dealing with other people seeing it as a tool of oppression, barbarism or even liberation. At the time I didn't consider any of those aspects, but rest assured they made themselves known to me, soon enough.

I didn't quite comprehend how the political environment had changed for Muslims. I knew that people would probably stare, but I was used to that, being brown in the suburbs in Brisbane. Now people on the street would know for certain I was Muslim too, but I didn't see that as a problem. That was who I was, so why should that bother me?

It was probably a blessing that I chose to become a Hijabi so early. If I had waited until I understood all the 'external' implications, perceptions and connotations associated with the hijab, I may not have been as brave. Furthermore, my identity would probably have started to be formed around my body and what I looked like, like most teenage girls. Wearing a hijab at that point then and having to reinterpret my identity – internally, but also externally, to my other non-Muslim teenage friends – would have been much more difficult.

I woke up determined that Saturday morning, having decided the night before that tomorrow was the big day. I marched up to my parents where they were busily preparing breakfast in the kitchen.

'Mama, can I borrow a scarf? I am going to be *Mahajabah* [a lady who wears a hijab] from now on.'

My mother looked at me out of the corner of her eyes. 'Just go into my room and there are some in the cupboard.'

I left the kitchen and turned right, down the hall to the master bedroom. Opening Mum's cupboard was like finding a window into Narnia, with all the wonderful colours of her dresses and scarves. She had so many scarves, hundreds perhaps, colourful, textured and neatly folded in columns in her closet. My mother wears the long rectangular scarf that Sudanese women traditionally wrap around their heads. Her preferred style is a cotton wrap, about two metres long and half a metre wide, lined with thin tassels on the shorter edges. I remember standing behind Mum countless times growing up, watching her wrap the scarf around her head with practised ease, her natural but well-kept fingernails making a pleasing scrape against the cotton as she elegantly brought it around her head. Standing in front of the mirror, she would place the scarf flat on her head, a third on the left side and the rest on the right, swing the long side beneath her jaw, bring it back up and over her head, and secure the material with a long pin just above her right ear. The top of the scarf would sit halfway down her forehead (she always says I put mine too far back and make my forehead look huge: 'It's all about proportions!') and frame her face in a smooth oval, a line interrupted only by the arms of her glasses. She never ties it too tight and always looks beautiful. If she was in a rush she would simply throw the long end of the scarf over her left shoulder, tassels swinging.

Accustomed to my white square school scarf, I was opting for the classical 'Arab' look sported by most of the Lebanese girls I went to school with and the style that was considered quite 'cool'. Rather than wrap the scarf flat against your head, the Arab style has more of a structured body, the fabric forming a peak at the forehead. I scrounged around the options for a square scarf that morning.

There was just the one. It was white cotton, plain with a faint striped pattern in the stitching design. This was perfect!

I ran back down the hallway, past the kitchen and straight into my bedroom. The scarf pin that my friend had lent me would have to do, I thought, as I picked it out of my small jewellery box, a teal-and-fuchsia plastic love-heart container. One of my primary school friends had given the pin to me as a gift a few months earlier when I mentioned that I wanted to go full-time. I had kept it safe for this very moment. The box had a hinge and a purple tray insert that held a couple of special rocks I had found, a few pairs of small stud earrings, and the scarf pin. All the valuables that my ten-year-old soul held dear.

I stood in front of my mirror, the cupboard door providing me a full-length reflection. My fingers groped with the material as I tried to fold it in half into a triangle to place over my head. The scarf was huge. It was much larger than my usual school uniform hijab, which was a polyester design a quarter of the size of this cotton piece, and much easier to handle.

Once I had a triangle, I positioned the scarf on my head with the long edge on my forehead, roughly in the middle, lifted up my chin and gently pushed the pin into the scarf right at the join of my neck and jaw. Looking back down into the mirror, I almost choked. Too tight! I hurriedly readjusted.

Because it was such a large piece of material, the scarf covered my entire upper body down to my waist. *This won't do*, I thought, unpinning it to fold it in half once again. That didn't work either. The folded scarf was far too thick to drape gracefully and be pinned effectively; it was like wearing a blanket on my head. I sighed, and reverted to my original plan. I had rejigged the style numerous times before my mother came in and asked if I was ready. I looked back in the mirror. 'I think so.'

As I walked out past the kitchen, Dad came towards me and pinched my chubby right cheek.

'*Ah, Khalas, ah?*' he said, which roughly translates to 'All right then, are you?' His face was unreadable, but that was nothing new. 'You've decided to wear the scarf now?'

'Yup!' I grinned proudly at my father.

'Are you sure?' he asked, his voice a mixture of pride and concern.

That seemed like an odd question to me. Of course I was sure! I was wearing it already, wasn't I? I wore it every day at school alongside the other girls, after all, so it felt no different to that. The only change would be that I wouldn't take my scarf off on the bus after school.

'Yes, I'm sure!'

'Okay, *Mabrook* [Congratulations]! Yassmina is growing up.'

As we went to the election booth that day, I strode down the street with my head held high, looking at people who walked past me, wanting them to notice. I had changed! I was now officially a *Hijabi, Mahajabah*, a woman! I had arrived.

Later that week, on the bus home from school, I talked about my newly hijabied status and a few girls on the bus laughed: 'You won't last! People always take it off and give up after a few months.'

Right then and there, I vowed not to. *Challenge accepted*, I thought, defiant. I was always someone who stepped up to a challenge, especially when I thought it was within my grasp. This one definitely was. This tendency has probably got me in more hot water than any other. On the other hand, this same stubbornness has given me the sticking power to learn new skills, try new experiences and generally push the boundaries to see how far they can go. My parents and family call it *Raas Zalata*, which literally means 'head of rocks', or that I'm stubborn. I call it determined and driven. Just different sides of the same coin, perhaps?

Either way, I had made up my mind. This was my new status quo.

Hafsa put the hijab on with me as well, but she capitulated to her parents' pleas to remove it after a few months.

'They didn't want me to be a target,' she muttered solemnly, relaying the news as we hung from the tree in front of her house in a leafy southside suburb of Brisbane. Hafsa said her parents were worried because a girl wearing a scarf had been attacked for being a Muslim a few days earlier on her way to school. 'Plus,' she added, 'they think it's something Arabs do, and we aren't Arab.'

The issue of being a target because of my hijab wasn't something my family had talked about. Being visible was simply part and parcel of practising our faith. Their general attitude was that they wouldn't let their values be compromised by external factors that they couldn't control, but this was never explicitly uttered; it was implicit in everything we did. Being visible but remaining true to our faith was our *Jihad*, our struggle. The world is what it is. When you live for an afterlife, sacrifice and difficulty are easy to understand and justify.

That is at the crux of why, as a Muslim, I will continue to do something that I feel is an expression or requirement of my faith even though it might be uncomfortable in the society I reside in.

If you believe that there is more than just the life we have now, you can accept sacrifice, compromise and struggle in the name of faith because you know that there is more beyond your years on this earth. If you believe that this is the only chance you've got, it may cause you to approach challenges differently. So in the case of my family, because we believe that this life is simply one stage in the journey of our soul, a little bit of turbulence is worth the plane ride.

My reasons for wearing the hijab started off pretty uncomplicated. My reasons for continuing were less straightforward.

From a religious viewpoint, I felt there was an imperative in the scripture to wear the hijab, but not necessarily for the reasons that people usually expect (although there are some who will disagree).

When discussing the hijab, it is important to see it as being something for women instead of something for men.

Very often the conversation about the hijab is conducted and controlled by men, in relation to the male gaze, or in some way centred around men and maleness.

Muslim men in particular will say things like 'women should wear the hijab because otherwise it is a trial for men', 'men can't control themselves' and so on. Understandably, with men having the conversation, it becomes about the men.

Nahhhh, mate. Have a look at the following verse from the Qur'an:

Oh Prophet! Tell thy wives and thy daughters, as well as [other] believing women, that they should draw over themselves some of their outer garments [when in public]: this will be more conducive to their being recognized [as decent women] and not annoyed. But God is indeed much-forgiving, a dispenser of grace! (Qur'an 33:59 Muhammad Asad)

There is a lot of variation in the interpretation of this verse, but to me what is interesting is *why* it was revealed. At the time of revelation, women were being harassed in public, and were at risk of being assaulted simply for leaving their houses. The hijab (with the focus not necessarily being on covering the hair but covering the body!) was brought in to allow women to feel more comfortable walking around in their own cities. It was *not* brought in for men but brought in as a tool to allow the women to participate more in their own societies.

It is also important that we ensure that the language about the hijab doesn't become one of victim-blaming. If we say wearing the hijab is about modesty (and for some women it is), that is fine.

However, extrapolating that concept and saying not wearing the hijab is the same as being immodest, and that is somehow linked to the behaviour of men, is excusing men from being civilised and that is *not* acceptable. The statistics show that clothing and a woman's attire have no impact on the likelihood of rape and abuse. Misogynist viewpoints are right at the root of such behaviour, and those are what need to be tackled, not the attire of the women in the street.

Why do I continue to wear the hijab?

I've been asked this question so many times I barely know what to say anymore. Religious imperatives aside, the hijab is truly part of my identity. It says to the world, I am Muslim and I am proud and I can do anything I damn well please, just you wait. Sometimes, it's because I feel super close to Allah. Sometimes, it is just my everyday way of sticking it to the man.

Chapter 5:

Back to Sudan

Sitting in my economy aisle seat in late 2001, on our way to Sudan, I dinged the bell for the hostess. My mother looked over at me with a warning glance. 'I don't think you will be able to go anymore, *Habibti* . . .'

Post 9/11, it felt like all of my favourite treats were being taken away, one by one. On our trips to visit the extended family, I always used to ask to see the pilots, to get their signatures and check out the cockpit. I loved those moments!

Today I was no longer a ten-year-old child interested in the skies, but a young Arab-looking, hijab-wearing Muslim asking for access to the plane's cockpit only a few months after four planes had been publicly hijacked. It was no wonder the air hostess's face dropped so significantly when she arrived, and my request was duly denied.

My family and I travelled to Sudan every two years until I finished high school. Once I hit university, things changed but up until then my father made it a priority to go back, meet the family, see where we were from, and gain an appreciation for our 'original culture'.

My early memories of Sudan are hazy and not just because we were young. Almost every single time we went back, I would get thoroughly ill, due to the change in weather, the food, something. Each time I found myself in bed with some illness – whether it was a cough, a fever or bowel movements that flowed so fast they made the Nile river jealous – it was typically something that meant I wasn't able to go on the big family *Ri7la*, the trip they always took to the Sudanese outback – and by outback, I mean the Sahara Desert. We would go out for a day's picnic, climb a small mountain that was a feature of the area or visit relatives that lived outside the main cities. Rather than the focus being the destination, though, the fun was all in making the trip and having an adventure with family.

For my parents, visiting Sudan was about reconnecting with their families. For my father in particular, being connected to family is a religious duty, and it has always been important to him that we know the people we are related to.

★ ★ ★

'What was it like when we went back to Sudan?' I asked my dad recently, trying to scrape together bits of memory.

'It's hard to say what you kids were thinking and feeling,' he replied as he continued to move around the house, shutting all the windows. It was 3 pm and Dad has a regular schedule for airing the house out on the weekends, based on what he thinks is best for holding heat in or keeping the house cool, depending on the season. I followed him from room to room as he reminisced.

'*Tab3n* [of course] the best memory must have been in 1997, when we were living in Robertson . . .' My dad was referring to the suburb we called home on the southside of Brisbane.

'When you and your brother saw our house, the house you recognised – whoa, you jumped up!' He laughed at the memory. 'You jumped so high. You couldn't believe you finally saw something you knew, something you recognised, after a month of everything being new and strange. Your mother and I laughed so hard our stomachs hurt!' I smiled at the thought: we would have been so happy because we had just spent a month in a world that was so different and foreign, even though it was technically where we were 'from'.

My brother and I usually stayed in one of two places on our trips home; either my father's family house or a few suburbs away with my mother's family.

My father's home was more rigid, similar to my father's personality. His father, whom he called Fati (the nickname a shortened version of 'Father' in German), was an intimidating figure to us small children, with large ears and wild black and white hair. We always called him Gidu, which means 'Grandfather' in Arabic. What I did not learn until much later was that he was a giant in the community, politically and academically, and that my father holds him in the highest esteem. Gidu's room was closest to the front door, and when he woke he would sit in one of the two seats right outside the door of his bedroom, resting his arms on the deep mahogany arm rests, a coffee table in front of him and a wall of books behind. That bookshelf, which spanned the entire wall, was the pride and joy of the whole house. I would gaze up at it, thinking about all the knowledge it contained. The books were in Arabic, English and German and talked about everything from science to history, even babies! It was a wall that forever entertained and where I found my first *Tell Me Why*, but also my scariest Hercule Poirot story, one that sent me into tears.

Habooba, Gidu's wife, would come out and serve him tea in the traditional Sudanese manner, a ritual they repeated for years. Gidu would have grapefruit for breakfast every single morning, and Habooba would ask us if we wanted any. I tried it once and scrunched my face almost immediately as the bitter taste of the grapefruit juice came into contact with my taste buds. The texture was deceptive, I thought – it should taste nice, like orange or lemon, but this! I politely placed the grapefruit piece back on the tray and smiled at my grandma. '*Shukran*, Habooba! I think I will just leave the rest for Gidu . . .'

Our days in the Abdel-Magied household were regular and easy. We would wake up for *shay* [tea] with Gidu and Habooba, then help get breakfast on the table, usually *fool-u-bayd* with whatever else my grandmother felt like, but always accompanied by fresh bread.

My dad would then take us to see one of the Abdel-Magied family businesses. The extended family used to own many businesses in Sudan, including a series of factories that produced everything from macaroni to candles. To ensure he had instilled in us a good work ethic, Baba would take us to visit the factories and then to the engineering office in the city for work experience. After all, we were a family of engineers.

Habooba would pack us some sandwiches in a small plastic bag, usually white cheese and tomato, give us a bottle of water and send Gidu, Baba and me on our way – my little brother was too young to come to the office. The sandwiches were always sumptuous, the key being Sudanese bread, which is like a short French loaf but much softer and always fresh. Preservatives are uncommon in Sudan so the bread would usually go stale in a day or two; fresh was the only option.

Dad would take me to the office of the engineering company and introduce me to the many people who worked there. We would walk past the tea ladies sitting on the broken tiles out the front of the building, fanning their teapots and crooning at passersby. Baba would let me push open the glass door, dusty from the street, and the tinkle of a little bell would announce our arrival.

'*Al Salam-u-alaikum!*' my dad would say, instructing me to say hello to the receptionist, the lady who took care of the books, the man in the office who did the logistics . . . Baba would instruct me to say hello to every one of them, and to be genuine about it.

'It's very important to greet everyone,' he would tell me, as we walked up the stairs towards Fati's office. 'Even people who are not family, or who are doing service jobs. You must show respect.'

For all my father's idiosyncrasies, he has always been consistent about respecting everyone, no matter what their social standing. It may have not even been about kindness, but more about duty, your duty to the community. Either way, it made me believe that no matter what your standing in society, you were to be treated with respect. Whether it was due to his father's socialist influence, or simply a deeply rooted principle, it set the example for us kids.

I would spend my day either reading some paperwork (a manual or similar), which at the age of ten I only barely understood, helping file documents or simply entertaining another engineer or officeworker with my stories, perched on the bench of the desk, legs swinging.

When we weren't at the office we spent our time reconnecting with family; my memory is littered with countless visits to houses I could only identify through strange landmarks – the house near the water tank, with the empty lot in front, with the nice garden, and so on. We would be welcomed in, sometimes by the family member and sometimes by the maid, ushered into the salon and plied with soft drinks, sweets and tea while my mother and father made conversation, with the occasional question about what we were up to or how we were liking Sudan. If there were other kids we would be out of the salon in a flash, playing tag and sharing childish gossip. I was a well-behaved joy of a kid to have around, or so I had thought. When I asked my mother, though, her recollection of the early days weren't quite as rosy.

'It was a little embarrassing,' she said with a sheepish look on her face.

It wasn't the answer I was expecting, and the rest of her answer only shocked me further.

'You were little Aussie kids who weren't used to being around lots of other people. You wanted your own things, you weren't used to sharing and, well, you weren't exactly quiet about it. You also didn't have the other kids' awareness or dexterity! One time we took you to the *souq* [the market] and there was a puddle of water on the ground. Of course, everybody else was walking around this big puddle but you walked right into it and tooooooosh!' My mum mimed falling. 'You slid over in the mud, on your bottom, and just started to cry.'

I burst out laughing at the image. Sudan's streets are full of random puddles of water as there is no real functional sewage system, so Sudanese kids were used to deftly avoiding them. An Australian city kid like me had no idea.

'You cried, and then everyone rushed to pick you up, to take you to the car, help clean your hands.' Mum was on a roll now. 'We would go visit people in their houses and you would just say whatever was on your mind. Things like, "Mama, why is everything so yucky and dirty? Why does no one have nice things?" You weren't used to things in Sudan.'

'So we really were spoilt Aussie kids?' That had never crossed my mind, but I guess we were those foreign children who spoke English, were used to toast and Weet-Bix, and wanted to play with our own toys. It was a little shameful to think I was one of those 'Western-bred-kids' with no manners who I would later laugh at on my trips to Sudan, because they didn't know how to act. It also made me really grateful that my parents had made the effort to teach us, so we didn't remain those kids who grew up overseas without connection or appreciation for where we came from.

'Yes, you were those spoilt Aussie kids who didn't understand this new world just yet. But it wasn't all bad. Do you remember when you and your brother used to sleep with your uncle on the ground in the salon? He would lay the straw mat down and you would all just fall asleep on that under the fan, then wake up in the morning nice and early with the sun and have white tea and biscuits with Habooba.'

I remembered; it felt like a lifetime ago.

'He would take you to meet his friends and show you and your brother off! The two little kids who talked a lot in English, so fancy and cool.'

I liked that we were able to provide our family with some street cred, regardless of the embarrassment we'd caused.

'You loved Arkaweet [my mother's family home]. The front garden wasn't paved so you'd play in the sand outside, put the sand in your hair, roll around in it – you loved it! You would say, "Habooba Saida's house is in a sandpit! Can we stay in her sandpit house?"' My mother smiled. 'That was so bizarre for people in Sudan, because they had no idea what a sandpit was. They couldn't understand that here in Australia people build pits and put sand in it for kids to play with. In Sudan, there was sand everywhere. The whole place was a sandpit. Why would you want to build one?'

I could only imagine the general confusion when my mother's English-speaking baby spent her time playing in the sand, which is the one thing that annoys Sudanese people uniformly.

'You also spent a lot of time fighting with your cousins, Esmat and Jamal,' she continued.

'OMG – but he used to pinch me, all the time!' I remembered Esmat's exquisitely painful but oh-so-sneaky pinches, and the innocence he would feign when I yelled at him.

'But then one day when you were playing in the bedroom he ran out crying and yelling. You followed behind him, smiling like this . . .' My mum's face arranged itself in the perfect imitation of the cat that got the cream, satisfaction oozing out of every pore. 'You'd bitten him on his bottom!'

I let off a peal of laughter, having forgotten that memory.

'He never pinched you after that.'

I am proud of my younger, still sassy self, showing my cousin what was what. It looks like I learnt how to defend myself in a scrap very early on. Although I was a bit disappointed to hear we were known as spoilt kids, as outsiders, which I told Mum.

'That's true, but every time we came back, people remarked on how much you had grown up. In Sudan, it's not easy to survive. You have to please everyone, serve the elders, and navigate the complex social web that is your extended family. It teaches kids skills that you don't learn here in Australia. Once you started to grow up, you developed those skills, and as you became familiar with the environment you began to thrive. Now you are better off for those experiences.'

Although my time in Sudan as a child feels blurred and like it happened to someone else, I have no doubt the visits had an impact on my connection with the country.

Thinking back, I didn't notice major differences being in a Muslim country because at that point all my friends and family in Australia were Muslim too, so I knew no different. Mainly, I just had culture shock from being in a world different to what I knew – chaotic, loud, dirty, full of people and demands that I couldn't understand.

I asked my little brother how he felt about those trips, and after much cajoling he said that Sudan was like a vacation for him, because he got to play soccer all the time. But when I pressed him about visiting family, going from house to house, his tone betrayed his irritation: 'I just didn't know what was going on! I couldn't understand!'

Whether it was to do with the age or personality, I think the culture shock may have been more difficult for my brother. He wasn't born in Sudan and didn't speak as much Arabic as me, so communication was challenging. His discomfort manifested itself in strange ways: he would only eat one type of food – *Ta3meeya*, the Sudanese version of falafel – and so my cousins became experts in making that dish for the little koala, as they called my brother. He also spent a lot of time running away from the endless kisses or hugs from aunties who hadn't seen us for two years. As happened with me, as he became older he grew into his personality, finding an identity as a Sudanese man, taking cues from the many uncles and cousins he would meet.

The early trips back to Sudan set the scene for who we were to become. They also gave us the ability to live between both worlds. Having experienced life there, I was able to do what this modern world allows: take the best of both and create something new. It was easier as a child, when navigating between the two worlds was simple. Things got trickier when I visited as an adult, when everything became as clear as a puddle of Sudanese mud.

★ ★ ★

'Hey, Mama! Look at the ground! *Al-balat* [the tiles] are so cleeeeeeeaaannn!' I squealed in delight as I spun around and swept my feet across the white tiles, pretending I was a ballerina, skipping back in forth in front of my parents, who sat crumpled in the check-in area at the Egyptian airport, surrounded by luggage, my little brother cradled in my mother's arm.

'*Mush'kida* [Isn't that right]?' My dad chuckled. 'Everywhere looks clean after al-Sudan. Remember when we got here a month ago and it looked so dirty because we were coming straight from Australia?'

I paused halfway through my swirl, casting my mind back to Sudan's sepia tones; no filter needed, just a side effect of being in the desert and having everything constantly covered with a thin film of dust or sand.

'You're right, Baba! Sudan is so dirty! There's sand and dust everywhere. Here is so clean!'

'Wait until you get back to Australia, Yassmina.'

I'm sure I was embarrassing my parents, yelling about the dirtiness of our home country, but who was going to quieten a six-year-old? I giggled and resumed dancing, excited to be going home.

Chapter 6:

High School

At the end of grade seven I left my comfortable and familiar community at the ICB, saying goodbye to Hafsa at the same time. She was moving to Rockhampton with her family as her father had found a new job up north. I couldn't imagine life without my best friend, and the tears flowed freely at our farewell.

'We'll write to each other,' she promised, and for years we did. In those letters we shared all that was important to us. I would explain how different the kids were at the new school and she would tell me what it was like moving to a country town that didn't even have a mosque. We were both adjusting to a world that didn't understand us, doing our best to make our way.

It wasn't an easy transition for either of us, although I didn't realise how much it affected me at the time. I tackled the move in the same way I do everything — I just did it and reported everything to Hafsa as it happened, from my crushes on boys to my developing love of cars, sketching Jaguar E-Types, Dodge Vipers and Corvette Stingrays into my letters.

The change in school meant a change in worlds. I was thrown from my cocoon into a realm where the rules were different, for me *and* my family. My parents went from being known and respected in the school community to virtual nobodies in this larger, more established pond. The things I cared about, like spending time with family, weren't cool or even normal and so it forced me to adapt. I had to learn to survive and then try to find a way to thrive in a foreign environment, a skill that I've used ever since.

My father selected John Paul College (JPC) with characteristic rigour, the decision made following the principal's positive response to my request to wear the hijab. Unlike other schools, which took weeks to send lukewarm responses to the idea of altering the uniform to fit my requirements, JPC quickly got back to say they were happy for me to wear a hijab as long as it was in school colours. I was going to study at a Christian ecumenical school, the largest school in the state, and be the first girl in its history to wear a hijab (although there had been a few Sikhs before me, wearing their turbans). All in a day's work.

I wasn't sure what to expect of JPC. The brochures showed a campus that seemed beautiful beyond belief, like a TV advertisement for a resort we couldn't afford. My father and I drove in a few days before my first day of school to do reconnaissance. As we rolled up, I noticed that the street leading into the grounds was John Paul Drive – named after the school! *Damn*, I thought. *These guys have sway.*

But we hadn't come to admire the scenery, check out the ovals or suss out new buildings: there was a class list, and I wanted to know who I was going to share my new adventure with. As I scanned through the names posted outside my future classroom door, I encountered a dilemma. 'Baba, I can't tell if they're boys or girls!' My father laughed.

After going to school with Mohammeds, Ahmeds, Laylas and Kausars all my life, names like Alex, Kenny, Chris and Ashley confused me. Who was I going to sit next to? What would they be like? Would they care about my scarf?

That night I asked my mother whether she thought I should stick with my decision to wear my hijab at my new school.

I had been thinking about what I'd seen on the news about Muslims, and the stories I'd heard through friends of how people treated Muslims on the street, especially women who wore the hijab. All this was running through my mind, as well as how difficult it could be starting at a new school and looking different to everyone else.

Then I remembered why I was doing this. I wanted to please Allah. This was for a higher purpose, right? I remember thinking, *If Allah is making this hard, I'll get extra brownie points*. The hijab was a part of me now. My identity had become Yassmin, the loud academic kid who wore the hijab. I had shown my parents I could do it, proved my staying power to my friends and started to experiment with different coloured scarves. My interactions with the outside world were already shaped by my clothing, which indicated to the world that I was Muslim. I had become accustomed to the associated biases, ready at any moment to explain not all Muslims were terrorists. I had adjusted to people assuming I was an expert in my faith, explaining polygamy, the oppression of women and the meaning of Halal food, all at the wise old age of eleven. My lived experience no longer included the freedom and the naivety of a young child, not because of the hijab, but because of what it seemed to say to people. There was no going back.

I made the decision myself. 'Actually, no, Mama, it's okay. I will wear it, *Inshallah*.'

Mum shrugged, nodding her approval. I left feeling surer of myself and my decision to stay true to the hijab.

There was a lot I didn't know about living in mainstream Australia after my sheltered primary school years, and moving schools highlighted how different my upbringing was from my Anglo-Australian classmates, and how my world-view was shaped by very different experiences and histories.

My father's attitude towards the West reflects the pain of historical wrongdoing coupled with a desire for progress. On one hand, he appreciates that the West has helped the human race advance in many areas; after all, we moved here to take advantage of that development and safety. On the other hand, the West has also been responsible for so much hurt and historically has had such little regard for other civilisations, yet continues to act like it is morally superior. The hypocrisy of that grates. That superiority is linked to the idea that the West does not want to accept there are other ways of being. Western culture also prioritises the individual over the communal, and this is something my father could never abide. The discussion about these issues and value systems is so important to our family because my parents had a real and well-founded fear of their children losing connection with their culture and the religion we all believe in. My brother and I were growing up in the West, in a world that was progressive but also problematic. How would my parents ensure we retained the values they deemed important?

Our family understanding became that as long as our actions are religiously above board, 'culture' should not be a barrier to what we can do. So if it was traditional in the Sudanese culture to get married early but not required in Islam, then there wouldn't be an issue with not following the Sudanese cultural expectation.

Culture, my family decided, was created through our habits, so we could create our own family culture that took in elements of Sudanese, Egyptian and Australian culture and, as my dad called it, 'being progressive'. Being progressive meant striving for education, leadership in the community, the betterment of those around us, all within the framework of our religion. 'Liberal' or 'Western', in my father's mind, meant being individualistic, and placing less value on family, elders and women. My brother and I are continuously working on finding the balance, along with migrant kids in various diasporas around the world.

My mother sees no issue with being called Western. 'You guys are Western,' she's told Yasseen and me, 'but why is that bad? The Western world has done a lot of good for the globe; we must never forget that. We can disagree with some of their actions and foreign policies, but ultimately they're the society that has reached self-actualisation!'

Mum often referred to Maslow's hierarchy of needs when we were growing up, to illustrate how people make decisions based on their circumstances. If a person is at the bottom of the pyramid, their focus and drivers are primitive: food, water, shelter. Once these are sorted, people have the mind space to think about concepts beyond sustenance: critical thinking, philosophy and culture.

'No one can invent something if they are at the bottom of the triangle, Yassmina,' Mum would say.

I'd sigh. 'So we should be thankful that at least someone is thinking?'

'Why did we move here,' she'd ask, 'if we didn't want to be part of the system?'

That was something my father agreed with, but he took it a step further.

'We chose to come here,' he once said, 'to escape the oppressive Islamist regime. If anyone wants to come here and do the same thing, we will also fight them.'

'So you would fight with Australia over Sudan?' I asked.

'If it was in self-defence, of course I would.' Fighting in self-defence is allowed under Islamic law.

The beauty of living a faith-based life in an individualistic Western society is having the freedom to practise your faith as you see fit. The Muslim communities, like many other communities, hold their members to account not through formal means but through the accepted social norms. In an individualistic society like Australia, you can choose to live your life as you please regardless of what the community may think of your decisions. You may pay the price with reduced social capital, but life goes on. It is not as easy in communal cultures, where going against the grain of the unwritten rules can have significant and very real consequences.

The simple response to finding a balance between the individual desire and communal obligation is to say 'take the best of both worlds', but that isn't so easy. I don't think any community has found the balance yet, though some are getting close. Even when I am doing well finding the balance in how I want to live in Australia, true to my 'values' – a mix of communal, individual, Sudanese and Western – I find that sometimes when I go back to Sudan I default back to 'traditional' gender norms.

I had no idea what I was getting into when I started at JPC.

It was the small cultural things that made me stand out. When we were introducing ourselves in class someone asked if I had any pets. Naturally, I was compelled to share a story from my recent trip to Sudan: 'I don't have any pets here, but I do have a cow!'

My grade eight classmates frowned. 'You have a what?'

'A cow!' I said, beaming, sure it would be more impressive than a dog or cat. 'My uncle gave it to me last time I was in Sudan.'

'Do you have it at your house?' The girls giggled as they nudged one another in a shared language I didn't understand.

'Don't be silly. It's still at the farm in Sudan.'

I grinned, impressed with myself. *How cool am I*, I thought to myself. Hafsa would have been stoked.

When they found out they couldn't come to my house to pet the cow the conversation soon moved to other topics I had no grasp of: boys, parties, songs with nonsensical lyrics. The most popular girls sang Khia's 'My Neck, My Back (Lick It)' every day for months and the words didn't seem rational at all. I often had to ask Caroline, my new Greek friend, for translations. Caroline was also loud and understood the commitments of family, so when we hung out she needed fewer cultural explanations.

Being cool in this white world was very different to the Islamic school, where kids got cred for their religious piety or because of their family influence. At the ICB, parents who were active and volunteered a lot, or who had tertiary qualifications like my parents, were well respected and well liked. I quickly became aware that social currency at JPC was based on individual decisions and choices. Another buddy of mine, Bridget, was on the fringes of the cool group. To my surprise, when she introduced me to the Queen of the Cats, I was embraced with open arms – not what I'd expected, given my nun-like attire. *Perhaps I am cool*, I thought. Later, we approached the cool-cat huddle as they gossiped near the toilet block, all long sleek hair and high ponytails, socks low and skirts short. The circle opened to let Bridget in, but another girl threw me a sideways look and stepped back to close it off.

'C'mon, girls,' Queen Cat chastised. 'Yassmin's new, let her in!'

The second girl looked me up and down. 'I don't think so,' she said, turning away, and just like that, I was dismissed.

I took a step back, shocked. I had never been pushed aside in that way before, and for what reason? At least at my primary school if you didn't fit in it was because of your ideology. Here, one look and I was out? Their leader just tittered and made space for me on her side, but I have never forgotten that experience: the difference a simple kind gesture can make, and how completely crushed being left out can make you feel. It also taught me about the currency of coolness, and how everything about me (my colour, my religion, my looks) did not fit in.

The school itself had done its best to help me fit in. They lengthened my sleeves and skirt, and away I went – a fully hijabified private school kid, covered head to toe in maroon, hat precariously perched on my hijab. Neat. The school even had a multi-faith reflection room, although I rarely met anyone else there, possibly because any other Muslims weren't comfortable praying regularly at a Christian school, and possibly because I was not always consistent with my prayer times, preferring to delay my *Dhuhr* prayers until I got home. It took courage to pray regularly during lunchtime when your friends are out having fun. I had bouts of regular prayer then would fall out of the habit. I always found my way back, though, like a homing pigeon, and when I didn't, my missed prayer weighed on my mind. The trickiest part for me was *Wudhu*. Having to do ablution in the communal toilets was too much for this young girl to handle every day. A few weeks into my first year I decided to try it out and began the ritual, washing my hands, face and arms. A cluster of grade nine girls walked into the bathroom as I was halfway through washing my right foot. I froze, toes wriggling under the stream of water, and a silence descended on the tiled room.

'What are you doing?'

I took my foot out and shook it slightly, placing it back onto the top of my sock, which was lying on my brown school shoe.

'I'm washing my feet. It's part of praying, 'cause I'm Muslim,' I said.

The girls glanced at each other and then back at me. 'That's *so* weird,' said one girl, giving me a pitying look; then they forgot me and began talking among themselves.

'I wash my feet five times a day, so technically that means my feet are cleaner than your face,' I muttered quietly, not brave enough to make an enemy just yet.

The embarrassment was acute enough that I completely avoided doing *Wudhu* and tried to keep my ablution from the morning until lunchtime, so I could pray without having to wash all over again. I was okay with being weird, but I wasn't game enough to be the weirdest kid ever. There were limits, and I had found mine.

I wasn't the type to remain feeling inferior, so with a combination of naivety and willingness to learn, I found my way. It was definitely uncomfortable for others; there were other Muslim girls who joined the same year as I did who didn't feel as confident talking about or even revealing their faith. This could have been for a number of reasons, but coming from a Muslim school meant I wasn't ashamed of my religion. I knew it was sometimes publicly contested, but I felt comfortable in who I was, which I put down to my primary school experience, my family and my connection with Sudan. Feeling comfortable also meant that I retained my loudness and my determination to be heard.

'Ya nincompoop!' I would retort at any boy who insulted me or did something I disapproved of. I saved most of my 'swearing' for one particular lad who had the misfortune of sitting next to me. He was the cutest new kid on the block and the grade eight girls swooned all over him, which made him the target of boys who weren't happy the new guy was cutting their grass. He was olive-skinned and well developed, with dark hair, a little attitude and enough height to make him seem manly. Todd was the boy every girl wanted, and he sat next to Yassmin Abdel-Magied, the fully covered Muslim chick from Sudan.

I didn't get Todd Fever, which wasn't to say I didn't notice the cute guys in the grade. I thought every second boy was cute; it was just something I kept to myself. In fact, everyone thinking Todd was good-looking made me decide not to like him. A guy knowing his own universal desirability – it smacked of arrogance, and I couldn't stand being one of the masses chasing a boy. It gave him such power! My gut reaction to guys expecting deference because of their inherent qualities has always been simple and clear: no. Find someone else to stroke your ego; you won't be getting that from me.

Placed next to each other, we chatted a lot, which gave our classmates plenty of ammunition. 'Ooooh, Yassmin! You liiiiike Todd, don't you?' the girls would taunt.

'Eww, no!'

Unfortunately it was one of those situations where denial only exacerbates the situation.

Being his girlfriend was never my aim, but I did want his respect. Todd was the sort of bloke who other boys wanted to be like, and other girls liked, so if he was friendly with me, it meant that the other cool kids had permission to like me too. He was the key to my legitimacy. I was determined to make him see I was just as capable as him, particularly in the fields where he thought girls didn't belong. I knew that was how I could get his respect. Despite this, our friendship was begrudging, but it existed. Todd would ask me pointed questions about my faith, sometimes making fun of me like any other grade eight boy, but sometimes out of genuine interest.

Walking to the bus stop one afternoon, in the middle of an argument about something superfluous, he went for the jugular: 'How can you be cool? You can't even go to the beach!' he yelled as we walked through a roundabout in front of the school. We were on opposite sides of the road, people milling around us, all privy to this public argument.

'What do you mean?' I yelled back, my bulging maroon backpack slung over one shoulder as I tried to be nonchalant, while my thick, ankle-length skirt swished with every step like an Imam's robe. 'Of course I can go to the beach! My family goes all the time!'

Which was a lie – we mainly avoided the beach because we couldn't be bothered and burkinis hadn't been invented yet.

'Oh really?' Todd said accusingly. The people around us had started listening in, heads swinging back and forth as they followed the action, their very own Melbourne Open. 'What do you wear then? Like, a full-length nun's outfit or a wetsuit?' He laughed.

'Yes!' I stammered out, not knowing what else to say. 'But so what?'

The conversation ended shortly after as we converged onto the same path to walk side-by-side. 'You're such a nin,' I said, the shortened word for nincompoop, which I'd been pushing to make part of the school slang all year.

'I just don't get how you do things, you know?' he said. Post-

9/11, it seemed like no one did. But we were on good terms again and I felt like I had won: he saw me as a person and not as just a girl or a Muslim.

It wasn't until the end of the year, during a basketball game, that I truly felt like I earned Todd's approval. It was nearing the end of the match and tempers were as high as the temperature, which is pretty damn hot in Brisbane in November.

The ball was passed to a boy on Todd's team and he made a run for it down the centre of the court, while Todd peeled off to the side to set up for a shot.

'Pass it, man!' he yelled. Not only was he good-looking, he was also a great athlete. Typical, urgh. It was not his day for glory, though – his teammate looked over his shoulder, decided against passing and took a shot at the hoop.

The ball sailed through the air . . . and missed.

Todd was devastated. '*You nin!*' he yelled at the guy crouched on the ground in defeat and embarrassment.

Caroline and I turned to look at each other and then looked back at Todd.

'*OMG, yes! Todd* called him a nin!' We pumped our fists in excitement. All year we'd been derided for cursing that way, and here was Todd, the coolest cat in town, using our word. We felt like we'd won the lottery.

My high school taught me how to survive in the 'outside' world, to learn the language of the people I was engaging with, and how to rock the boat in a way that wouldn't make people feel too uncomfortable. Usually it was about using humour to point out an inequality, or sharing a story that described a personal experience of discrimination without apportioning blame to any one party, allowing people to draw their own conclusions. Sometimes it's as simple as asking a question from an angle they may not have considered, so I am not telling them what to think but allowing them to come up with the answer themselves. Like when a white friend suggested someone shouldn't be offended by a certain comment about people of colour and I asked, 'Well, who gets to choose what is offensive – the white person or the person of colour?' Their pause was all I needed to know a seed of thought had been planted.

Sometimes, though, I wonder if people do need to feel slightly uncomfortable in order to grow and change. These days my aim is to use the platforms I am given to ask some unsettling questions and create just enough unease that, without thinking, people slowly shift their perspective to become more inclusive.

I learnt how to speak to haters; to never rise to the bait but to be patient, understand where they are coming from and meet them, if not in the middle, then in their court – all the while wearing your team's colours.

My Muslim primary school taught me who I was; my Christian high school taught me how to be that person in a world that wasn't ready to accept me just yet.

Chapter 7:

Jumping In

My father encouraged me into debating as soon as he saw my speech at the grade seven graduation. '*Khalas*, Yassmina. Do you want to speak on important issues?' he asked me on the way home, and I nodded.

'*Tayib* [okay]. When you start at JPC, make sure you join the debating team. If you're going to speak, you have to learn how to debate properly. The people you'll come up against will be great speakers – you have to be better.' With that, my speaking career began in earnest.

I joined the school team the following year, and immediately loved it. I had found a way of expressing myself that people would listen to, which crystallised when my grade nine debating coach, Mrs Lepp, taught me the power of the anecdote. Even now, I try to start almost every speech with a little story, to hook people in straight away.

I relished using this technique at every possible opportunity in our debates and it became my competitive advantage. Often the opposition speakers would use the traditional structure we were all taught: greet the people in the room, introduce and define your topic and theme, signpost your arguments and then get into the body of the debate. Who needs a traditional speech structure when you can start with a story?

When the timekeeper called my name, I'd take a moment to gather my rebuttals and summary.

Head down, I would pause.

Head up, face the crowd.

Let the silence build.

'Imagine a world . . .' I would say.

I discovered that I could make an audience lean in if I whispered, and sit up and take notice if I changed tone. I learnt how to command a room, to use my voice as an instrument, what it meant to hold a silence. I found there was power in simply standing up straight. My love for the art of oration was born.

Soon after we started, Mrs Lepp moved me to third speaker, so from the age of twelve I learnt to listen to an opponent's argument, understand the underlying concept and then shred it to pieces, eloquently and resoundingly.

My father was right: debating gave me clarity of thought about difficult moral issues, and an appreciation for the art of discussion and dialectic. It also taught me that any topic has two or more angles, depending on your perspective: I could argue that we most definitely had to change the voting age to sixteen then vehemently and convincingly argue the opposite.

Debating has served me well throughout the years, particularly as a technical person. There is a dearth of technical minds and voices in the public space and so policy debate has become dominated by people with moving oration skills, like lawyers, but they may not have the technical grounding or scientific knowledge to be able to provide the context and content required for deeply informed debate. It is important that those with technical backgrounds involve themselves in public discussion so that members of the public can be legitimately informed and ensure their decisions at the checkout and the ballot box are made accordingly.

At the same time I was learning how to formulate an argument, I began building connections with the social justice world. The Amnesty International Camp I attended at thirteen forms my first memory of being involved in social justice work. I was in grade nine, a little younger than most of my classmates, but I wanted to fix the world's problems; poverty, lack of education for girls in countries like Sudan and the treatment of asylum seekers all drew me to the space. There may not have been a lot of world-saving happening at the camp, but it was the first time I'd been around young people who shared my views and were equally into world issues.

★ ★ ★

'Yassmin Abdel- Uh . . . Yassmin, please come to the office.'

It was like high school all over again, where no one ever knew how to say my name.

I logged off my cash register and stepped out from behind my platform of newly found freedom.

In 2004 I'd signed up online to work at one of the Coles Myer stores, clinching a spot at my local Kmart. Not only did I now have autonomy, I also had something to talk about at school.

I'd had enough of being left out of conversations because I lacked the shared experience of having a part-time job. My friends talked about being on shift, having annoying bosses and hanging out at the shopping centre afterwards, and I was missing out. All I did on the weekend was family chores, go to barbecues with the Sudanese community or volunteer with the Islamic Women's Association of Queensland (IWAQ). None of my friends wanted to hear about Sudanese community gossip and they couldn't relate to the aunties' critique of my tea-serving skills (an important accomplishment for any respectable Sudanese lady). As a practising Muslim with strict parents and an even stricter curfew, I couldn't get up to the same shenanigans as everyone else, but at least as a Kmart checkout chick I'd witness some of the action.

I lasted a total of three days.

When my name was called over the loudspeaker, thoughts of what I could have done wrong ran through my head as I approached the store manager's office. Maybe I was too loud? People always say I'm too loud, but I had been trying so hard to keep my laughter at a respectable decibel range.

'Yassmin, please come in.' The store manager, who was probably in his mid-twenties although he seemed *so old* at the time, turned around in his chair and gestured at the seat in front of him. 'When is your birthday?'

'Uh . . . March?' I had an inkling this wasn't going to end well.

'That means you're too young for us to hire you, I'm afraid. We just didn't check because you seemed older.'

My gamble hadn't worked out after all, and he let me go. I got fired and my father was so pleased, because he didn't want me taking the job in the first place. How was he always right about these sorts of things?

The store manager offered an olive branch before I left.

'How about we give you a call when you turn fifteen so you can come back in and work?'

I watched him put my birthdate into his calendar, but I never did get a call. I was too busy fighting the world to be a checkout chick by that point, anyway.

★ ★ ★

My major break came from a little closer to home. As my mother had left her architectural career behind in Sudan, she needed an alternative outlet and threw herself into community work. She channelled her passion and skills into developing the capacity of communities from the ground up and creating opportunities for my generation to contribute fully to the society we lived in. She convinced two other ladies in the community to start the first group for Muslim girls and women in Queensland, naming it Al-Nisa, which means 'The Women' in Arabic.

Al-Nisa became the part-time job I'd been hoping for. It wasn't the same as a department store gig, and it wasn't paying me, but being involved in a youth organisation set the scene for the next few years of my life by introducing me to the world of community organisations, social issues and the skills required to run a not-for-profit. Mum was the agitator in the organisation – she had the big ideas while her co-founders brought the operational ability and community networks. The organisation was revolutionary for its time: we ran sports programs, had forums where we discussed the issues facing us and submitted recommendations to government, and we even ran 'meet and greets' for ministers who wanted to engage with real young Muslims.

I was selected as secretary in a bid to keep me busy, so I attended all the meetings with my mother, recorded the minutes, organised the events, and was given more responsibility than

I ever would have had at my Kmart job. Although I didn't realise it at the time, I was seeing aspects of organisation management and leadership that fourteen-year-olds don't usually get exposed to, which meant I was comfortable with the language of management, leadership and strategic thinking from a very early age. As I grew, so did my responsibility. No one coddled me; I was treated as an equally contributing member of the organisation, and so I went to facilitator training, wrote a strategic plan and helped deliver the first Brisbane sports day for Muslim girls, all thanks to the support of the women around me.

Being involved in community organisation wasn't considered too unusual for the girls and women who joined Al-Nisa, since migrants are often involved in community events and organisation. For migrant communities, these activities bring families together, allow people to stay connected to their heritage and provide the social interactions other people get from hanging at the pub. My experience at Al-Nisa meant starting my own group from scratch, as I would a few years later, was nowhere near as scary as it could have been.

The ladies in Al-Nisa were some of my best friends, and I'm so grateful I spent my teenage years surrounded by independent, confident Muslim women. Women like Salwa, a Lebanese girl a few years older than me who dripped punk-rock cool and was an activist through and through. She had a skateboard, smashed the guys at basketball, was an amazing graffiti artist and wore silver rings on her fingers and a plain white hijab but her clothing was always political, with badges shouting 'Close Gitmo', 'Rights for Aboriginal People' and a Palestinian flag. Or Sara, who studied make-up even though she did really well at science at school, because she wanted a challenge. Nadiah was an academic and Islamic scholar; she was the first to help me understand that there were different interpretations of the Qur'an, and how they varied depending on the world view of the translator.

Being involved in Al-Nisa meant that I was part of a healthy community who never doubted the capacity we had to create change. If doubt ever did arise, my mother, as one of the leaders of the organisation, would stamp it out. 'We are not victims!' she would remind us. 'We can't just blame everyone else. At some point we have to take ownership.' Al-Nisa was the realisation of that desire to take ownership.

That being said, the environment made it difficult for Muslims not to feel like the odds were stacked against us. We were still in the shadow of 9/11, and the Bali and 7/7 bombings. The West had undertaken military activity in Afghanistan and Iraq, despite public protests and weak evidence. The emotive language on TV, on talkback radio and in our newspapers was divisive.

As a Muslim, it took no stretch of the imagination to believe that all white people thought we were terrorists: when you turned on the TV, the only people on the news who looked and dressed like us were terrorists, even if the accusation wasn't explicit. We all joked about ASIO tapping our phones; on some level we all believed there was truth in it. There was the possibility of any Muslim 'disappearing' without reason because Guantanamo Bay existed. We knew that if anything did happen, for example, if we went to the 'wrong' mosque class, spoke to the 'wrong' people or made the wrong joke in the airport, justice would not be on our side and we would be presumed guilty until proven innocent. Ultimately, we understood that no matter how 'Australian' we were, different rules applied to us as Muslims in this society.

The language being used and the stories being shown by most media outlets made us feel like we didn't belong. The media constructed Muslims as 'the other'. Islam and Muslims were often correlated with Arabs, but the language used by the media othered an ideology, an entire faith. Muslim men were labelled as terrorists, women as subjugated by the patriarchal oppression of their own faith. The word *Jihad* was hijacked and turned into a colloquial reference to any violent act committed by a Muslim, instead of its actual meaning: to strive, struggle, persevere, usually in the context of one's faith, trying to be a good Muslim. Holy War doesn't exist in the way the media portrays it, but this is difficult to communicate. There was a dangerous lack of nuance and comprehension in a lot of reporting, and that made issues of faith and culture difficult to debate. The terms 'Muslim dress', 'Muslim attitudes towards women', even 'Muslim leaders' made it seem as though the Muslim community was one homogenous group, which is far from the truth, and made it hard to break away from that single story. The implication was that Islam was fundamentally incompatible with 'the West' and that all Muslims were just biding their time.

We were forced to choose one of two camps – moderate or fundamentalist – so we had to call ourselves moderate, even if that word didn't sit comfortably with most Muslims.

'I believe in the fundamentals of Islam, which are all good things, so that makes me a fundamentalist, right?' said Nadiah as we prepared for a Fair Go For Palestine protest. 'But I couldn't possibly say that, or they'd call me a terrorist!' If you were labelled an extremist or a radical sympathiser it was the end of your legitimacy in the mainstream. The War on Terror made people pick sides, and the media clearly demarcated the sides.

In early 2015, a young Anglo guy was arrested after a

homemade bomb containing shrapnel, ball bearings and fishing sinkers was found in his house. You can bet your bottom dollar if his name was Mohammed his actions would have been attributed to terrorism. The police statement simply stated 'this is being investigated as a one-off incident, there were no threats made and no person was put at risk by this incident'. The twenty-two-year-old had a criminal history but was only charged with 'possession, supply or making a prohibited device and possession of a prohibited device', not with terrorism-related offences, which may have been the case had he been Muslim. It seems not much has changed since my time at Al-Nisa.

I spent all my spare time during high school with the Al-Nisa ladies. They were strong female friends going through the same battles that I was. My parents trusted them so I was allowed to spend time at their houses, discussing politics, eating and occasionally playing sport. I was a young girl trying to find a group to belong to, and I had found one: this was my community, my grassroots.

I never spoke about my Muslim friends or activities at school; I didn't think anyone would be interested, and I was uncomfortable talking about my achievements. Australian teenagers aren't keen on people who boast about how good they are, so this was also instinctual self-preservation. I kept my worlds apart, even at the beginning.

Al-Nisa set me up for years of running organisations. As well as marketing and logistics, I learnt how to manage a group of diverse people and personalities – foundational skills I still use daily. I had to learn to manage up, to control a room or table of people older than me, and that facilitating a collaborative environment meant listening to other ideas before contributing my own, bringing quieter people into the conversation by directing questions at them, and diffusing tense situations by finding common ground.

Al-Nisa also introduced me to working with government. It was an amicable relationship, driven by my mother, who knew how the world of grant applications and ministerial appearances functioned from her job with the state government. Unlike many young Muslims at the time, I didn't see the government as the 'enemy' or 'out to get us', but more as bumbling older people who didn't understand what it was like to live as a Muslim, but who could provide support and funding. They used the wrong language and made the wrong assumptions, but I saw the effort being made and appreciated it. Engaging with government from an early age played a crucial role in setting up my beliefs and expectations of political institutions. Rather than viewing the government as an amorphous, malicious system that loathed Muslims, I saw it as a collection of individuals with biases but with whom we could work and influence, although this belief has been sorely tested lately following recent rhetoric that has been immeasurably damaging.

The realisation that I could have influence was astounding! Running events with Al-Nisa, consulting with government departments and realising we could directly talk to people who could change policy taught me I could potentially make a difference through legitimate pathways. That was a powerful realisation for a young migrant kid whose parents come from a place where change requires anarchy. Here, anarchy was seen as uncivilised and people made change through articulating their cause and then speaking to the right people, and I began to form an ideology around working from within the system. Some grassroots groups view working within the system as selling out. I guess there is purity in anarchy, but I am not sure purity on its own will get us the results society needs – and who gets to decide what is pure? Each of us chooses a different mode of change and for now, I had chosen mine.

My involvement in Al-Nisa ended a couple of years later. I was untethered again, but it was my final year of high school, so I had other focuses.

A number of things were happening around the world: Israel was entering another conflict with Lebanon. Australia's involvement was another reason for Aussie Muslims to be angry. Young Muslim women, particularly those who wore the hijab, continued to be a visible minority, copping hatred for violence happening on the other side of the world. People were speaking *about* us all the time.

I was in Sudan when word of the 2005 Cronulla riots reached us, making the news in Khartoum! Imagine. My grandfather's brother turned on the TV while we were visiting, and *Kahk* [biscuits] were passed around in front of visions of Anglo-Australians clashing with the Lebanese lads by the beach. Cousins, aunts and uncles were all concerned about our welfare, asking how we dealt with that kind of racism. I understood this part of our nation's dysfunction. It was a reflection of the world I had personally experienced at school and on the streets. 'Ah, it's unfortunate, yes,' my father would reply, 'but Sydney isn't the same as Brisbane. We are different types of communities.'

The size and density of the Western Suburbs makes Sydney's migration politics different; large cultural groups aren't forced to interact with the wider community in the same way my family was. There weren't enough Muslim Sudanese people in Brisbane to even consider forming a gang. However, it is misleading and offensive to call Western Sydney 'ghettoised'. There may be some subcultures with those elements but today the region has thriving metropolitan cities, fourteen local councils and 2.5 million people. It is a wonderful world of its own.

The Cronulla riots informed the impression that the world had of us. I was torn: on one hand I saw myself as Australian and neither race nor religion changed that, but the government and media demonised people who looked like me. Not only did I have to deal with puberty, migrant identity issues and parents with high academic expectations; but I also had to justify my belief system to every Tom, Dick and Harry (or John, Bruce and Shane)? Oh, life!

There is this strange dissonance when I write about my time as a teenager, because on one hand there was frustration and anger at how unfair it all was, but I had also started to understand that I needed to be measured in my response to the vitriol. So, although I was mad, I felt like I couldn't express it. Did I really want to play into the angry black woman stereotype?

It was a fun smorgasbord of issues that I was trying to understand. Why did I care? My parents constantly discussed issues, and I was surrounded by people who campaigned, lobbied against, and decried what was happening to our society. My environment was politically active.

Outside Al-Nisa, I found an outlet through charity groups like World Vision's 'STIR' platform online, a forum where young people signed up and talked about international issues, poverty and ways to save the world. I was one of the first to sign up globally, and my friend Katie and I would sit in class refreshing the forum page to see if anyone had replied to our messages. Katie was on my debating team so she got things like social justice, and she was from South Africa so she understood Africa and the impact of inequality in a way that most people in my school didn't.

I also flirted with several other groups: I attended various Oaktree events, went to my first national conference for young Muslims, checked out Oxfam events, volunteered at the local Islamic schools as a support teacher during my school holidays. I played with the kids and tried to help them learn the content: English, maths, science and general primary school subjects. I wasn't allowed to do part-time work, but my parents wouldn't let me lounge at home either, so I had to find ways to keep myself busy. All my activities were social but all had meaning.

When I wasn't volunteering, my parents would help me organise work experience; this was their way of introducing me to different life avenues so that I could figure out what I was interested in. I found myself in all sorts of fields: marketing, marine policy, graphic design, composite manufacture and aged care. I even tried to get into panelbeating, but the workshop owner didn't think I would 'fit in'.

It turned out that I liked building things and making things work. I liked hands-on projects and problem solving. Dad must have loved it; his daughter wanted to be just like him. She wanted to be an engineer.

Chapter 8:

Building Stuff

Woodwork class in grade ten introduced me to a whole new world. Walking into the workshop felt like coming home: the smell of varnish and wood shavings imbued the room with a feeling of industriousness, like things were *happening*. It was a world where only the tools and the pine mattered. I could leave my stress at the door. This is where I learnt that the simplicity of the physical, mechanical world is my panacea for the burnout-inducing complexity of social change.

With my love of palaeontology, rock and random diseases, I had always wanted to be a scientist, so when we got to choose our subjects in the first semester of grade ten I chose chemistry, biology and physics without hesitation, and design and technology for a bit of fun. I'd always thought building stuff would be cool.

There were a couple of other girls in the class, but it was dominated by boys – and these weren't sensitive, book-reading boys; these were the rugby boys, the players and the jokers. The kind of boys I'd never hung out with because, well, girls like me didn't hang out with boys like them, although they mirrored the masculinity approved of in Sudan.

I had a few things going for me that made fitting in slightly easier. By this point, I was totally obsessed with cars, ever since my brother rented *Catch That Kid*, a B-grade bank heist movie that introduced me to the world of go-karting and racing. It was the beginning of a love affair with the sport that would take me to Barcelona, Malaysia and even Monaco.

I announced to my mum that I wanted to be a Formula 1 driver – the first black, female, Muslim on the grid. Then I started researching cars, borrowing basketfuls of books from the library, collecting pictures, and covering my walls with posters of Lamborghinis, Dodge Vipers and Supras. There was no way my parents were going to fund a driving career because they said it wasn't 'serious', but I could love cars anyway, right? I spent hours trawling online forums and learning about engines. SeriousWheels.com was my favourite haunt because it gave me the specifications I was after for almost any car *and* listed all the new models hitting the market.

I often get asked what I love about cars, which highlights an unconscious double standard because we *never* ask guys the same question or expect them to justify their interest. When I saw *Catch That Kid,* I fell in love with speed and all that it represented. The kid in the go-kart looked like nothing could stop them. Something in the simplicity of perfecting a drive was entrancing: a person and a machine, going faster and faster around the track each time. My love of cars persisted because there was so much to learn and it was such an exciting world. Structurally, cars are more or less the same at a base level, yet there's enormous variety, every possible type of expression in their shape, the way they drive and the amount of *power* some have. Every detail, every flourish – every car has a story.

I learnt to reel off names and statistics about Formula 1 drivers, fastest production car specifications and the best set-ups for getting the Nissans and Toyotas to drift. I had no practical experience yet but I could hold my own among the boys when it came to our knowledge, which it often did.

I had a father who got me involved in home maintenance early: Yasseen and I would be called upon to lug out his toolbox whenever something needed fixing. Baba's toolbox was a tan briefcase filled to the brim with tools from his university days in London. It was beaten and worn shiny from years of use, but it was more than double my age, so it was treated with respect, love and care. As he worked, Dad would tell us the story of each and every tool and how his toolbox was the target of many a theft attempt in Sudan. I never got tired of those tales.

In between stories, he would talk my brother and me through whatever process we were undertaking. Fixing leaking taps was a common task; firstly we would go to the shop and find the jumper valve, o-rings and washers we needed, then we would all crouch in front of the water main control panel sunk into our lawn to switch off the house's water supply. Yasseen would try to get involved, despite my overbearing body language, but I was too wrapped up in my own world to pay him much attention. My brother had a heart of gold and he looked up to his sister, so I regret how I often treated him as a competitor rather than being a caring older sibling. My idea of being nurturing at the time was setting up a mini-blackboard to teach Yasseen basic literacy and numeracy skills.

After we'd watched my dad replace a washer or change the

oil in the mower engine a few times, Baba would hand the tools to us: '*Yalla*, Yassmina! *Khalas*, you're a big girl – it's your turn.'

I could have had an alternative career as a plumber or a handy-woman. Dad never treated me differently because I was a girl; he shared his love of engineering with both his children in equal measure. He took us to science museums to explain the history of technology and how the world works. One of the first gifts that I remember making a real impression on me was a microscope I used to investigate objects around me, comparing strands of my hair to my neighbour's, looking at flies and ants up close. When my brother got into Meccano, Dad always encouraged me to get involved building those worlds as well.

Although these things didn't make me want to be an engineer, they did divorce my interests from my gender. The social cues and expectations we get as children have an enormous impact on how we see the world, whether we realise it or not. In some ways my father is quite a conservative man; he is more right wing than left, more capitalist than socialist, and he believes in traditional gender roles within the social and family context. Despite this he actively encouraged me to be independent and resourceful from a very young age, because he doesn't believe gender roles apply to your intelligence or career path. My father saw education as the great equaliser, and didn't think that it should be confined to men, whether that was learning complex mathematical equations or how to fix a tap. His teaching me practical skills from an early age also meant that I had a head start in woodwork class and so I was more than able to hold my own.

Another woodwork teacher may have thought girls didn't belong in the class, but Mr Stumpf's encouragement was instrumental in shaping my positive experiences. He was one of the first of many mentors who have pushed me.

It turned out I was pretty good at building stuff, partly because I wanted to prove that I was more than the academic chick I was known as. My father often talked about how many academics were divorced from society, and about how important it is to know how contractors and tradies work, as they create the world engineers design. Many years later, this is what drove me to take a hands-on operator's role in the field rather than an engineering role when I graduated from university. I wanted to understand life in the 'trenches', and also be able to gain the added respect and legitimacy from having experienced that perspective.

The workshop benches were pitted and marked with years of high school student abuse: chips from dropped chisels and planes, budding artists' graffiti and varnish stains. Beside the doorway were the bench drills, and large windows let in natural light and air. The back wall was an enormous pegboard that stretched from the floor to the roof, home to all the hand tools – wood saws, metal saws, screwdrivers, various sizes of chisels and wood planes - each outlined so it was obvious if anything was missing.

The workshop was hidden away from the rest of the school and before class we would mill out the front, generally ending up in a big circle, exchanging verbal blows.

A new part of me thrived on being able to speak the language of the lads; I had access to a new club, and with it a level of legitimacy and social currency. Diverging from social expectations gave me leverage and connected me with others outside of my usual groups. I've always been super curious about how people who aren't in my world live and operate, fascinated by characters from worlds where I don't feel I inherently belong, and the workshop was filled with those.

One of the first guys I met was a short blond surfer with a false front tooth that he would wiggle menacingly to freak out the girls. He always hung out with the leader of their group, a tall brunette with a smart mouth who I often had good chat with.

Then there were the 'lads' – the guys who dated the pretty girls and strutted around like they owned the playground. They either wouldn't say much to me or were total jokers, and I loved seeing these seemingly unflappable lads at their goofiest.

One of the coolest guys in the class was a football player who wandered around with his socks sagging and a swagger that belied his private-school white-boy background. Even though he was too cool for me, the nerdy Muslim girl, we both liked cars and so when I saw the ride he had as his laptop wallpaper I couldn't resist asking him if he actually wanted a 180 SX, as I preferred Supras. We'd never had a reason to talk before, so he looked slightly taken aback. 'Yeah, it's the first car I want to get,' he replied cautiously, and with that began a strange, secret sort of friendship. We would email during class, passing notes about the different kind of rides we were interested in and what had piqued our interest in the motorsport world. It was the end of Michael Schumacher's era and the beginning of Alonso's, so a lot was happening, and it was nice to have someone to share it with. And it didn't hurt that he was kind of cute.

My fourteen-year-old self would never have imagined that within a decade I would be travelling to the very races I watched on TV.

Once this car-loving football player established my credibility at the beginning of that first conversation, he never again questioned it. He took me seriously as a fellow car lover, and his early acceptance allowed me the confidence to feel like I could claim the space as my own. I learnt that if you establish credibility as a car person, the usual identifiers of race, religion, gender, sexuality and able-bodiedness become unimportant. All you need to do is speak 'car'.

The rest of the woodwork class were gamers, skaters or kids from the usual high school groups.

One boy in our tech class was new – not instantly cool but not a write-off either, jostling his way up the social ladder. However, I was the partial cause of a sudden drop in his status after an incident one afternoon.

The boys were standing in a pack a few benches away from where I was working when I heard sneers aimed at this new kid: 'What, are you gay, man?' It was a common high school taunt in 2005. The laughs were mean, glinting with a hard edge and echoing around the high-roofed workshop.

'Oh, man, you just love the D, don't ya?' More laughter.

I wasn't having it; these guys were just being bullies. I left my work and walked into the conversation, interrupting and standing in front of the lads. 'Oi, idiots, shut up, will ya?' They turned as one to look at me.

'What's your problem, Yass*man*?' one said, twisting my name meanly. 'Oh, dude, you're such a faggot you need a girl to come to your rescue!' he called out as the guy I'd been defending walked away.

'Hey, don't be a douchebag – just leave him alone!' I scolded and the boys fell silent and returned to their design projects.

I followed the kid into the next room, but when I tried to console him he didn't meet my eyes, just muttering, 'F*** off, Yassmin. I don't need your help,' as he pushed past me.

I froze, confused. Why did I feel like I'd done something wrong?

We live in a masculine society where girls are seen as weaker and less worthy, particularly by many teenage boys. The new kid felt ashamed at being saved by a girl – he had to be bailed out by a chick so he was no better than one, a feeling legitimised by the reactions of the boys around him. This is an insidious type of inequality, and the only way it will change is if we teach our boys from the get-go that women are equally as strong and powerful as men, even if their strength may manifest itself in differing ways. To show boys how to respectfully treat women as equal members of society, we need to look at redefining what it means to be a man, which is a conversation men have to lead for each other.

I learnt the banter that has allowed me to negotiate these masculine environments early on from my dad, who loves a healthy dose of ribbing and would encourage us to be quick with our wit by getting everyone else in on the game. The first time my new best friend Chandni visited he told her, 'Anyone who takes the mickey out of Yassmin is welcome in this household!' Chandni's parents were Indian and Dad was happy I was friends with the daughter of a fellow migrant, even more so when he found out she was born in Nairobi. This was lucky because Chandni and I were inseparable from grade nine until the end of high school.

Chandni was a complete romantic and unlike me she was comfortable with accepting the seeming inevitability of our parents' cultural scripts: women being the primary caregivers and homemakers while fathers play the patriarchal breadwinner role. We loved the same silly music, and like all teenage girls we spent a lot of time talking about our many crushes; even though I would never do anything about mine, I was her wingman through a few Bebo dates. Chandni was my refuge from the masculine waters I found myself constantly steeped in, an antidote to the battle I didn't know I was fighting.

★ ★ ★

Mr Stumpf left at the end of the year, and although the new woodwork teacher was outwardly supportive, his jokes made his unconscious bias clear. I was now the only female in the class and whenever I made a mistake he'd point it out and say, 'Maybe that's why they shouldn't let girls in the workshop!'

The boys might chuckle but I'd just call it out with an 'Oi!' when he made those kinds of jokes.

'Oi what? You know I'm only joking,' the teacher would say, and maybe he was, but it wasn't conducive to making me – or any other female – think that this was a place where we were wanted and belonged. In previous years, the boys thought I'd been the favourite because I was a girl. Now I was the only female in the class and their prayers had been answered; this teacher was never going to show a girl favouritism.

This was the beginning of an ongoing internal conversation I still have about what kind of joke I'm comfortable with in a workshop environment and where I should draw the line. Up until that point, the ribbing I'd been involved in had been good-natured, the jokes about me as an individual. All of a sudden, the jokes became about who I represented: a female in a male's world, a Muslim, a migrant.

There was quite a bit of teasing about me being a Muslim, particularly as the boys got more comfortable in my presence – and the challenge to their hormones I presented. I remember standing on one side of the bench, drilling some pilot holes into my shelving set, when a couple of the lads approached me.

'Hey, Yassmin, do you have sex with your clothes on?'

I laughed dismissively while they continued, the ringleader miming the actions while the others milled around, preening and laughing: 'So, do you have to, like, hold up your skirt to let the dude in when you're doing it?' They looked at me for a response.

'Nah, guys, of course not. I don't cover up in front of those I can't get married to: women, young kids, my family and stuff. When I get married I'll take my clothes off in front of him like normal or whatever.'

'So you can't have sex before you get married?'

'Nah, man. That's the way it goes.'

The guys looked at each other and burst into laughter.

'How are you going to know if your husband's any good then?'

I shook my head and picked up my drill. 'Don't worry about it,' I replied. 'I won't know any different!'

* * *

Banter is how I navigate difficult situations, but Mum isn't a fan and tried to talk me out of it more than once, saying, 'Yassmina, in my house, kindness and gentleness were the most important things, not signs of weakness as others think.'

Rightly or wrongly, I've not adopted this attitude. Gentleness is as rare as hen's teeth in engineering. Where it does exist people see it as an opportunity for exploitation, while more traditionally masculine characteristics are seen as the hallmarks of a leader. Our society needs to have a much broader conversation about what traits are identified as masculine or feminine, powerful or weak, but in the meantime I have to find a way to navigate the divides, so I use wit and repartee to speak to the masculine in a way that doesn't silence my feminine. The balance is in finding a way to be kind in a cutthroat, capitalist world, while not being manipulated and subjugated. How do you ensure your kindness isn't mistaken for weakness? How do you be vulnerable and yet strong? The women in my family epitomise strength but are not afraid to show affection and vulnerability with their family and loved ones, so I do try to draw on their example.

It is unusual for me to talk about love and care as these are areas I tend to avoid. Admittedly, I have always been a 'tough cookie' and so asserting authority through joking around has been my dominant style in masculine environments. I am learning, though, that this is not the only way and I have started to follow the model of kind but firm leaders, including men in the oil patch, who are respected despite their gentler, more caring leadership styles. It makes me believe that we should encourage more leadership with kindness.

Banter will always play a role in my life as a language that helps me connect with people, but I've started to embrace the strength in kindness, and the power and influence these gentler traits can achieve. To create real social change we need to use every tool available to us, so kindness is a weapon we can't afford to leave behind.

Chapter 9:

Boys? Inshallah

Grade nine was the first year that I became aware of having any sort of sexual value – I borrowed a friend's Roxy shirt and almost immediately noticed a change in the way the boys in my class looked at me. The shirt was tight, showing off my figure like I never had before, and I didn't know how to feel about the type of attention I was getting. It was certainly different to the kind of stares I got in my hijabi outfit.

As I walked back to class that morning, past a group of boys lounging outside the room, one looked down at me from his perch on the step. His eyes wandered all over me and his lips curved up into a smile. I wasn't quite sure what was going on, but something told me I was meant to enjoy this. His eyes eventually looked up to meet mine and then flickered down again. He stared at the logo on my chest as he spoke. 'Roxy, hey? We should call you Foxy to match.'

I laughed and started walking up the stairs. My friend nudged my shoulders as we made our way to our bags and grinned. 'He's cute!' she said.

He was, but damned if I knew what to do about it. I avoided him for the rest of the year.

* * *

I have had plenty of schoolgirl crushes in my life, religion notwithstanding, as any of my close friends can attest to, but I never let myself turn these feelings into a relationship. I was the kind of Muslim girl who didn't have boyfriends, because well, ain't nobody got time fo' dat. Yassmin's relationship status? *Inshallah.*

My mum saw dating as a gateway activity; she was vehemently against the idea of me doing things like going to the cinema, particularly if we were going in a mixed group with any of the boys from high school.

'One day, you're going to the movies, next minute you'll be wanting a *boyfriend*!' she said accusingly. I still feel guilty about denying that statement during our argument because she was right: I did have a crush on one of the boys who was going to the movies that night. My mother was adamantly opposed to activities that weren't aligned with our values, like tight clothes or boyfriends, and I felt like a hypocrite for having allowed some of those things into my life, and ashamed for not admitting it to her – or myself.

The closest my father came to talking about boys with me was once pointing out that all my close friends were male. 'You do know they're only looking for one thing, don't you?' he asked after I told him about a new mate I'd just bonded with over a love of Formula 1. I was aghast that he was implying something more than friendship could be happening. How did he even know about those sorts of things?

Aside from those brief conversations, I didn't discuss love or marriage with my parents until I graduated university. I was twenty and had just finished my thesis when my father started making noises about me starting my own family. Somehow, Baba still thought I would follow all the traditional Sudanese norms! Bless. There are other norms that I do choose to adhere to, customs that are more important to me than the appropriate age for marriage, such as bringing up my children Muslim. I've also always planned to marry a Muslim, but that ain't no easy feat in a country with less than half a million of us in total.

'I just can't find any good men,' my friend groaned over dinner one night as the topic of relationships came up. It was something I had started thinking about more, having recently started working full-time and realising how much slimmer the dating prospects were in the workforce compared to my previous safe university environment. It didn't help that many of the people I now spent the most time with were either married, or divorced and nursing their hurts. The work environment in the oil and gas community can put a lot of pressure on relationships.

I looked at my friend, incredulous that she was complaining about her lack of options. 'Are you kidding, gurl?'

'I know, I know. They're all either superficial or unavailable . . .'

I sighed. I was winning this race to the bottom. '*Habibti*, let me break it down for you. Try finding a Muslim bloke to marry in Australia. That gives you like maybe 200,000 men to choose from –'

My friend interrupted. 'Wait, do *you have* to marry a Muslim? What's up with that?'

I sighed a little that I was having this conversation again. 'Yeah, I do.'

'Yassmin, that really surprises me. I expected you to be different, you know? You're so different in all the other ways to other Muslims. What if you love someone and they're super respectful of your religion or whatever?'

'Babe.' I stopped her. 'I take my fundamental value system from Islam. If they don't share that, then we're not starting from the same base, which might be okay while we're young and independent, but what about when we have kids and I want to raise them Muslim? Or if we're arguing about something that meant a lot to both of us and I quoted the Qur'an or the Prophet and was all "the Prophet Mohammed (PBuH) says you have to treat your wife with the utmost respect". He could turn around and say, "Yeah, but I don't agree with that anyway." A Muslim man would never dare to go there. If we're both Muslim, we'll sing from the same song sheet; I can exercise my rights with Allah's backing.

'Oh, and if I married a non-Muslim, my family, along with my community, would probably disown me. There are high stakes. The thing is, he'd have to be a hell of a man to replace my family, community, network and support system – and, potentially, my afterlife. That's a lot of pressure.'

My friend was taken aback. 'Okay, right, yeah, I guess that is a lot.'

I smiled. 'So, back to the maths. If I'm looking for an Aussie Muslim bloke, that gives me maybe 200,000 men to choose from. Let's say a large chunk of those are already married or too young, and you're looking at around 50,000 lads. Around 30 per cent of the marriageable ones I grew up with wanted a wife who was willing to stay home and satisfy traditional gender roles, so they went back to their parents' country to find one. Those aside, I'm hoping for someone slightly taller than me who isn't threatened that I'm an engineer and could most likely bench press him, so we're probably left with about 300 guys, scattered around Australia. How do you like them apples?'

And with that, my friend finally capitulated: 'Yeah, okay, I don't have it that hard! But I still think that you could fall in love with someone who isn't Muslim. Just keep an open mind.'

So many friends share this sentiment, and I get the feeling it's because they don't understand that my religion isn't something I just say I am; it's the way I see the world.

It was only in high school that I realised almost everything expected of me at home contrasted with what my non-religious mates did: Aussie popular culture didn't usually fit within the boundaries of what was morally acceptable to my faith. My practicing religious friends, whether they are Muslim, Christian, Jew or Hindu, tend to agree that for some young religious people, mainstream Australian society can be excluding, and occasionally feel tense. It's all about walking the line between worlds.

Muslims believe in fate, the concept of *Naseeb*, which is someone's share in life or their destiny. Your *Naseeb* can also be a person, a partner that Allah has destined for you. There is a freedom in knowing that you just don't have to worry too much about finding someone – that when the time comes, you'll meet the right person.

The flip side is Allah expects us to work at things. It isn't good enough to sit back and think Allah is going to sort you out. Laziness isn't going to get you anywhere.

A bloke named Anas ibn Malik reported a *Hadeeth* that explains this perfectly. It's about a man who asked the Prophet (PBuH), 'O Messenger of Allah, should I tie my camel and trust in Allah, or should I untie her and trust in Allah?' The Messenger of Allah, peace and blessings be upon him, said, 'Tie her and trust in Allah.'

Growing up, we were taught the phrase *A3kila wa tawakal*, which, loosely translated, means 'Do your thang, do your best, and the rest is up to Allah'.

$$* * *$$

All through university, I had almost complete control over who I hung out with. My mates, often male, were from my classes, from the race team and occasionally from boxing. 'Hanging out' was often just chilling at someone's place, going out to eat or taking our cars for a drive up the nearby mountains. Because my friends were mostly from university, my time hanging out could all fit under the guise of 'university work' and so I didn't have to justify and explain anything to my parents like I had to when I was at high school. I thought I had gotten away with it, not needing any difficult conversations about who I was allowed to hang out with, but that wasn't the case. When I graduated from uni, my mother sat me down and informed me that I was no longer able to hang out with my male friends one-on-one because members of the Muslim communities would assume we were in a relationship, and an illegitimate one at that. According to Mum, it was inappropriate now that I no longer had the excuse of university work. If I was seen to be with different men all the time, particularly at night, it would ruin my reputation.

I was infuriated at the insinuation and the expectation that I was going to abandon the lifestyle I had established and that I loved. I captured my anger in a diary entry titled Hectic Vent, July 2012:

Ah!!!!! Just had the most ridiculous conversation with Mama about something I never thought would be an issue but *honestly ya Allah, why.*

So, I am telling her I am going out for lunch with Dan tomorrow and she's asking all these probing questions and I am like, dude, what is the deal? What's with all the questions? She ums and ahs and eventually comes out with it: now that you've graduated, the rules have changed.

What?

Cos apparently if the community sees me meeting one-on-one with different boys all the time, my reputation is *shot*. My reputation is everything, apparently.

Are we serious right now?! What are we, living in Sudan all over again?

Man, I am so angry right now. Apparently it was fine when I was a student but NOW I'VE GRADUATED SO I PRETTY MUCH CAN'T HAVE FRIENDS.

GAH.

ALL MY FRIENDS ARE GUYS. WHAT AM I SUPPOSED TO DO?

This is definitely an FML moment.

Edit: Maybe I should just have stayed at uni.

I was enraged for weeks. How dare she even suggest that I change my behaviour because of what people would think, especially when I purposefully ignored what people would say when making so many of my life decisions.

I knew Mama was attempting to protect me from the reality that people would point to my behaviour as evidence that the West had corrupted me. That in training to be an engineer and an activist I had lost my Islamic values.

If that happened, my friendship choices could be used to delegitimise the work I do, and that would be a real tragedy.

Since that argument, my parents and I have a 'don't ask, don't tell' agreement, reaching an unspoken truce — we just never talked about it again. I am now an adult, they said, and so they leave it up to me to decide who to hang out with, knowing that I understand the implications of my choice to be with male friends — that people may think I have lost my way as a Muslim woman and that the freedom I have been allowed in choosing an unconventional path has led to me losing my values. I always knew, on some level, that my mother was only trying to protect me because she understood how quickly communities could turn on someone if they behave in a way that is perceived as not appropriate, regardless of whether or not that perception is accurate. It took honest reflection, an appreciation of my mother's perspective and the decision to own whatever consequences occur in order for my anger to subside. It was part of becoming an adult, I suppose.

Knowing that people are watching me and judging my actions has changed my behaviour a little, but I can't live my life in fear of what the community may think. Muslim communities as well as societies in general need to challenge the idea that a woman's worth is based on her 'appropriateness'. Until then, I do what I feel is comfortable and hope that, *Inshallah*, Allah sees my intentions fit within an Islamic framework. After all, that is the framework to which I am held to account.

Chapter 10:

On Being Strong

I've always been a bit obsessed with the idea of being strong. I wanted to have muscles, to be able to handle myself in any environment, to thrive in independence. Strength of character, strength in convictions, strength in faith – I've built my life around ensuring I'm strong enough to make the absolute most of the one life I have been given. I was also taught I needed to be strong enough to avoid sin. Growing up, there was also an understanding that we, as migrants, Muslims and people of colour, had to be resilient. My parents were incredibly resilient throughout their lives, making sacrifices and tough decisions for the sake of their children. Their fortitude was something to aspire to and I wanted to emulate that strength in any way I could, to gain that grit of character. The gym and the world of debating were the two areas where I found those values, and although they may seem like an unusual combination, both spoke to me in unique, but equally important ways. Being a good debater requires resilience and an ability to communicate your values with conviction, and developing your body at the gym requires learning the mental toughness to push yourself physically when you think you cannot keep going. The gym is also a place where you can see tangible evidence of your growth and the physical manifestation of the effort exerted. Strength of mind, strength of body.

For years, my mother, Yasseen and I would drive by a big sports centre on the way to my brother's football training and I would stare at the building from the car window longingly. I had only ever seen gyms on TV, and the appeal was to do with what they symbolised: power and independence.

I had never considered myself as sporty; I saw myself as the girl with her nose in her books. You don't get to be nerdy *and* sporty when you're young: you're either one or the other, right? Well, not quite. I guess I never stick to the done thing.

Sport tapped into the competitiveness that pervaded everything I did, although I competed more against myself than anyone else. There was a time when losing even a small contest felt like a personal failure but as I matured, winning became a motivator, not the main purpose. This was something I consciously worked on as I learnt that the person I became when competitiveness took over was not someone I was proud of. I reminded myself to be grateful for all opportunities that arose and that as long as I put my best foot forward, the result was what Allah desired, meaning I could learn something from the experience either way. The outcome was not a reflection of my worth as a person, but just how life worked out sometimes.

I began to mellow out when I started to get involved in collaborative spaces through community work. Striving to win was actually a disadvantage in certain sectors. This was particularly the case in the social space, where competiveness reduced the overall impact because the work was not about the individual doing it, but about improving the community and empowering others. When I started Youth Without Borders and as I went through university I worked to channel my competitiveness so that it became about finding ways to be better for the sake of better results, not for the sake of beating others. Competition became about individual capacity – it was a driver I used to push myself to find out how much I had in the tank. This is something I do regularly: try to push myself to reach the end of the tank. I like to think the tank gets bigger the more you push.

As a child I did Little Athletics, played tennis and dabbled in soccer. I was tall and strong enough that, although I was never the best, I did just well enough to be picked in teams. But this was not good enough for my own standards, as I knew that I would not be competitive enough to reach the upper levels.

I soon turned my gaze to the gym, that place where you could visibly build your strength and to which I felt I might be better suited.

Alanna of Trebond, the female knight, was responsible for the revival of my obsession with being physically powerful. She was a Tamora Pierce character from a novel assigned to me during a reading competition I'd been enrolled in at school, after someone noticed I was into books.

My pre-tween passions had been more typically girly: The Baby-Sitters Club (I loved that Claudia never wore the same outfit twice), The Saddle Club (before it became cool, naturally), Nancy Drew (she never listened to what she was told!), the Hardy Boys (the good-looking roosters that they were) and Agatha Christie (I forced my school library to buy every single book she ever wrote).

I wasn't inspired looking at the reading list, but two books caught my eye – a book called *Stormbreaker* and *Alanna: The First Adventure*.

Alanna had a terrible cover and I immediately judged it: a worn out, old-fashioned image of a young girl holding a sword. Boring! The year of publication? 1983. Yawn.

I left it for spy heart-throb Alex Rider in *Stormbreaker*. A well-built blond who did missions for MI6, the CIA and ASIS, he was the teen equivalent of James Bond – he could speak several languages, was unbeatable at karate and could scuba dive. What I wouldn't do to be a spy with his language skills, I thought, and made a mental note to investigate martial arts after I finished the book, just in case I followed in his footsteps.

It turned out Alanna of Trebond was even cooler. A fierce young noble lady who wanted to be a knight, she switched places with her twin brother so she could pretend she was a boy while she trained. She made up for being physically weaker and smaller than the men with her absolute determination and her ability to control magic.

Alanna had her own style of femininity even though she lived in a hyper-masculine environment; she was vulnerable and had relationships even though she wanted to be tough and impenetrable. For some reason her boyish looks were attractive to all sorts of powerful men, even though she didn't try to make herself typically good-looking. She was a formidable swordswoman, overcoming her initial weakness to claim renown throughout the lands. But it was not her swordsmanship that allowed her to connect with various different tribes, it was because she showed them due respect, learning their languages, behaviours and customs. She was disdainful of the elitist way her society functioned and she did whatever she chose to make it better. I wanted to be Alanna: doing good things for society however she wanted, while still being respectful, feminine and strong. She made sense to me.

When the reading competition ended, I signed up to the school gym. I was twelve.

How I loved being a chick who went to the gym! I worked to be strong enough to swing a sword, just like Alanna. When I first started as a young teenager, I could lift just as much as the boys. How good was that?

My desire to keep up with the boys seems to be an unconscious reaction to the fact that men hold the power in society. I've felt that to become powerful, I need to be as good or better than them at their own game. Initially this was a product of my competitiveness, then it was about proving my worth, which merged into wanting to feel like I was making the most out of what I had been given in life, physically and mentally. Drawing from interactions in the world around me, I correlated physical strength with societal power. I wanted some of that, and to be part of something bigger, so I would have the capacity to make positive changes. If I was physically strong then men would have no leverage over me. To my twelve-year-old self, physical strength was the only visible difference between men and women.

If you're thinking this all sounds a little drastic, think about the social cues we are surrounded by as children, as a teenage girl: don't 'play like a girl', 'cry like a girl', 'be weak like a girl'. I didn't want to be like a girl because, apparently, that wasn't as good. At the time, I was too young to read between the lines, unable to see this language reinforced the system I was trying to fight.

I also liked that the gym allowed me to be mates with the boys as well as the girls — it gave me choice and varied experiences. Hanging with the boys gave me social mobility but also social capital; I was the girl who was 'in' with the lads. I felt like I belonged, even though technically my membership of various marginalised groups should have excluded me from this particular club. I was comfortable in the environment of banter and boys, and I used the skills my father had taught me to find my place in the world of iron and steel.

At my first gym session I was introduced to the machines I would faithfully use for the next five years, and the board that held the gym's record results. I'd eventually take out the chest-press record for fifteen-year-old girls (ten reps of 52 kg). I met the lads who inhabited the space, white guys in rugby shorts, who looked scary with their bulging veins and sweaty muscles, but who acknowledged the brown girl in long sleeves, trackies and a head-thingy nonetheless. The gym was a leveller.

At the end of the induction, the coach wrote me up a circuit program. 'Now, do you want to work on cardio or weights?' he asked.

'Oh, definitely weights!' I said.

He paused, program held in his right hand. 'See, the thing is, Yassmin, weights will make you quite big and a lot of girls don't really want to be big.'

I remember thinking, *Imagine not wanting to be strong so you can stay skinny!* Ludicrous.

By the time I left school I could bench almost as much as the boys, and that trainer was right – doing heavy weights at an early age did change my physique. At twelve, I was as lean and wiry as the rest of my family but by the time I left school at sixteen, my body shape had made itself known – I'm the strongest and heftiest by a long shot. My size is something that has had an unusual impact. Being tall and strong means I have a larger physical presence, bestowing me extra legitimacy in male-dominated areas like boardrooms and on the rig. It also means

I am less likely to cop abuse or be walked all over by others. Sometimes being an 'intimidating Amazonian-like woman', as I have been described, has its advantages.

My gym buddies changed: early on I hung out with two of the prettiest girls in my grade who wanted to stay fit. White girls with shiny hair and blinding smiles, they had that elusive social capital and knew how to handle boys. We became friends almost by accident, and they taught me how to hang with girls.

By the end of senior school, I went to the gym with male friends from my classes, an eclectic group of jocks and geeks. I would usually have to initiate the gym-based friendship because the guys would never have approached a girl. Working out together gave us a lot of time for one-on-one conversations, and I began to learn the value in having 'deep dive' chats with people in order to find out who they were. It's a skill I still use and find invaluable, as it gives me the ability to better understand the world around me and the perspectives of those whose lives are so different to mine.

We would chill on the grass outside after our gym sessions, or lounge on the carpeted area used by gymnasts and cheerleaders, discussing topics we wouldn't have broached at lunchtime: politics, society, economics, the meaning of life. Being away from class and the usual structure in our lives opened this beautiful window of freedom where the barriers came down and we felt at ease with each other. It was a safe space, a place where I connected with folk that I may not have otherwise.

It's sad how my relationship with the gym has changed. When I was still too young to be very self-conscious, being at the gym was invigorating and imbued me with a sense of power. Today, if I'm not careful, despite my best efforts, gym visits can be infused with guilt about my worth as a woman, because I sometimes feel that by working out I'm giving in to wanting to look a certain way, when I don't like capitulating to society's expectations of what I 'should' look like. Gyms today target people with a promise of making you look good, or of fitting into a mould, rather than focusing on keeping the body and soul healthy. Fitspo fashions itself as a movement that cares about your soul, but it seems to me that it only applies if your body fits a certain norm, so once again, the focus is on the aesthetic. To me, that motivation seems warped, and it frustrates me that exercise is promoted – implicitly or explicitly – as being about how you look instead of how you feel. Society took a place I found empowering and made it a prison for our minds and souls.

I still love lifting iron, but I prefer places without wall-to-wall mirrors. For me, the gym remains a place to work on strength of body and mind, not to stare at my reflection. That, I leave for my bedroom!

★ ★ ★

When the coach suggested I take up boxing I was wary. He had also suggested I get into sprinting, and I'd joined the athletics team, but I'd been nowhere near excellent so I stopped running when I finished school. I left this boxing suggestion percolating in my mind until I graduated school in the summer of 2007. The day I received my final school grade I looked up local boxing clubs. As luck would have it, one had opened near my house called The Boxing Shop, owned and run by former rugby player, Gareth Williams. The Boxing Club was his baby, and I had joined right at the beginning of their journey.

My mother didn't approve at all: 'Don't you know one punch can kill, Yassmina?' Even my father thought it was bizarre, but I loved it. To my mind, brawling is violent – but boxing is much more than that. Boxing training is one of the most intense forms of training there is – and I revelled in the challenge, in the mix of mental and physical, in the dance. I was getting good at something that was about pure physical strength: it needed speed *and* stamina, strength *and* agility – balled fists and a brain. It was about the mind game, the shuffle around the ring, the flick off the rope, the quick 1-2-3-4-5-6 that they weren't expecting, the right hook to catch them unawares – that was always my favourite. I also liked that I'd be more capable of handling myself if I ever encountered someone in a dark alley, the independence that confidence brought.

I met all sorts in that ring. My first real opponent at my weight looked intimidating, her jet-black hair swinging in a high ponytail. We stood at opposite ends of the ring and I slipped my headgear over my mini-hijab bandana, keeping my mouth tightly shut over my mouthguard. The black-and-red leather padding covered my entire head and face, leaving holes for my ears, eyes, nose and mouth, so I'd be protected if I got punched in the head.

I pushed my hands into my white 16 oz gloves and hopped on the spot from foot to foot, shaking out my nerves.

'Ready?' coach asked, motioning for us to come in close.

'Touch gloves!' he instructed, and we fist bumped to promise a fair fight.

'Take it easy on Yassmin, okay? She hasn't sparred in a while; just go light!'

The timer beeped and the punches came almost immediately. My hands weren't fast enough to understand what was happening. A left–right to the face, followed by a few body shots and a finishing hook – she wasn't holding back.

I threw a standard left–left–right in response, but I hardly got a look in the entire three minutes. I was stalked around the ring, punches raining down at every possible opening; blows with weight behind them I had never experienced before. She knew what she was doing, efficiently breaking down my defences in a clinical and professional manner but I couldn't recover fast enough to think let alone respond. My muscle memory resorted to defence mode, hands up in front of my face, protecting my body with my elbows as I walked backwards, skipping at times, trying to avoid the ropes.

It was three minutes that lasted a lifetime.

The beep called time and I collapsed against the ropes. She retreated to her corner, the way she strolled betraying her self-assurance in her utter domination.

'Are you okay?' Coach approached me from the other side of the ring, his face concerned. I pushed myself off the ropes and turned to him, puffing. After my weary nod, he then turned his attention to my defeater.

'Hey! I said go softly! What was that?'

I saw her shrug.

'I tried to hold back, but ya know . . .'

For the first time in my life, I realised that having the ultimate strength didn't always garner the respect of your opponent. Rather, I resented the arrogance that had led her to hurt me unnecessarily. It was a training spar, not a fight, and my coach had warned her to go light. Instead of respecting that and my more junior level of ability, she chose to show off, a selfish act of aggression that belied the collaborative nature of training.

Although we may have strength, the use and display of it should be commensurate to the situation. I had thought the way to earn respect, particularly in the ring, was to go as hard

Our first official portrait
as a family of four, living
in Singapore.

One of our first flights to Sudan, featuring retro
headphones.

One of my favourite things, and a privilege we lost after 9/11, visiting the pilots in the cockpit.

A good representation of my father's family in Sudan. We are a jolly bunch.

Beaming with pride in my class at the Islamic College of Brisbane.

The carefree life of a girl enjoying primary school.

It's official. I have chosen to wear the hijab.

Me, holding my best friend Hafsa's hand alongside some of her relatives, preparing for a traditional dance at a Pakistani event. I was an honorary Pakistani that night.

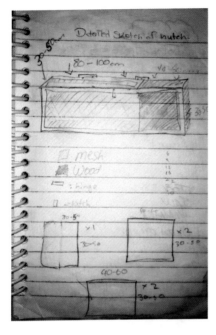

Even in primary school I was showing an aptitude for technical drawing. I designed a hutch for my guinea pigs.

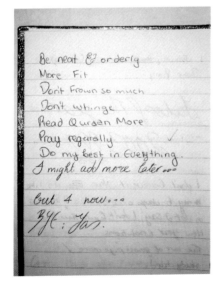

I have always kept a diary, but I haven't always been honest with it … (age 12)

High school days
at JPC.

My fellow students
when I was
studying in Sudan.

My unbeatable UQ car-racing team.

I had the privilege of speaking with His Holiness the Dalai Lama in front of a crowd of thousands at a conference in Sydney.

Receiving the 2010 Young Queenslander of the Year award from Anna Bligh, then premier of Queensland.

Receiving the 2015 Queensland Young Australian of the Year award from then premier Campbell Newman.

Meeting Lewis Hamilton on my first trip as a Formula 1 journalist in Malaysia, with Nico Rosberg doing the sneaky photobomb in the background.

Yes, that is Monaco behind me, home to the world's most amazing grand prix.

Visiting the Williams HQ on my trip around the UK following my visa disaster.

If it has wheels and moves fast, I probably love it.

Representing Australia and the United Nations Alliance of Civilisations in Vienna, Austria.

Being on the organising committee of the 2014 Youth G20 Summit was an honour and a ball.

My TEDx talk on unconscious bias has proved one of their most popular.

Some of my fav peeps from UN Youth Australia after the Q&A show on International Women's Day hanging with the Hon Julie Bishop backstage.

InStyle
#womenofstyle

Don't go stereotyping me. Cars are cool, rigs are satisfying and a bit of glamour can be fun.

The launch of the 'Shinpads and Hijabs' partnership with our local Federal Member Graham Perrett MP, some of the girls from the Islamic College of Brisbane and a couple of national level futsal players.

The Governor-General, herself a Queenslander, is an inspiration to many women, myself included, and has given me great advice over the years.

I was proud to be asked to join the board of Our Watch.

Speaking to schoolkids in Cooktown on a tour of schools as an Australia Day Ambassador.

Life as a field engineer on oil and gas rigs is not always as glamorous as it sounds.

Learning how to swing a tong! Still need to work on my technique …

as possible, to show my opponent and coach all the strength I could muster – demanding respect.

Instead, I learnt that sometimes the best way to build allies is by showing how you control the power you have, bringing the right amount to the situation. Where is the strength and nobility in beating down a weak opponent, when you know they will be unable to retaliate? Sometimes you can gain respect by simply meeting people where they are at, dancing the dance, and holding fire until they can meet you in the middle. If my opponent had reined it in that day, I would probably have enjoyed the spar and found an ally. Instead, I was bruised, literally and metaphorically, and chose to never train with her again.

Strength is like a flame – it has the potential to be a bushfire that drives people away or a campfire that brings people together. It's all about finding the appropriate intensity.

Chapter 11:

Learning to Lead

'The only thing I've learnt at school is how to throw a right hook!' I said defiantly to the forty or fifty people who had turned up to hear me speak at the Socialist Alliance headquarters in the Valley. This was one of the first real speeches I had ever given and I wasn't nervous; I knew what I had to say. I was exaggerating, of course – I'd never been in an actual physical fight because of my race, religion or political views, but I was stretching the truth to what I thought people wanted to hear. I certainly spent a lot of time at school defending Islam, but always with words, never with fists. My classmates liked to question me disdainfully about Islam being a terrorist religion and I would have to suppress my eye roll, smile and painstakingly explain that no, in fact we were not taught to kill all the infidels. But it never got to fisticuffs . . .

Perhaps it's no surprise that after being constantly asked to explain my personal beliefs I got involved in political organisations outside of school. There was one that consumed a lot of my time, energy and passion as a teenager, my true activist beginning: the 'Fair Go For Palestine' movement. Online petitions and World Vision forums weren't quite doing it for me, and I wasn't allowed to attend the large NGO events, run by groups like Amnesty International, because they were usually held in the city at night. My father was concerned for my safety, and didn't approve of the drinking and illicit substances that might be going around at protests.

To allay those concerns, I volunteered with organisations from the Muslim communities, like Al-Nisa. The ladies from Al-Nisa encouraged my participation in groups like Fair Go. I trusted their judgement and got involved. It was nice to branch out from activities that were only about our community and rally against global injustices and feel like I was part of a movement. Because many of the people in the movement were also from Al-Nisa, my parents knew that there would be no alcohol; they also understood that the issues we protested would be relevant to our family, rather than those chosen by a 'well-intentioned-but-misguided' Western view, as my father would often say. Whether it was people advocating for organisations that travelled to African nations to deliver a service that the locals hadn't asked for, or even the Northern Territory Intervention, my father often referred to Western interventions that damaged communities as something we had to be wary of – and not replicate ourselves!

The Fair Go For Palestine (FGFP) crew fit the bill. Mum would happily drop me at the houses of the organisers so we could discuss the issues facing Palestinians, ways to fundraise and how ludicrous we thought Israel's policies were. A few of the organisers were Lebanese, and so when Israel invaded Lebanon in 2006, the FGFP crew was mobilised to make some noise.

I purchased one of the shirts, not quite understanding the wording written on the back. What was an 'anti-semite'? Who knew? I wasn't one, I thought, and no one told me otherwise, so I wore this and other slogans with half-baked knowledge but fully cooked conviction.

Oh, the simplicity of being angry about an issue you only partially understand.

With this, my era of being a street activist began. My friends were protesting so it seemed like the right thing to do, even if I wasn't exactly sure of why. Yelling at the world was a satisfying way of releasing pent-up emotion: yelling in the streets at an imagined enemy that was all around us. We would meet up at one of our houses and get prepared there, then travel to the starting point of the event, usually a park, where we would collect banners, buy badges for our bags and shirts and gee each other up before we hit the streets. A change of banners and we could have been preparing for a music festival or a soccer match. It goes to show how the desire to be part of a tight friendship group, bonding over an exciting activity and being involved in an event that kicks up the adrenalin, is something that is common to us all.

I started off attending incognito: not yelling too loudly, just absorbing everything around me, but a couple of protests in and I was wearing the shirts, yelling the slogans, marching up the front, holding the banner and making myself heard. By my third protest I decided I needed to get up and say something, to be useful, to share my anger at the injustice in the world. I felt like I had something to say and I was keen to share it – I just didn't know what it was yet. Even though the specifics of my message were hazy, I instinctively felt that if I was given a platform, I should take it.

In some ways this moment was the catalyst for an attitude I have embraced throughout my life – if there is a microphone available to you, use that opportunity to say something. You may never get that chance again. If you're from a marginalised group, using that platform is profoundly valuable because it's likely a voice such as yours has never been heard from it before. I subscribed to this policy for years, until I couldn't physically utilise all the platforms I'd been given and had to become more selective. Up until then, though, I was indiscriminate in where I chose to share. These days, I've learnt that being effective means being discerning about where you choose to lend your voice, and that my credibility, which is what allows me to influence change, is something I must guard in every way possible.

'Anyone else have something to say?' the man with the microphone asked the 150-strong group that had just marched, asking the government to support Lebanon and, for good measure, to back the Palestinians as well. I had carried a banner at the front and was feeling the power of being part of a movement course through my veins.

I motioned for the mic.

What was I, a fifteen-year-old, going to tell a pack of passionate protesters?

I'd had some experience with public speaking, but this was not the same as debating. I had to draw on a different skill, one that came from my Sudanese roots.

In a collective culture, every family is a big crowd, so everyone gets informally trained to speak in front of a sizeable audience, and as a child you learn how to cajole grandparents, parents and cousins using different intergenerational influencing styles. I'd seen enough family drama by this point to understand that, as a speaker, the emotions you drew out of people were often more important than what you actually said. Growing up in a communal culture is actually a lot like being part of a volunteer organisation – people have different roles and responsibilities, decisions need to be negotiated and agreed on by a majority or even by consensus, and there are unspoken rules you need to pick up on to be able to effectively function.

Spending time in Sudan frequently meant I was able to acquire some of these abilities, like how to deal with different generations in the one 'organisation'. I found ways to share space and make my voice heard when everyone wanted the floor and also instinctively began to understand how to have influence when people have different motivations and drivers. So, as I bounded up the stairs and turned to look out over the protesters, I might not have known what I was going to say, but I knew exactly how I wanted to make people feel.

'Everything that needs to be said already has been ...' I started nervously. I paused. '*But that doesn't mean it isn't worth repeating!*' The crowd roared their appreciation as I ran through phrases I'd heard during the day, injecting impassioned fervour into the delivery. It was a performance; I had found my stage. '*We won't let the government get away with this!*' I yelled into the mic, gesticulating wildly. 'They stand by while *young children die!*'

It was only a few minutes, but they were enough for me to understand the power in a crowd. I knew that I had said the 'right' things, and by doing so in such a public manner, I had proved that I belonged. The connection and impact I had that day as a teenager with nothing but passion says something about the nature of protest and its dependence on emotion over information; how well I knew my content didn't matter in the face of my fervour. At the time, I believed passion was enough. Today, my thinking has changed. Passion plays a role in driving change, but depth and knowledge are important for meaningful, lasting transformation, and that takes time and dedication. Every movement needs a combination of all the different types of people: passion people, doers, thinkers, deep divers and implementers. Bill Moyer, an American activist, talks about four specific roles that are needed in any movement – citizens, rebels, social change agents and reformers – and how without all of the elements, change is incomplete. This does not stop people from moving between these roles; I started out as a rebel and now fit somewhere in between social change agent and citizen. The role I am in changes as I do, but the constant is my desire to make things better.

It amazes me that I had such gumption. The naivety of youth is so potent. I'm glad I went through the 'vocal activist' experience and had the freedom to explore that mode of change without fear of long-term reprisal from the broader community. It did a number of things: I gained grassroots credibility, learnt from the experiences of those who had spent decades in the activist space and I saw what life was like as protester.

Being part of a physical movement of people was intoxicating, and I understand why others dedicate their lives to being activists. You become part of a world untainted by the realities of our status quo and the restrictions that we have placed on ourselves. Part of me misses the ideological purity at times, but as with every path there are pros and cons. Life is about picking what is right for you at certain points in time and not looking back in regret. Every experience I have had has led to new, occasionally different types of opportunity. Grasping these opportunities is how I have grown and evolved, allowing me to lay down a solid foundation on which to build – and every engineer knows a concrete foundation is strongest when reinforced with some steel, a bit of something different.

Later that day, a fellow protester from the Socialist Alliance approached me to congratulate me on my speech and offer me an opportunity.

'We'd love to do an interview with you for our newspaper,' he said. 'Would you be interested in speaking at one of our events?'

I couldn't believe my good fortune. Newspapers! Speeches! How awesome. This wasn't debating class anymore, this was real. I gleefully relayed the good news to my parents, who were lukewarm in their support, but I knew I would show them.

★ ★ ★

'What's the address, Yassmina?' Dad asked as we drove into Fortitude Valley. It was a weeknight and the Valley was the 'dodgy' part of town.

'There!' I pointed at a door plastered with posters and graffiti.

'Hmm, okay.' My father didn't sound impressed. '*Yallah* – let's go.'

A small sticker next to the door handle printed with the Socialist Alliance logo announced that we were in the right spot and we followed carpeted stairs down to a much larger open space that looked like an underground hideout. The walls were covered with posters of old men and multicoloured flags; I wasn't sure what it all meant but it felt like I was joining something exciting.

'Yassmina, do you know who these people are?'

'Who?' I asked Dad distractedly, eyes roaming around the room, taking in the threadbare couches, desks overflowing with paperwork and an area set up with chairs and a lectern.

'Do you know who Karl Marx is?'

'Who, Baba? Baba, what are you talking about?' I asked.

'Yassmina, that is Marx –' Dad pointed at one of the posters. 'Do you know what he stands for?'

I shook my head.

'Yassmina, you should go home and read his work. It is important that you understand the viewpoints of these people before you support them.'

'Whatever, Baba. I am sure he's all good.' I trusted these people; they'd taken me into their fold, right? I had protested alongside them and they had embraced me. They gave me badges for my bag, let me know what the right slogans were and had now asked me to speak to the whole group. I was in!

I'm ashamed to say that I embellished my problems with discrimination and being accepted in society to gain approval from the Socialist Alliance group. I played up to their expectations in my speech, when we were protesting and at any opportunity. It was my way of showing that I, too, understood the anger and I, too, belonged. That guilt has sat with me for a long time, but I wanted them to take me in, and they were angry, so I thought I should be angry as well.

I was a young teenager looking for a place and I joined the first group that made me feel important. This was before the age of Facebook. It was fortunate that I joined a relatively harmless group, and had parents who encouraged me to think critically about who I was following and what I was getting myself into. What if I had been drawn down a completely different path? It's important that as a society we don't demonise kids who are looking for a place to belong, but recognise what is really going on. I lived in a time when I was semi-free to make mistakes without them being held over my head. Sure, we joked about our phones being tapped, but it's not like it is now. Surf the wrong sites too many times, hang out with the wrong people or follow the wrong religion, and you might find your house being raided. Or, you know, just be a brown guy, and you might find yourself on the front page of the state's newspaper, described as a terrorist. All part of the life of a regular ol' brown person in Australia. Criminalising people at a young age puts them into the justice system and legitimises their anger.

Groups like Daesh are particularly cunning in the way they target people, tailoring their recruitment strategies for every individual with whom they interact. They focus on the young, the marginalised and those looking for meaning in a place where they don't feel they belong. And there are people who feel like they don't belong. If you are born and bred (or, like me, simply raised) in Australia, you have nowhere else to call home. But imagine this: whenever you turn on the news and there's a picture of someone who looks like you, that person is being called a terrorist. Kids at school tell you that you don't belong, or to 'go back to where you came from'. The country you call home invades the country your parents came from and there is nothing you can do about it. Your family back home is terrified for their lives and suffering from the fear and violence that comes with warfare, but there is no space for that conversation in the Australian landscape – you're accused of defending the terrorists. You protest but no one listens.

These events become part of a cycle, a story of identity and lack of belonging. We cannot underestimate how important identity and belonging are, and what young people will do to find them. We need to provide the right kinds of support so that people don't see the attraction in sacrificing everything for a path that may lead to destruction. My support network was strong enough to protect me, but not everyone is as lucky as me.

The Socialist Alliance loved my angry talk, but I never returned to their HQ, partly due to the chat I had with my father in the car on the way home.

'Yassmina, you have to think about the kind of people you associate with and what kind of change you want to make,' he said to me.

'Those Socialist Alliance people are doing what they need to –' I started to protest, but Dad cut me off.

'*Asma3i* [listen]. People like that are on the fringe of society. They'll yell and yell and yell but no one will listen to them because they are considered too alternative, not connected to reality. If that's what you want to do, then fine. But if you want people to listen to you, people who have the power to change things, then you have to think about how you're seen.'

That conversation was immensely influential, shaping the decisions I made about my chosen career path and affecting my choice concerning the types of organisations I would volunteer for in the future. It biased me towards believing in more traditional modes of transformation, like influence through boards, although that is something that may change with time. The conversation certainly reflected my dad's world view, which had been imprinted onto mine – a view that privileges further education, security in life and a stable profession, because a safe and secure life is so important for migrant parents.

I am now in the role of changing things from the 'inside', learning and understanding the system that requires changing and then looking at ways to transform it. I've embraced my chosen path and although I understand that it's not everyone's cup of tea, it's one that I am comfortable with for now. There may come a day where I am not okay with that choice. If that day comes, I'll find another path, *Inshallah*.

A second reason to rethink my mode of activism came shortly afterwards when the principal of my school stopped me one morning after our weekly assembly. 'I saw you on TV the other day,' he said, his voice betraying nothing. 'You were at the protest on the weekend?'

It turns out my antics on the front row of the march were broadcast on national TV and the news item had caught the eye of some students and their parents. I could vaguely remember yelling towards some cameras while we were marching. Who knew they were actually filming?

'A few parents have phoned me, concerned. In fact, one family called me up saying that if we had students like you in the school they would actually take theirs out.'

'Oh gosh, sir!' I was shocked. I hadn't realised my actions were going to somehow have implications for my other identity, my driven, fairly law-abiding academic self. Then I started to feel annoyed. What did 'students like me' mean: Muslims? Protesters? Why didn't these parents care about the injustices in the world? Hearing people had complained seemed to give legitimacy to the impression some of the Al-Nisa crew's rhetoric – that the mainstream just didn't quite get it. If parents were telling their kids that people like me shouldn't be at their school, what kind of attitudes were their kids going to grow up with? One of my friends told me her mother had complained to the school about me wearing the hijab. Even our friendship wasn't enough to break her mother's prejudice, which gives you an idea of how powerful negative media and stereotyping can be.

My headmaster's next words surprised me: 'I told them you were one of our best students, and that if they were going to act this way their kids shouldn't be at our school in the first place.'

I was lucky to be at an institution led by someone with such a uniting vision. That headmaster was my first sponsor; he put himself on the line for me in a way white males of privilege rarely do for young brown and Muslim women. I didn't fully appreciate at the time the way he normalised this kind of support at a wealthy, largely Anglo, Christian school, but I am forever grateful for his backing and his foresight.

I still left that conversation feeling slightly uneasy, recalling the exchange I had had with my father. Did people really see me as an aimless, rowdy troublemaker? I didn't see myself as different, but my actions were obviously having an effect on the people around me in ways I didn't fully comprehend. I guess I didn't exactly understand my actions either. It's frightening how vulnerable we are at such a young age, and also how I could be so affected by the response of some parents.

I feel fortunate to have dabbled in ideologies as a teenager, as it allowed me to find my feet, to be fully aware of the path I chose and to figure out what I believed in, independent of my parents' and friends' beliefs. My parents, realising that I had energy, sought to also find outlets for it, and after a fairly varied start, Youth Without Borders (YWB) became the main one.

It never occurred to me that I couldn't do something because of my age, which partly comes down to my belief in fate. In Islam, everything happens for a reason, and even if the reason is not clear at the time, it is ultimately for our best. The certainty that you can face every challenge and opportunity means that, rather than questioning every event, we spend our time looking for the message, the test or the meaning and then get on with dealing with it.

We also deeply believe that Allah does not test us with things that we cannot handle, which means that whatever adversity we face, we know we can make it through – we just have to figure out how. It's like being in a game and knowing you have all the weapons and potions to get you through the level; you just have to find the right combination.

That may be why, *Alhamdulillah*, I haven't had to struggle with anxiety over whether I could do something, even when people questioned my capacity, age or skills. In my mind, this was meant to be – Allah has blessed me with opportunities, so I have a duty to a higher power to make the most of them.

Not everyone is comfortable with the fact that my motivation is religious. Does my motivation matter, if I think it comes from a good place and the results are virtuous? If people have a problem with organised religion, should they have a problem with the work I do? I don't think so. But then again, you can't please everyone, and I have work to do.

So, that's the driver – wanting to serve the world and in doing so serve Allah in whatever way I can, using the skills I've been blessed with. I understood from a very early age that my family was privileged because we had moved to Australia, and we were well educated. I knew that I wanted to somehow use that privilege to pay it forward, to give back. I recognised the need, and then found a way to do something about it.

Chapter 12:

Back to Sudan: Teenage Struggles

'Yasseen! Oh my god, can you move your elbows? You keep hitting me with those bony things!' My brother was squeezed next to me on the intercontinental flight from Australia to Sudan. This would be my last trip back to the homeland with my entire family, although I didn't know it at the time. I was fifteen.

As we walked out of the plane down the steps and into the bus to take us to the terminal, I could smell the sand in the air and feel the dry heat I was taking into my lungs. Oh, Sudan, you bittersweet land – I missed you.

My family and I stood in the citizens' queue with our green passports. I was proud to have both Sudanese and Australian passports; I liked the idea of having as many passports as possible. Each one was an identity I could slip into when it suited me: I could be the 'cool brown Aussie chick' in the United States, the 'demure and slightly aloof Sudanese woman' in the United

Arab Emirates, and anything in between. I kept begging my father to apply for an Egyptian passport so I could as well, but he was never interested. 'I'm not Egyptian!' he'd say, not seeing the point of another green passport. The Egyptian passport would only give us bragging rights and cheaper tickets into the Pyramids, but I got those anyway by smiling sweetly at the guards . . . Hijab or not, a smile from a lady seemed to go a long way!

The wait for the visa desks was exhausting and dreary, hundreds of passengers forced into three lengthy, disorganised lines. Families around me had dressed their young children up in little suits and fancy dresses: for some, plane travel is still a luxury that you should look classy for. A film of fine dust covered every surface, a characteristic of life in Sudan. The tiled floor felt cool through the thin soles of my sandals and as we inched forward I pushed my hand luggage across the ground with my foot. The queue snaking out of the women's bathroom made me glad I'd taken care of business on the plane. Flushing public toilets were now filed to a memory: squatting was the name of the game, and although it's reputedly better for your bowels, I prefer a porcelain bowl.

I tried to avoid people's eyes as I looked around; making eye contact with strangers has different connotations in Sudan and I hadn't yet readjusted. Eye contact, particularly from a woman towards a man, is a strong sign of interest – or at least it invites people to approach you. But any teenager wants to have a bit of fun, so even with my parents standing next to me, I scanned the room, deciding who was cute. The trolley boy caught my eye and smiled. I quickly looked down, acting the part of a demure Sudanese girl (I was dressed the part too, in a long skirt and flowing top), but was smiling as I looked away, knowing he'd be watching. Yassmina was learning how to flirt! Cheeky, and definitely not very Islamic!

It was eventually our turn to be dismissively called to the counter and my father passed our passports over to the officials behind the counters.

He checked each photo against the individual and when he got to mine, he lifted his eyebrows. 'Are you sure this is you?'

I looked at the photo. It was from when I was nine, a turquoise scarf hastily wrapped around my head and a childlike grin beneath a nose and forehead shiny in the studio lights.

I nodded and he shook his head slightly in disbelief. We waited until he was done with the paperwork, the two-fingered typing uninspiring. Although the computer was aged, the passport scanner looked brand new: not so behind the times after all.

We walked through the turnstile to a hall of baggage carousels surrounded by huge boxes, cling-wrapped and duct-taped suitcases, and assorted bric-a-brac. When Sudanese families travel, they bring back everything they possibly can: gifts for every single member of the extended family, furniture, bedding, machinery. You name it, someone has brought it in. This is largely because good quality items often can't be found in the markets in Sudan, so travelling is an opportunity to buy the things people in Australia take for granted. When someone announces they are travelling overseas, they're usually inundated with requests. Shoes, underwear, baby clothing and toys are the requests we often get: simple, everyday items. Online shopping is out of the question. Not only do people not have mailing addresses (houses don't have numbers and streets don't always have names – and I don't think I have ever seen a postal service), but credit cards don't work in Sudan. Sanctions make the life of the average Sudanese person much more difficult than one would expect.

As I waited, my fellow travellers hurtled past me, rushing towards the carousel for their luggage, and, hijabs *Jalaleeb* (the plural of *Jalabeeya*) flicking me as people whisked by. I was overwhelmed by the kaleidoscope of colour that the Sudanese around me wore, and the diversity of the people who called this country home – a diversity that meant a different definition of beauty than the one I was used to. Here, I fit the stereotype of beautiful more than I did in Australia, and I was still skinny and short enough at fifteen for people to not be intimidated by my size. By my next visit, after I finished university, my increased size and height would make me much less desirable in Sudanese terms. It was nice to fit what was normal for a while; as much as I revelled in being a novelty at school, it was sometimes wearying.

Luggage in hand, we walked out and were almost immediately greeted by an enthusiastic group who had forgotten what we looked like but loved us all the same – aunties, uncles and cousins, who ushered us to the car, babbling excitedly about having us home.

'Faiza?' My mother's sister called me by my mother's name and I shook my head, laughing. '*La'a*, I'm Yassmina!' I said in Arabic, smiling at her shock over how I'd grown. We all piled into a couple of cars and drove to my maternal grandmother's house.

The main road was now bitumen, an improvement since our last visit when Khartoum only had a single asphalt road. We cruised along until our turn-off onto a dirt road, or '*zugag*' as it's known in Sudan. These roads are more like alleys, paths created by the repeated travel of cars, donkey-drawn carts and trucks. I recognised the right-hand turn-off to my grandmother's house, preceded as it is by a large empty lot covered in desert shrub and thorns, the long spikes catching rubbish from across the area. Piles of plastic dot the landscape as far as the eye can see, every crevice witness to the strange juxtaposition of poverty and consumerism.

The surface of the alley is rutted and potholed but also familiar. The rattle of the vehicle as it navigates the terrain is almost soothing. If a car lasts in Sudan, it can last anywhere, my mother always told me. When you think about the amount of stress the suspension and shocks go through on a daily basis, you can understand the sentiment.

The wheels create a dust cloud around us as we drive. This fine brown dust settles on all surfaces in Khartoum. This isn't the sand of the beach or the Dubai dunes; it is a fine silt that covers everything and anything, and means the air ducts in the cars are never opened and the house must be cleaned every single day. It is also why wearing a white *Jalabeeya* is a mark of cleanliness and a point of pride for men. The *Jalabeeya* is a cotton, floor-length tunic, usually with long wide sleeves, that both men and women traditionally wear. It's airy and comfortable, and can be worn as pyjamas or as a classy, traditional event outfit, depending on the design. For men, it's the Sudanese version of a suit, and having a *Jalabeeya* that stays white in a dusty world means you take pride in your appearance and come from a clean home. The *Jalabeeya* is an equaliser; the simple cloth is something even the poorest man can wear with respect and pride.

The uncle who picked us up is wearing a bright white *Jalabeeya*. With one hand on the steering wheel, he lifts his right hand off the gear stick to gesticulate at the kids running in front of the car as they play soccer in the street, yelling at them to move and be careful. We pass three or four houses on the right, all fenced in by large walls topped by hooped barbed wire. The walls, although towering and thick, are made from mud-based brick and rendered with paste that cracks almost immediately in the harsh Sudanese environment. The weather chips the paint on almost all houses, giving even the most well kept building a slightly worn look.

We pass the local mosque on our left, right across the alley from my grandmother's house. This fence is sturdier, and the green dome and minaret of the mosque stand high above the neighbourhood, an obvious landmark. A few neon light bulbs are affixed to the side of the mosque, spelling out 'Allah' in Arabic. Their glow flickers as we drive past.

Town planning seems non-existent in this neighbourhood. My first memory of my maternal grandmother's house is of a single, tall brick building in a large, empty space. The block, as is traditional in Khartoum, is a number of storeys. Three, to be exact, topped by a flat roof, on which are a couple of beds where we sleep in summer under the night sky. The structure of the house is similar to the one I lived in for the first year and a half of my life in Sudan; the main family house is downstairs and the next two levels consist of small apartments for the sons and daughters and their families, as is traditional. My mother designed this house when she was working as an architect in Sudan, although she insists they used the wrong plans. 'They wanted a design straight away so I sketched something super quickly and gave it to them. I was going to change a whole lot of things. Open up the kitchen, all sorts of other modifications, but by the time I got a chance they had already put down the foundations!'

The houses on the block grew with the community. Every time we returned to Sudan, there would be another new house on the street. Although it meant the area was growing, I slightly resented these newcomers. Who were these people, building in the open spaces where we'd previously played soccer? There's still one block left open and undeveloped adjoining my grandmother's house; there's nothing between the left side of the house and the mosque apart from shrubs, meaning the flickering light bulb spelling out 'Allah' can still be seen from my bedroom window on the second floor, reassuring me with its faint light. We turn at this empty lot and drive alongside the house, past the first gate, permanently blocked by an old rusted VW, and the *Zeer*, the Sudanese version of a public drinking water fountain – two deep clay pots filled to the brim with water, held half a metre off the ground in a simple metal frame. The top is covered by a small mesh roof, the whole contraption placed in the shade with a metal drinking cup, or *cause*, on top. The clay pots are wide open at the top and cylindrical for half their length, tapering down into a soft point, to keep the water cool throughout the day, so that anyone at all can come drink if they're thirsty. This includes people walking by, *Raksha* [tuk-tuk] and taxi drivers, family members, street children and the like. The water is topped up daily by the owner of the *Zeer*, often the people whose house it sits in front of – in this case, my grandmother and her family. In the fifty-degree summer heat that Sudan is accustomed to, the thirty-litre pots are filled up two or three times a day.

As soon as we had parked the car, I leapt out: 'HABOOBBAAA!' I squealed as I came through the door.

'Yassmina,' she crooned in her soft voice, ribboned with age. She pushed herself up from a lying position on the bed and opened her arms for a welcome hug. *Habooba*, which is 'grandmother' in the Sudanese-Arabic dialect, is a proud woman who brought up eight children; my mother is the fourth.

Habooba Saida was a beauty in her time and still holds herself with dignity, styling her grey-and-white hair in braids that reflect the traditions of her youth. Her hair is long, a source of pride even though it's now thin and often covered by a scarf and a *towb*, the traditional outfit for Sudanese women. The *towb* is similar to the Indian sari, a piece of cloth that is wrapped around the body and head, covering her modestly, and seen as very feminine in Sudan, usually only worn by married women. Habooba wears only *towbs*, with a *Jalabeeya* underneath to match. She keeps them stored in a cupboard locked with a key she guards closely, sleeping with it under her pillow. When we have visitors she sends for one of the grandchildren to fetch a 'good' *towb* — new, neat and pressed — from the cupboard, and wraps it around herself with careful, measured movements.

She looks after herself this way even though she's bed bound, due to osteoporosis and the various other illnesses that plague the elderly in poor nations. I can remember when she used to be able to walk around on crutches, then on one trip back to Sudan she was in a wheelchair, and since then she's been in bed, but she's still the woman of the house and won't hesitate to tell anyone how it is. Her white, thin skin is wrinkled and frail but the parts of her body that are always on display — her face, hands and feet — look surprisingly firm. She sits in a cross-legged position on the bed, rocking back and forth, or lies with her head on the pillow — medicine and money stuffed underneath, out of reach of meddling fingers. Her bed is in the main area of the house — Sudanese beds are used the way Australians use couches — in full view of the television and kitchen, positioned so the rest of the family can sit around her. The windows aren't close enough for her to see the outside world, so family and friends coming in with stories is what brings her vitality and connection. Although she is physically disadvantaged, she is still a strong, commanding presence and a matriarch, and despite being a woman who grew up in a village with very little formal education, her passion for learning, initiative and excellence is unbridled.

Habooba believed if her daughters were educated they would never be completely dependent on a man, an attitude that would have been considered progressive even in Australia at the time. She was proud of mothering a doctor, two architects, three engineers, a scientist and a pharmacist.

* * *

That trip to Sudan was the last time I went as a child; I was still in school so there was no pressure from my parents to consider my marriage yet, as there would be when I visited after university. Even though my parents would never pressure me to get married immediately, they were asked about whether or not I was interested in marriage in almost every house we visited because I looked older than my fifteen years. My mother would just laugh. I would only find out when someone made an 'offer' if I happened to overhear my parents talking about it later. It was kind of exciting to think that someone wanted me to marry their kid, but only because I knew that my parents would never agree to it, which made me feel special. I just wished that they told me when it happened! I suppose it came from wanting to know that, despite the fact that I was 'different' in this world, I was someone aunties would want their sons or nephews to marry; perhaps I was searching for reassurance that I was acceptable by Sudanese standards. My parents never told me because they, like their parents, thought education was the most important thing and that experiences like marriage would come later on in life. All in good time.

My maternal grandmother would tell me that I was the right weight for a woman and that I should watch my figure, because that was important in marriage. 'Look at some of the women in this country who get old and let themselves go! Your mum is good, though, she stays slim. Be like your mum,' she'd say and I'd look down at my thighs and vow to myself that I wouldn't put on any more weight. Although I would like to think it didn't matter to me, I did 100 push-ups a day on my dusty bedroom floor for the whole trip, finding any way I could to stay trim. Even back in the gym in Australia I would occasionally think of those moments. 'Don't let yourself go, Yassmina; don't be one of "those people".' How uncharitable.

Days were spent lazily that summer, waking up and having tea, playing with the cousins, watching TV. It was one of the last summers that I would have without obligations; I had yet to begin university, yet to start Youth Without Borders, yet to step up to the plate. A simpler time, enjoying a childhood that would be over before I knew it.

Chapter 13:

Check Your Bias

I've never been one to blame my race or gender, an attitude which is largely a product of my parents' mindset. *Work hard and you will get the result you deserve* was their mantra. We were privileged enough for that to be true, a privilege that is not always bestowed on those who migrate.

Let's unpack the concept of privilege. Reminding myself (and others) to 'check my privilege' is such a normal part of my vocabulary that sometimes I forget it's not so familiar to everyone.

Privilege is, by definition, 'a special right or advantage granted or available only to a particular person or group'. What privilege means in *life*, is, as the blogger Franchesca Ramsey so eloquently put it, 'things you will not experience or ever have to think about just because of who you are'.

Because of the way power is structured in the West, there are many things people belonging to the white and male groups don't have to think about. Male privilege allows men to go through life never having to consider their safety when walking home alone at night, never needing to prove their legitimacy as a leader due to their gender, and choosing what they wear without others making a moral judgement about them.

Those who benefit from white privilege are never asked to speak for *all the people* of their racial group, can buy toys and magazines and watch TV shows featuring people who look like them and can buy 'skin tone' beauty products or stockings that actually match their complexion. They can turn up late to a meeting and not have it be attributed to their race, be pulled over by the police and not worry about their ethnic background working against them, never have to think about racism affecting them at *all*.

There are many different types of privilege and they are not all equal. There is able-bodied privilege (not having a physical disability, which means not thinking about how to physically access a space), cisgendered privilege (pertaining to my identification as a straight, heterosexual female), the privilege of education in a world that respects Western institutions, the privilege of having a stable job, the privilege of wealth that allows me to access technology, food and media freely, the privilege of a stable childhood. All of us reading this book benefit from a level of privilege – at the very least, we all share the privilege of literacy. Discussions about privilege are about a *system of oppression* rather than about the individual people within that system. For anything to change we should all be a part of dismantling the structural inequality that exists, which we can do by recognising its existence and becoming effective allies to those with lesser privilege than ourselves.

It was due to the privilege of education and our Western accents that my brother and I were able to access spaces in Australia without too much friction. My parents instilled in us that we were capable of going wherever we wanted to go, so I was forever optimistic and often forgot about my visible difference. I acknowledged the problems that people like myself from visible minorities faced, I just felt like they didn't apply to me. I didn't feel any different to my classmates, so why would anyone see or treat me differently? This changed as I began to understand the distinction between self-perception and actual perception. However, this was not until grade twelve, when my self-perception was challenged by my mother, no less, at a Lions Youth of the Year competition.

I had made it through the local and district levels and was now at the regional finals in a small country town in rural Queensland.

The competition consisted of an interview then a public speaking element. The interview took into account your previous leadership accomplishments and you were asked five questions about global current affairs. The public speaking was quite demanding: two impromptu speeches and a longer prepared speech. The impromptu sessions were designed to test your on-the-spot thinking. You would stand at the podium and be given a topic that could be as specific or abstract as the judges chose; one year the topic was simply 'circles'. Another year, it was on the Israeli–Palestinian conflict and the two-state solution. You were then immediately required to speak for two minutes, in a coherent manner, on that topic. The longer speech was a five-minute monologue on your subject of choice.

I was so ready for this. I didn't usually prepare speeches much in advance, but this time I had written my monologue (about the future of society) and had begun practising and memorising it days before. During the three-hour drive with my mother and Chandni I repeated sections of the speech, over and over out loud, watching the dry countryside slide by. Memorising speeches in a short amount of time was something that I had become known for in the debating team at middle school. I would receive the speeches from the first and second speakers in the team on the Thursday before or sometimes even the Friday morning of the debate and memorise them by the afternoon. I would print out a copy of the speech and repeat it over and over, sitting on the bag racks in front of the classroom, legs swinging, muttering the words under my breath.

For me to write the speech over a week in advance and practise it for days meant that every single word was analysed, scrutinised and mulled over. It meant every hand gesture was deliberate. I rarely write my speeches these days. I usually plot out a framework in my mind about what I want to talk about, using the same structure I was trained in as a child:

Anecdote
Signpost (tell the audience what you are going to talk about, like an agenda)
Deliver the body of the speech or argument, try to keep it to three main points if it's technical, or a story arc that's easy to follow
Share three lessons learnt
Recap main points
Finish with a strong conclusion.

It is a structure that's worked well for me over the years and I recommend it to others, although my main tip is to find whatever format works for you.

When we arrived at the competition, we knew we looked different. It was a small enough country town that two Muslim women and an Indian girl wouldn't go unnoticed. I was used to being a visible minority, though, and took it in my stride. *They're just staring because of our great beauty!* I thought, half-believing my own story. I don't know how or why I started thinking like that. It definitely wasn't due to the influence of my family, as we never discussed looks. I think it came from retaining the sense of worth I had as a child, simply believing that I could do anything. There was also a common narrative in the media that told me pretty people were often stared at, so I put two and two together and ran with it.

The interview process for the competition was strange. I was accustomed to being able to connect with people when I met them; cracking a joke to set them at ease, making eye contact and sharing a warm smile. It had worked with all the previous panels, but this time I kept hitting a brick wall. The panelists were constantly looking away when I attempted to make eye contact; they didn't seem to appreciate my sense of humour and didn't seem impressed with any of my answers. *Hmm*, I thought. *This is going to be a challenge.* I answered the questions the same as always and left the room knowing I had given it a pretty good shot. I never did quite find out why they acted the way they did and it might not be fair to speculate. All I know is I wasn't able to establish my usual rapport and the demographics of the panel members were the same as always – older Anglo-Australians. The only obvious difference was geography, which plays a part in limiting people's exposure to different cultures and faith groups.

Even in retelling this story I am reluctant to imply that the judges had some sort of bias or prejudice based on colour, ethnicity or religion. My every fibre is rebelling against making an accusation, and I am trying to find ways to couch my language in soft, inoffensive tones. Such is the power of the years of avoiding racially charged conversations for fear of being ostracised – a manifestation of an internalised migrant postcolonial identity.

The speaking and judging event was on that evening, in a local restaurant. As my mother, best friend and I walked in we commanded the attention of all in the room, some fifty or sixty attendees. Were they judgemental? I paid no attention. *Embrace it!* I thought to myself as I took my seat. Hijabied head high, shoulders back, game on.

The impromptu questions were first, and their abstract topics could have been tricky, but I sailed through on the advice of a speaking mentor: 'Break it into threes,' she had told me. 'Use a structure, like Past, Present, Future, or Local, National, International. If you have a simple structure in mind, your talk will always make sense.' I recommend this structure to people who are starting out in public speaking, particularly if you're ever expected to provide an articulate and sensible answer on the spot.

I nailed the impromptu speeches that night, and an hour and two courses later, it was time to deliver the monologues.

As I stood at the lectern, I surveyed the faces of the crowd. *All here to listen to me*, I thought. *What an amazing moment*. The crowd was full of older, mostly white faces. This wasn't my community in the traditional sense of the word – we weren't born in the same country, didn't share the same history, faith or upbringing – yet they were willing to hear me, to listen to what I had to say. It was a world away from my first speech in a public forum at the Socialist Alliance. This was no fringe group – the Lions Clubs were truly an institution. Had I made it with the group my father had defined as the 'right people'?

The room was silent as I moved away from the lectern.

I wanted nothing between myself and the crowd, I wanted to be able to connect directly as I shared my story. Microphone in hand, I began.

Five minutes later, I put the mic down to thundering applause. I was in the zone; it couldn't have gone any better. I had perfected my hand gestures, planned pauses so pregnant they were almost rushed to the emergency room, and altered my tone to bring people in and send them out. I'd taken everyone in that room on a journey they hadn't realised they had tickets for.

I sat down with relief as the response of the crowd continued to swell around me. Mum looked at me, beaming. '*Mashallah, habibti.* Good work!' She rubbed my back. The others seated with me nodded and yelled their congratulations across the table, over the applause that just kept going.

'You took that out! That was the winner for sure!'

I grinned, pleased.

The lad up next was decent, I thought, but nothing spectacular. He was mild-mannered, articulated his points and smiled charmingly at the judges. 'Not bad,' I thought, unruffled by the competition.

As I got up in between speeches to head to the loo, people stopped me on the short walk across the room to offer their support.

'What a great speech! You had me spellbound.'

'You did so well, and look at you, you walk so tall!'

Men, women . . . even a kid greeted me and I smiled. Whatever happened with the overall prize, it seemed like I had the speaker's prize in the bag.

Shortly after the last contestant spoke, it was time for the announcement of the winners. We were called towards the podium to stand in a line behind the lectern.

'The winner of the Regional Lions Youth of the Year for 2007 is . . .'

The name was not mine. The young lad who had spoken after me moved forward to claim his prize.

I pursed my lips and looked at my mother. 'It's okay,' she mouthed from across the room. She motioned for me to wait.

Then came the second presentation, the one for the best speech. 'The public speaking award goes to . . .!'

Again, it was the young man who had spoken after me. I felt a pang of disappointment. Really? Him? I checked myself. *Yassmina, you gave it your best shot and it wasn't enough, so this is what Allah must want.* With that sorted, I grinned and shook the winner's hand. *He must have worked hard too*, I thought. He deserved it. Good on him.

As I rejoined my table, the support was resounding. The chorus of 'We definitely thought you would win!', 'Oh, but you did so well,' and 'I'm proud of you anyway!' all served to soothe the soul further, and I had made my peace with the result. 'Onwards and upwards!' I said, smiling. 'It's okay, his speech wasn't too bad.'

It wasn't until my mother and I were walking out of the restaurant that she said something that blew me away: 'You were never going to win it because you are a brown Muslim woman and he is a white male. There is no way the judges would have let someone like you represent their region.'

'Mama, you can't be serious!' I recoiled at the suggestion. It was the first time in my life she had blamed racism for anything. This was not how we rolled – we were beyond that.

'Of course I am, Yassmina. Some people in towns like this are still racist, whether they realise it or not. It simply wouldn't have happened.'

I was completely taken aback. It felt like such a cop-out,

like something 'other people' in the community would say – people who spent their time being victims rather than taking control of their narrative, people who were not proactive in trying to change how Muslims were perceived. We were supposed to be the family that believed hard work could overcome all barriers, not one that blamed external factors.

I almost instantly dismissed the possibility racism had affected the result; it didn't fit with my world view and it challenged my belief that hard work would prevail. If my best effort wasn't enough, what else could I do? I disregarded it because it made me feel powerless.

It was only years afterwards, when I began to reflect on later experiences that were occasions of blatant racism, that I considered the possibility that my colour, race or religion played a part. Even now, I doubt the judges' bias was conscious – or I would like to believe that it wasn't. I prefer to think that people are better than that.

This reflection came as I began to understand structural inequality, institutional racism and unconscious bias. As I read more, I started to comprehend how the systems in which we are brought up take away our power as individuals. It is frightening to realise that you may have to work harder in life, just because of who you are, in order to overcome the prejudice of people around you. The reality is life is deeply unfair and we need to do all we can to level that playing field a little and make it less of an uphill battle for those coming after us.

Unconscious bias has popped up in various forms throughout my life. One memorable moment was the announcement of my year's high school captains. I was in the running, but I was the first hijabied Muslim girl who had attended the school and I wasn't sure they would let someone like me lead.

Prefects voted for who they thought should be captain and, although the actual process was always kept secret, the understanding was the boy and girl with the most votes became school captains, those with the second-most votes became vice captains and so on. Even though it was a vote, the school principal and board always had a say.

I knew I was in with a pretty good shot at one of the top spots, based on my speaking skills, academic marks and general willingness to get involved. People in my classes were amping me up, telling me they thought I had a real chance and it made me a little nervous; I didn't want to raise my own expectations just to have them smashed. I kept my mind modest, and responded with warm thanks for all the support.

On the morning of the announcement, my home room teacher made a curious comment, saying, 'You've got great potential for school captain, everyone thinks that. It will depend on how the board sees it, though, and they might not want someone like you as the face of the school.'

I would like to say I was shocked by her words, but they rang true. 'It probably won't happen, will it?'

My teacher shrugged, but her meaning was clear. I wondered how many other teachers thought the same thing: that I had the skills, but not the right look for the school.

That morning, I prayed to not become school captain because I didn't want to be involved in the politics. It was the same feeling that I would later have in the Lions Youth of the Year competition – an unwillingness to bring my colour, race or religion into the conversation and make others uncomfortable by saying 'Has this been a factor in your decision making?' *What would be the point of making waves?* I thought. Up until that time I had always minimised my differences and didn't want to be seen as that person from a marginalised group who talked about it all the time. How that has changed!

That was 2007. These days, Muslims and people of colour are in more positions of influence. The school now has a multicultural leadership team, but at the time appointing me to the position would have been seen as something of a statement. Remember, JPC is a Christian ecumenical school. To have a covered Muslim girl as the school captain would need to have been justified to the religious community – I can't imagine a Christian girl being the school captain of a Muslim school. I did not want this battle.

Knowing which battles to pick is important, and this was definitely not the last time I would have to make such a decision. There is rife injustice in this world, and as a woman of colour and of faith, injustice affects me on a daily basis, but if I got frustrated or tried to fight every single inequality, not only would I burn out, but I'd be ineffective. This is why I won't pick a fight with every single guy on the rig who says something misogynistic, or every random colleague who's a little racist or sexist. I will try to find ways to influence those situations, but my focus is on battles that deal with structural inequality. It is important to persuade individuals, but the system is a lot harder to change. If you're going to take on the system, you want to make sure you're prepped.

★ ★ ★

Which battles to pick became a decision I had to make almost everywhere I went, whether it was school, the rigs or the sailing club. I had thought things might be different, more professional and less biased once I joined the workforce and 'grown-up' sporting clubs but it turned out that I was mistaken.

★ ★ ★

I never had any desire to sail until the opportunity presented itself. I was a few years out of university by now, and my colleagues in Perth were part of a sailing competition and invited anyone interested to join in. I thought, *Why not?* I was curious as to what type of people I'd meet in the sailing sphere.

As to be expected with any sport that combines water and a desert-born human, there was an adjustment period. There was a 30-knot wind for my first afternoon on the water, which wasn't the perfect environment for beginners but I was not to be dissuaded. Committed to learning this new skill, I wriggled onto the boat, locking my feet under the strap and heading out towards the buoy.

As my boat sailed faster, the hull started flying. I was right in the middle of the pack, loving the feeling of the wind rushing over my hijab. *This is easy!* I thought, and glanced over at the drilling engineer on the boat beside me.

'Hey!' I yelled. 'Look how fast I'm going!'

Max smiled, but the next moment his face changed –

THWACK!

My boat careened into the front of his and launched me up, across and into the water. My boat capsized, I put a huge dent into the front of Max's boat and I ended up at the bottom of the river. I gave the sailing instructor heart palpitations that afternoon. It was the start of a strange love affair with sailing.

★ ★ ★

Sailing the surf cats became so addictive I joined the local yacht club – fancy indeed. Apparently you're supposed to find someone to introduce you so you can gracefully enter the society. Not me, no, sir. I simply went online, looked up a course that would teach me how to sail, and registered myself into a sailing club course.

People ask why I constantly put myself into situations where I don't quite belong, and the answer is that I love the adventure of novel experiences, of trying something new in an unfamiliar environment. I'm always fascinated by other people's lives and their stories. By gaining access to their world I get to learn how another type of person lives, thinks and exists in the society around them. In doing so I know that I'm also showing people the value of my perspectives and cultures.

I had a quite close friend who once said our friendship 'pretty much single-handedly knocked my views into shape'. When I pressed him on what he meant, it became clear that when he was growing up he had no exposure to Muslims and so his opinions were based on what he saw on TV. He was biased, and frightened of what he saw.

The reality for my friend, as for so many others, was once he met me – a real-life Muslim – and we began to connect, he moved past the one-dimensional view of Muslims he'd been fed by the media. When people are able to openly ask questions, their ignorance and hate is diluted – even if they don't come around to the ideology, something violent and dark is turned into simple disagreement. I hoped that if I encountered any bias at the yacht club, I could do something similar and open the members' minds as we became mates.

The weekend sailing course sessions were relaxing, picturesque and full of new skills to learn. We were taught how to handle the wind, how to jibe and tack, what beam-reach and close-haul meant and when to shout '*Starrrrboaaard!*' Once I befriended the instructors, they let me into their club, and when

I asked if there were any boats that needed an extra member I found my way onto a crew.

I met the team on a Saturday morning as they were preparing for the race: three older Anglo men who were brave enough to take on my fledgling sailing skills.

The skipper introduced himself, but when I gave him my name he said, 'I've got a terrible memory, and I won't remember your name. You remind me of Serena Williams, though, so I'll just call you Serena from now on.'

As I laughed along I wondered if I should be outraged. I wasn't – but was that wrong? I chose not to be, storing his remark as a funny anecdote. This sort of casual racism happens all the time because banter by its nature often walks the fine line between edgy and inappropriate. I allow some of it to pass, picking my battles.

In theory, if you thought something was inappropriate you would explain why to the perpetrator and they would listen and adjust their attitude. In reality, the world is not so clear-cut and it can be more effective to influence the person's attitude by becoming part of their domain and then slowly asking questions that challenge their accepted world view. During conversations, I also like to insert stories and anecdotes that come from a completely intersectional perspective and subtly contest all the views previously articulated. Change from the inside, right?

I have also learnt to never take things personally. Australian ribbing is like a game of air hockey – lightning-fast back and forth – with points scored easily on both sides of the table; and points are how you climb the social totem pole in Australia, among men at least. How do you climb that greasy banter totem pole as a woman in a male-dominated space? When talking to a group of men, for example on a sailboat or on the rig, I occasionally choose to use 'the sassy black women' trope that most men would understand from music, movies and TV through the likes of Nicki Minaj, Miranda Bailey from *Grey's Anatomy* and the caricatures in *White Chicks*. Slipping into this character allows me to signal that I'm powerful without having to use the men's language. You could argue this isn't authentic and that using tropes is damaging, undermining a black woman's agency. But sometimes it's an invaluable way in for me, a way to speak in a language Australians have at least heard before. People already know that I am a brown Muslim woman. How do I come into a white male world and get respect? I show them that my sass and my wit and my banter game is just as good as theirs, and there is no getting anything past me. All of a sudden, I have established a place in the pecking order that they understand, and then we can go on from there.

Chapter 14:

Oriental or Official?

'So, Yassmin. Do you think you Orientalise yourself by allowing yourself to be used as a token on the councils and boards you're on?'

Ohhhhhh. I froze as my brain scrambled. I'd been thrown into the deep end and was going to sink, fast. 'Wait, what?'

'You know you're just there to fill the diversity ticket, so they can say there's a young Muslim person and that makes their decisions legitimate, right? How do you live with that?'

I was keen when a couple of Muslim ladies from Western Sydney said they wanted to interview me for their local Islamic radio show, especially since they suggested meeting at a local restaurant that sold Afghan halal food. I was beyond excited to be eating at a place that didn't just serve kebabs or Nando's – Brisbane still had slim pickings.

As we said our *Salaams* [hellos] and sat down, I wondered if this was going to be a tough interview. They were both smart and charming and it was clear they wanted genuine, considered answers to questions that went beyond the superficial. This was an unusual situation; more often than not I was explaining very basic Islamic concepts to an uninformed audience. This interview was likely to put me through my paces.

I paused, taking stock of all the times I've sat on an executive board. The very first was in 2008 when I had just turned seventeen and I joined the board of the Queensland Museum. For a long time, I didn't quite know how I made it onto the board. The invitation came entirely unexpectedly in a letter from the Queensland Museum and it took me years to understand the opportunity that I'd been presented with. A policy change requiring the Museum to have a stronger focus on engaging young people had brought my break. My name had come up through a board member who had seen my announcement as Young Australian Muslim of the Year in 2007. I took the chance without a second thought, the way I did most things then.

I was in my first year of engineering at the University of Queensland and I arrived at my first board meeting straight from class, board papers heavy against the calculus textbooks in my Country Road bag. Deep wooden double doors opened up into a chamber that would become familiar to me over the next eight years, but at that moment, I couldn't believe I had made it here. An enormous timber table gleamed in the centre of the room, overlooked by glass windows offering panoramic views of Southbank. The back wall was decorated with framed pieces of the Museum's collection. I strode in and took the first available seat – the seat, as it turned out, right next to both the Chair and the CEO of the Museum. My board adventure had begun.

It took me some time to understand my role. I would read the board papers but sometimes skip over the finances when I didn't understand what was going on. I just tried to see if anything didn't quite add up, making notes like '*Whoa, this looks like a lot for lightbulbs?!*' and '*What is this expense, anyway?!*' I felt the weight of responsibility and treated the process seriously even though I often felt a little out of my depth. I wondered if the others could tell, but years later, when I asked a board member for some insight into this time, she put a different spin on it, saying that the Chair of the board had appreciated my engineering training, which meant I often asked concise questions about systemic change. Thinking back on it, I began to appreciate how the Chair had created space for me at that table by asking my opinion and considering my contributions sincerely. These established professionals were listening to the thoughts and musings of a teenager, one who hadn't even finished her degree. I realised these board members used their privilege not only to sponsor me but also to actively enable me to contribute to the board. In fact, it was these board members who would later nominate me for Young Queenslander of the Year.

This is an example of how those with power, particularly wealthy white men, can use their privilege to enable people from marginalised groups without co-opting their voices. They got me to the table and legitimised my voice. The power had been shared and become more abundant, leading to positive outcomes for all.

For the first few meetings, I observed how people spoke, mirroring the tones and language they used. I'd discovered, through hanging with the boys at school, this was a good way of short-circuiting the assumptions people held when you didn't look like them, as using familiar language can give you credibility, and I've used this technique to great effect in many other situations since. I didn't know much about the museum industry, so I needed to figure out how I could be useful, and asking questions became my ticket. Trial and error taught me how to ask the right questions, but I still felt I needed to contribute more substance, so after a year, when my mother asked me how it was all travelling, I still wasn't sure. I felt like I didn't have anything to offer alongside the other board members' experience.

'Yassmina, they didn't approach you to be a copy of a fifty-year-old white man. They brought you on the board for who you are, so just be genuine. They want your voice – don't tell them what you think they want to hear, just tell them your thoughts.'

Ah, okay. Try to be myself and to not be embarrassed I wasn't like everyone else. I redoubled my efforts to understand the board papers, and then asked the questions I genuinely felt like asking, but using language that would translate in that forum:

'Why are we still doing this? Does it fit with the strategy we've agreed on?'

'Are we thinking about people aged thirteen to twenty-five in any of these programs? Why can't they become part of our demographic?'

'That doesn't sound like an event I would attend; it is more aligned for this other demographic . . .'

Sometimes, I let my own language slip through.

'Let's do that! That sounds awesome.'

I probably offended most of the people around the table at some point, but change takes some discomfort. Age didn't matter, and I was told that I was both fearless and funny, a combination that enabled me to say what I wanted and often needed to say, while still being taken seriously. It was one of the nicest pieces of feedback I have ever received.

But of course, finding my voice wasn't just about the language I used but what I contributed and the reminder came sternly from my father. During a conversation with him about my role on the Board of the Queensland Museum, he reminded me not to be a coconut.

Being called a coconut implies you are 'culturally white' even though you are black (or brown). It's an insult mainly used in jest, particularly between friends, when you participate in activities that only white people usually do: learning guitar, eating organic food or surfing. It's an innocent gibe, but saying that people of colour shouldn't do the activities white people do reinforces the notion that we are fundamentally different and not able to be upwardly mobile without losing our culture.

From my father, though, the term 'coconut' suggests failure – that you're not quite brown enough on the inside to be 'ethnic' and not white enough on the outside to be accepted as one of 'them'. Dramatic, I know, but it's all about representation.

'Yassmina, if you are there as a diversity representative, whether token or not, you can't let yourself be exactly the same as them on the inside. Remember not to be a coconut!'

'What do you mean, Baba?'

'You must keep connecting with *al-Sudaniya* [the Sudanese] to stay true to your roots. Remember that you are not a white woman. If you end up saying what the rest of the board members are saying and just learning their opinions and not adding anything different, what is the point of you being there? You are then just legitimising their position because they can say "Well, we had a young Arab African hjiabi woman on the board and she didn't seem to have a problem with it."

'You are there to bring diverse views to the table. Don't be scared to say something different – that is what you are there for. Remember to be grounded to the community, remember you are there to empower the communities we came from.'

I would have to find a way to be a Caramello egg – brown

on the outside, and a mix of white and brown on the inside. A mixture whose composition I decide. It is about adapting to change and finding a way to flourish in a new environment. If that meant going from being a Milk Chocolate Lindt ball – brown on the outside and brown on the inside – to a Caramello egg – then so be it. Everyone loves chocolate, anyway.

Chocolate chat aside, if you want roles like this to come your way it helps to maintain a level of visibility to those making decisions, then making sure that when an opportunity does come along you make the most of it so that other breaks follow. There's nothing more powerful than a good word or whisper between the right people.

My second major opportunity came on a mundane afternoon in an email with a nondescript title: Opportunity with Queensland Design Council. I was in second-year university at the time and the council was a new initiative whose remit was to influence the nature of design in the state – not simply product design, but the design of policy, infrastructure, communications. The email was an invitation to be on the board, which was responsible for instilling the principles of good design in everything the state did. It was an awesome opportunity and talked to me as a technical person; engineering is all about finding solutions to problems. I would go from focusing on the number of teeth on a gear in design class at university to sitting in a meeting discussing the future of design policy in the state. It was kind of cool to also be able to contribute more in line with my profession and area of expertise: being an engineer on a design council was seen as a slightly better fit than being one on a museum board.

The Queensland Design Council would also introduce me to a woman who would have an enormous influence in shaping my life for years to come: Julianne Schultz, the editor of the *Griffith Review* and then Chair of the Queensland Design Council.

Early on, Julianne suggested my name as a potential subject to a journalist friend for an article that appeared in *The Age* in January 2011. The headline used was a quote from the interview where I shared my dream of reaching Formula 1 and read 'Fired up to be the first female, Muslim F1 driver'. The article went viral. I got interview requests from the USA, the UK, Austria and further afield, along with messages from people around the world wishing me luck on my quest. I got recognised in the street in Western Sydney by another Muslim girl who was like 'You're that F1 chick, right?' At that point, I was a car enthusiast as well as a member of the University of Queensland's race team, which would design and build a specialised race car that would compete annually against universities in the Australasian region. I worked with my mates on their cars, replacing gearboxes and pottering around their workshops, I attempted to fix my own (but anyone who has owned an Alfa Romeo understands the futility of that ambition), and I would regularly (but unofficially) race my mates at any given opportunity, learning how to rip 'sick skids', trying to drift and generally having a mad time in anything with wheels.

One of the people who emailed me introduced me to someone from the Motorsport Masters in Cranfield University in the UK, which led to the offer of work experience at Mercedes F1, meeting some of the top people in motorsport in England.

Julianne was the catalyst for all of those life-changing experiences.

I followed the motorsport dream for a few years, until it didn't quite fit as a career path. I moved my focus onto other areas in engineering, but am forever grateful for the experiences I had; the networks and friends I made are something I will always treasure.

The second thing Julianne did led to writing this book. It was a couple of years after that *Age* article came out and shortly after I had waved goodbye to the motorsport dream that I walked into a Design Council meeting exhausted, having just come off the rig. Julianne was curious and asked what it was like out there with all those men. I laughed and stories immediately came to mind; they were part of the experience of being a woman on the rig, which I had become accustomed to. 'Well, yesterday, I walked onto the floor and one of the boys said to me "Hey, Yassmin, do you hear that ticking noise? It's your biological clock. Better get onto it!"'

Julianne insisted that I write a story for the *Griffith Review* about my rig experiences for an issue on women and power the following year. I wasn't sure if anyone would be interested but Julianne worked patiently with me and my dodgy internet connection at work, guiding me through three versions of the essay before it was ready for publication.

The essay was, to my surprise, a hit! We toured writers' festivals with the *Griffith Review*, which opened doors to a whole new world and the rest, as they say, is history.

And by history I mean my entire world changed! I secured a literary agent and wrote a book proposal. I later enjoyed a whirlwind couple of days meeting publishers and being awestruck at the idea that they wanted to publish *my* story. Here I am, and here you are, *Alhamdulillah*.

I've been included on or invited to join many boards and management committees over the years and count myself fortunate, as each has taught me something different.

Al-Nisa and Edgy Advisors taught me the importance of grassroots organisations. As I moved into university, being on the management committee of the Youth Affairs Network Queensland showed me the challenges faced by a peak body advocacy group that was trying to get the Queensland Government to change policy. My role with the Queensland Youth Council gave me an insight into advising government. I thought we, as the young people who had been brought in, would be asked what the main priorities were, but when we arrived the priorities had already been assigned. Indignant that my voice was being used to legitimise a list I didn't know if I fully agreed with, I argued to have my priority added to the worklist. Needless to say, not much happened on that particular issue throughout the year.

As the years went on, I joined and left various other groups. The Australian Multicultural Council in 2012 was my first ever federal appointment and one that catapulted me into a level of politicking that was above my non-existent pay grade. I was encouraged by some leaders within the culturally and linguistically diverse communities to apply and so I did. Another case of a sponsor or mentor opening a door for me I didn't realise was there.

Sometimes I took roles that weren't as obviously connected to my core passions. I accepted a role on the ANZAC Centenary Commemoration Youth Working Group because I had grown up in Australia with the stories of the ANZACs but they didn't seem relevant to me, and if I couldn't engage, I doubted too many other Muslim kids could either – barring Turkish kids, perhaps.

So why have I taken on this series of roles? It comes back to capitalising on opportunities that will make life better and easier for those coming behind me. Every board, committee or council is a chance to encourage another sector of the community to consciously think about how their decisions affect young people, women, Muslims, people of colour, and to then have that organisation engage and affect those groups in a positive way. I love thinking strategically in diverse teams, wrestling with problems that require layers to be peeled back before a root cause is uncovered – and then crafting the strategy for the solution. I am heartened by the potential for positive change and even more enthralled when we achieve it.

I'm currently sitting on the board of ChildFund Australia, OurWatch and the Council for Australian–Arab Relations, as well as Youth Without Borders, the organisation I co-founded. I've also recently departed the UN Youth Australia board, a group I returned to after being involved as a volunteer years ago. Each role has been an opportunity that came by working the long game and ensuring that I took every chance I could along the way and knuckled down to make the most of it. Sponsorship only opens the door – once you are through, you also have to prove your worth. Never forget to work hard to earn your place – that was what I always reminded myself. But no one had ever challenged me in quite this way . . .

★ ★ ★

Back in the restaurant in Western Sydney, when I opened my mouth to answer, my thoughts were just as much for myself as for the two Muslim ladies interviewing me. 'You know, there have definitely been moments when I have been the token person on a board. Being brought on as a part of some quota doesn't mean that I have to stay that silent symbol. Once I'm at that table, I have just as much right to get involved in the discussion; I can sway the debate as much as anyone else. I can't control the factors behind why they invited me on, but I can control what I do when I get there. If being a token is the easiest or only way in, then so be it. Once you're there, show them you're way more than they ever expected, hoped or bargained for.

'At least this way, we can influence, we can show them an alternate perspective; we're not sitting on the outside throwing rocks at the table but hitting the glass wall. We're inside the room, sitting at the table and dropping rocks so big they can't ignore them.'

It is tough constantly being a token contributor because you continually have to take into account the fact that you are not representing simply yourself as an individual, but the marginalised groups you are from. Even if you aren't in an elected representative role, it becomes your responsibility. I know people in the Muslim community who would reject an opportunity because they didn't want to be seen as selling out. These ladies were trying to understand how I was okay with constantly being on the edge of doing just that. I wondered if they thought I was selling out. They never said as much, but it was implied in their questioning. It is something I often think about. I guess constantly questioning ourselves, while having people around us who will keep us honest, is the best defence against betraying our own values.

'How else are we going to access these decision-making places? It isn't going to be by slowly crawling our way up the ranks – unconscious bias will take care of that.'

They may not have totally agreed with why I had chosen to live with the seeming compromise, but they understood and accepted my decision and believed I was working towards positive change. Those ladies are now some of my closest Sydney Muslim friends, and their perspective on life is always grounding.

As a member of many marginalised groups, I've just had to accept that, at the moment, we can't be choosers. I will take up an opportunity, no matter how condescendingly it is provided, and try to find a way to make it work and to provide benefit not only for me, but for those behind me. It's important to make sure that we pay it forward, so that the people who come after us can choose to be fussy about the packaging of the opportunity if they wish.

Chapter 15:

The Snowball

'Dude, I won!'

'OMG, no way! That's awesome!'

'I know! What on *earth*?'

It was 2007 and I'd just been named the Young Australian Muslim of the Year at a fancy event in Melbourne, so after the announcement, I'd snuck off to call Chandni in Brisbane. I couldn't believe my name had been called. What did this award even mean?

'We were very impressed by everything that you were doing at such a young age, and all in Queensland,' one of the judges said to me afterwards. 'It's much easier in New South Wales and Victoria, where there's already a lot happening. You brought the hijab to your school in tenuous times, you were a founding member of the Al-Nisa Youth Group, started the Amnesty International chapter at your school, were vice captain, and you're still so young!' I couldn't understand why people kept bringing up my age. Dude, I was sixteen. That was like, heaps old, hey.

This award was my first taste of the big time. Back in

Queensland, I was featured on the front of the local newspaper, written about in magazines and photographed on the lawns of my high school, my chubby hijabied face grinning while I held up my award. *I had made it!*

My mother, bless her soul, was always looking towards the next step. 'Okay, Yassmina,' she said, pretty much as soon as the ceremony was over. 'There's so much we can do with this opportunity. We can't afford to waste it!'

I had no idea what to do with it. I was already in a couple of other small advisory groups, off the back of my involvement with Al-Nisa. Being Deputy Chair of the Queensland Youth Council and sitting on the Ethnic Communities Council of Queensland (ECCQ), the Youth Affairs Network of Queensland (YANQ) and the Amnesty International Club at my school had been keeping me pretty busy. More importantly, I had my final high school exams coming up, so community work was taking a back seat while I figured out which career path I wanted to take. I loved technology studies and graphics, and really wanted to design cars, but thought law might be more useful, because then I could help people, right? Bond University's 'Law for a Day' trial literally sent me to sleep, so I crossed that off the list. What kind of a word was 'tort'?

I was scrolling through different course options when my mum gave me an application form for the Asia Pacific Cities Summit. For the first time, the Cities Summit was holding a youth forum alongside the major event. It was over four days, the four days before my QCST (Queensland Core Skills Test, the final year university entry exams), so the timing wasn't ideal. I hurriedly completed the application form and sent it in with a sincere apology as the due date had already passed: 'I only just heard about this but would *love* the opportunity.'

I got lucky. This was exciting. I'd never been to an international conference. The food would be halal, and because it was in my city my parents would let me attend! The biographies of the other attendees were all so inspiring. I felt out of my depth and giddy with anticipation.

I remember listening to the speech by the Young Queenslander of the Year, Lars Olsen, and being in absolute awe at what he had accomplished. He had set up an orphanage in Nepal – I couldn't believe someone so young could do something so big! I jumped at the chance to chat with him afterwards; I wasn't sure what I wanted to say so I just thanked him, and he was so kind and down-to-earth – I still remember the encounter clearly. *This guy was super important, but was still cool enough to chat with me.*

The rest of the conference wasn't as gratifying. I had multiple conversations with others who were touting their organisation's effectiveness, but they often felt disingenuous to me. I was struck by how many groups from similar areas were uninclined to work together. Whether young or old, people seemed more prepared to throw stones at other organisations than to share their resources. I'd realised this wasn't uncommon in the NGO community, but that didn't mean I needed to accept it.

As a forum, we discussed how crazy it was to have all these overlapping organisations. We talked about it at length, in between summit sessions and sandboarding. 'That's just how community work is,' people kept telling me. A few shared my indignation, but we weren't coming up with any workable solutions, and I was perplexed at the lack of motivation to actually *do* anything about an issue we all agreed was a problem.

It was only on the third and final night of the conference that I spoke to my mother. 'I wish I could join something like Doctors Without Borders,' I said as we sat at the dining room table, where we had been debriefing about the conference. I had recently discovered Médecins Sans Frontières and fallen in love with the message and ideal: travelling to far-off places, where I would face the dangers my parents had fled, to directly give back. Was this the migrant version of white guilt?

'I want to be able to help but none of these groups want to work together!'

'Yassmina, why don't *you* do something about it?'

'I guess I could try, but I don't have a profession!'

'What if you called it Youth Without Borders, and made your youth the strength?'

I sat back in my chair, considering. 'That sounds pretty cool, Ma. I could see who would be interested tomorrow and we could start our own thing – focus on bringing groups together to share resources. I'm sure if we pooled grant money we could do all sorts of projects.' My mind ran away with the possibilities.

Honestly, when I say I owe everything to my mother, it's moments like these I'm thinking of. My mother has been the ultimate sounding-board, since she has a similar moral compass to me. She's also an ideas person, so she synthesises what I vent and helps me come up with ways to alleviate the problem – even if sometimes all I want to do is vent! Even today, she still remains my favourite sounding-board, although our relationship has matured.

Occasionally I thought this dependence was a point of weakness or vulnerability, and I'd question whether I was just a young conduit for my mother's ideas. I was weighed down with guilt because I would receive an award and think, *I didn't do it alone; you should be giving the award to my mum.* The truth is the story of Yassmin and Youth Without Borders is incomplete without the story of Yassmin's mum. We are told to honour individual heroes – Mark Zuckerberg, Thomas Edison, Taylor Swift – but, in reality, each individual has a huge group of people behind them, supporting them, giving them ideas, guiding them along the way. The belief that one person can do it all by themselves is the epitome of individualism and I think ignores who we are as humans. As Derek Sivers, an American writer and entrepreneur, says in his impressive TED talk, when starting a movement it is in fact the first follower who transforms the lone nut into a leader. It's important we remember that the community and the people around us are those who enable us to do what we do.

The final day of the forum was a trip to Tangalooma Island in order to showcase the beauty of Queensland to our international guests. We played with dolphins – one of my bucket list items, along with skydiving and visiting every continent. On the way back from the island I sat on the boat deck, staring up at a night sky in full starry glory. I gathered my wits and went into the main cabin to throw my idea into the mix.

'We can't let this be another talkfest!' was a sentiment being bandied about by the group as they discussed where-to-next. 'What are we going to do then?' There was a general hubbub but not much focus.

'Hey, guys, I have an idea!' Some faces turned towards me, while others continued their conversations unperturbed.

'What if we set up an organisation that is simply about how to get us to work together and pool our resources? We're obviously all doing cool things –' I motioned to a couple of friends I had made over the last few days who were artists and social workers – 'and I'm sure we could learn from each other and do much bigger things if we worked together?'

My suggestion was almost instantly laughed out: 'Oh no,

it's so hard to start a new organisation. Do you have any idea how difficult it is?'

'We're all too different, anyway.'

'You want to start an organisation that gets other organisations to work together so people don't start their own organisation?'

'You're only sixteen!'

About ten people out of the hundred were interested. Three were from Brisbane and together we formed the first Youth Without Borders (YWB) group.

I pitched the idea on behalf of the Youth Summit at the closing ceremony of the Asia Pacific Cities Summit. Presenting the concept at City Hall meant that all sorts of dignitaries heard about the organisation and Brisbane City Council offered us free office space for three months at a location in the Valley. Only a few years after my big Socialist Alliance speech I was returning to the Valley in pursuit of making a difference, this time under my own steam.

Our first YWB meeting was on 16 September 2007. We used a non-traceable chatting service, well before that became cool, to discuss the objectives of the organisation.

One of my co-founders, Anthony, was a twenty-one-year-old Sri Lankan economics student, intensely interested in the economics of development, who brought a sense of rigour and evidence-based thought to the organisation. Anthony and I both lived on the southside of Brisbane, so he would drive us to the meetings in the Valley.

'I'm just going to warn you,' he said to me the first time he picked me up, 'I like changing lanes a lot.' I laughed. *I can handle speed*, I thought, but I had no idea what I was in for. As Anthony was ducking and weaving, he talked about the structure of

YWB and how we needed to make sure that we focused on collaboration as we had said that we would, rather than trying to come up with solutions ourselves. I nodded as my knuckles turned light brown from gripping the door handle.

Lucy, the other co-founder, was also twenty-one, and she was responsible for the inclusion of young people at the Asia Pacific Cities Summit. She was working with Brisbane City Council and had lobbied hard to have a youth forum or a youth contingent included in the summit.

I have so much love for Lucy, more than I think I ever expressed as we set up YWB. She held us to account and was never afraid to tell Anthony and me what needed to be done. She was thorough, and knew what was required regarding registration, our finances, the paperwork, and how to do things properly. She was also funny and had an amazing laugh that would fill the space with joy.

Lucy and Anthony were the best things that could have ever happened to YWB and I owe them a lot. As co-founders, we all brought something different to the group: I brought the youthful enthusiasm; Lucy, a policy and governance rigour that ensured we were all above board; Anthony, development thinking and often playing devil's advocate to ensure we tried to do things the best way possible. Even though they were both older than me, we were always peers.

What mattered most was that they believed in YWB as much as I did; and a strong belief is vital when you're building something from scratch – attending six-hour meetings every week, coming up with objectives and fundraising plans, and debating the structure of the organisation. I don't know whether Lucy or Anthony – or even I – knew what we were getting into, but we believed in it, particularly when it started taking shape.

My main recommendation to people who are launching a new organisation is to find people who believe in it just as much as you do. Not only will they bring different skills and perspectives to the table, but you can support each other through the tough times. It's also so much more fun with a team – partners in crime, fighting the good fight!

Our first project was the epitome of how we would work: haphazard, online, and on the smell of an oily rag, but somehow effective in the long term. One of the participants at the summit was Fathima, a fifteen-year-old girl from Depok, a city in Indonesia, and she had mentioned that she didn't have access to a public library. That had resonated with me, so when we had our first face-to-face YWB meeting, I pitched it as a possible option for our first project. Maybe we could set up a library in Indonesia!

It was tricky. We had no money, no direction and no reliable line to anyone in Indonesia. Fathima was only periodically able to check her email due to limited access to the internet. All we had was gumption.

Lucy was the main point of contact with Fathima, as she had worked to secure her position in the conference, and I set about finding ways to connect with other people in Indonesia. I emailed, randomly, various people I could find online until my mother suggested I contact someone who had links to the Australian Government.

I am not sure how those first emails must have sounded, but judging from my diary entries at the time, they probably weren't the most sophisticated pieces of writing. Genuine, yes. Nuanced? Hardly.

The government official with whom we made contact didn't know how we could make the library happen, but he suggested other organisations that could help and those were all the leads we needed. We collaborated with a large, student-based organisation in Indonesia, PPSDMS, to come up with a proposal. However, after we got it translated from Bahasa to English, we realised a few things. Firstly, that the idea we'd come up with was slightly different from what they proposed, but that their solution worked for them. Then we found out that they had forged ahead and started the project without our help! I also became aware there was so much that we hadn't thought about, down to what language the library books would need to be in. I thanked Allah for our local partners and mentally slapped myself for being just as bad as those well-intentioned-but-misguided-saviour-types my father constantly derided.

We set about fundraising for the project, named Kamar Buku (*The Book Room*, in Bahasa) through barbecues and concerts, but we were nowhere near as successful as we expected to be, and in the end our partners in Indonesia got the entire system donated to them – the motorbikes, the boxes fitted to the back of the motorbikes *and* the books – while we were still trying to raise money. In fact, while we were freaking out because we hadn't heard from them in a few months, they were getting things done their own way. It turned out phone calls were expensive and their internet wasn't fast enough or reliable enough to Skype, but one day, over a year after we had had our first conversation with them, we received a twelve-minute video, mainly in Bahasa, that showed our project had come alive. The video, which is still on YouTube, followed the motorbike as it travelled through the villages, and showed the volunteers sitting with classes full of children, reading to them and sharing stories. The young Indonesian students were clearly full of joy, their worlds broadened. It was hard to believe we had had a part in this at all, but it had actually happened and the evidence was in front of our eyes.

Kamar Buku became our showcase of how you could run community initiatives through project-based collaboration. Our most important realisation was that we didn't have to be there on the ground, as we weren't the important ones in the equation. Our role was about acting as a catalyst and empowering other young people to realise they could create the change they needed.

That momentum took us through the first few years of YWB. There were plenty of other little projects along the way. We put on small concerts, although we always forgot to advertise. We developed partnership programs and set up school holiday camps for young refugees and asylum seekers. We ran sports programs like a Ramadan football tournament for the African boys in the Brisbane community, and organised Shinpads and Hijabs, the fantastic collaboration with Football United where we worked with the Islamic College of Brisbane and all the girls in high school, teaching them how to play football. The awesome twist was that ladies from the Matildas and the Vikings (our national futsal team) got involved in coaching, and the Muslim girls began to see soccer as something they could do, and be quite competitive in! We supported other young people who wanted to start their own projects. *One Moon* was a project to send sanitary products overseas to women in East Africa. *One Hope* fundraised for the Haiti earthquake. *Masterchef Meets the Streets* was a cross-cultural awareness program where we worked with high school students from high socio-economic areas and taught them how to cook dishes from culturally and linguistically diverse communities, while explaining the cultural significance behind the food. It was then shared with people at the local homeless shelters. All of these projects, and many more, were only possible because we partnered with others. We didn't have the money, capacity or knowledge to do it all ourselves; collaboration was the only way.

People often asked us what our specific cause was, but at the time we had no language to describe the concepts we were working with – youth empowerment, access to opportunity, and becoming leaders of positive change.

I was on the money that day at the forum when I realised the different organisations needed to do more to collaborate, but it was a much bigger problem than I could have ever anticipated and we didn't quite have the sophistication to tackle the structural problem it was and continues to be. In late 2015, the Community Council for Australia's chief executive officer, David Crosbie, publicly asked organisations to combine and pool their resources, eight years after we had said the same thing. We had been seen as purely idealistic. It will be interesting to see if Crosbie's push has traction.

YWB's focus has shifted to a slightly different area – using collaboration to get young people to realise their full potential. We still occupy the same ideological space but aim to get individuals working together, rather than organisations. Originally, we aimed to tackle long-term, deep-rooted issues. We wanted to influence organisations and create alternative models for philanthropy, rather than just the hands-on activities – those that people are often drawn to and that garner more immediate, tangible results. But we found that it was difficult to attract other teenagers to agitate for this kind of structural change.

The slight shift in mission also brought with it an increased focus on the idea of 'young leaders' of positive change. However, the concept of leadership seemed icky to me, conjuring up an image of people forcing their way to the front, demanding to be a leader, when I wanted us to be humble facilitators of change. I wonder now where that distaste for the word 'leadership' came from. Perhaps from my parents drumming the religious concept of humility into me. Islam is about being humble, communal, not focused on oneself. Maybe I was compensating because I was a confident, loud person who was often up the front, happy to volunteer and be the centre of attention, but being focused on getting attention has unIslamic connotations. With maturity comes understanding. My focus these days is on the intention behind my actions and in executing that in the most authentic way possible.

It may be that my distaste for leadership came from some anti-authoritarian streak. Being a leader seemed to imply following the rules, which I didn't always like doing. I liked setting rules for myself based on what I felt was important, which was often my own combination of Eastern and Western values. As the years have gone by, the organisation and I have become more comfortable with the concept of leadership. Perhaps this is because we have matured and realised that leading is the business we are in, creating leaders from diverse backgrounds who can guide their communities, young people who feel empowered – leaders who realise that sometimes the best way to take charge is to follow, the best way to communicate is to listen and the best way to empower others is to let them do something themselves. I don't know if the word leadership inherently implies all of that, but that is what it means to me.

It certainly isn't always an easy process. Something else that I was forced to learn along the way was that people have different reasons for getting involved and for caring, and not everyone's intention is altruistic. Once something becomes successful, people want in on it, or they want to take it from you. Leadership can also be about standing your ground, protecting what you know is good and being prepared to back yourself.

Chapter 16:

Failing, Learning and Finding the Spark

Running Youth Without Borders wasn't always going to be a walk in the park, which became clear when a fancy fundraising dinner I had been planning completely fell apart. We made a grave mistake by not requesting payment immediately when we sold our tickets. A few days out from the event when the time came to collect the money we got apologies left, right and centre. We went from 120 confirmed attendees to thirty-five.

The day before the dinner was a series of excruciating phone calls, starting with one to the event planner. When I ran her through the details on my way to an 8 am engineering lecture, she recommended we cancel the entire event, but I didn't want to hear it.

Arriving late and huffing with frustration, I slammed myself into a seat at the back of the lecture theatre next to a couple of mates, fuming, and faced with gear calculations. I was in my third-year advanced dynamics lecture, one of the most difficult mechanical engineering courses, but I couldn't hear a single thing over the volume of my thoughts. I willed myself to focus on the importance of how to calculate the ideal gear ratios for a system, but my will wasn't working. I needed to get out.

I tapped a friend on the shoulder: 'Oi, mate. Let's bail.' I collected my books, jumped the seat behind me and headed out. My mate followed, unaware he was about to become a punching bag.

'Dude, what's wrong?'

As I explained the situation to him, the enormity of it became more obvious and my voice kept getting louder: 'Oh, man, I'm going to have to cancel all these favours and we're going to be out so many grand . . .' I was getting more and more animated, totally wrapped up in the unfolding disaster.

'Dude –' He stopped me.

'What?'

'Dude, you're yelling. It looks like you're breaking up with me.'

I glanced around – we were standing in a main walkway at the university, people milling around us, staring at me as they passed. Something snapped in me and I burst into laughter; he just looked relieved that the yelling had stopped. *Way to go, Yassmin*, I thought. *Winning every day.*

The rest of the day was a lesson in humility. I made phone calls to all the dignitaries I had invited, informing them of the late cancellation and thanking them for their contribution. I made humbling phone calls to the YWB members, musicians, and my friends and family, telling them the news.

YWB taught me early on that we sometimes fail and make mistakes, and that it's important to learn from them. The realisation that I couldn't make everything work my way was a bitter pill for my teenage self to swallow, but every event has a lesson buried in it; it's just up to us to figure out what it is.

This time, beyond learning to collect money when you sell a ticket, the message was to remain humble. Failures like this are a huge part of being a start-up, whether it's a company or an NGO, but we never seem to really talk about them. It's not fun to talk about failure, but it is how we improve.

There were a few times when things got tough, people started leaving, things didn't turn out how I'd expected them to, and I'd contemplate just walking away, shutting up shop. There were moments in the dead of night when I asked myself why people were choosing to leave YWB and felt helpless to change it. As we were young, everyone had their life plans and sometimes YWB didn't fit with them. People left to travel overseas, because they got a part-time job or had found another cause that resonated – the reasons weren't personal, but I often took them that way. It took time for me to realise that this was just part of the process that had to be managed.

A particularly rough moment came during my second year of university. I'd just turned eighteen and was overseas on my first trip by myself and the organisation started to fall apart in my absence. At this time we hadn't yet heard about the success of Kamar Buku and a number of the long-term members had left the organisation. Meetings weren't being held, money wasn't being fundraised – we'd lost our momentum and I was wondering whether we should even bother to go on. Then a friend asked whether the reasons we started YWB still existed.

'Yeah, of course,' was my immediate response, 'nothing much has changed! Everyone is still competing for funding, loads of young people don't think they can change their communities . . .' I soon realised her point: if the problem was still there, then the organisation was still needed, right? We had started it for a reason and if that reason still existed, we needed to keep it moving forwards.

Our first real organisational breakthrough was inspired by my younger brother, who had just finished a life-changing vacation camp. The camp had kindled a love of aviation and aerospace in him, which eventually led to his mechanical and aerospace engineering career. I had been on a similar camp in grade twelve, and while chatting about it at YWB, we realised both camps were full of a very similar demographic to that of the big companies in Silicon Valley. In 2015, Google's employees were sixty per cent white and thirty-one per cent Asian – only nine per cent were black, Hispanic or other races. In a similar vein, only thirty per cent were women, with only eighteen per cent in the technical space. The engineering camps my brother and I had gone to had comparable percentages. Also, in addition to the lack of ethnic and gender diversity, everyone at the camp was from upper- or upper-middle-class neighbourhoods and schools, partly because it was prohibitively expensive.

When the YWB crew talked about the work we wanted to do, we realised we wanted it to be with kids who looked like us. We wanted to focus on students who faced a barrier in their life that we could help take down. Enter stage left: Spark Engineering Camp.

I've been told that learning happens when we're uncomfortable. Organising the Spark Engineering Camp was definitely one of those times – the steep learning curve and challenges I faced made me feel uncomfortable, proud and inspired, all at the same time.

Spark has evolved to be the heart of YWB. On the surface, it's an engineering camp for kids in grade ten to twelve run on university campuses through engineering faculties in Brisbane (University of Queensland) and Melbourne (University of Melbourne). In reality, it is an experience that empowers young people who face barriers (students who are asylum seekers, refugees, Indigenous, from low socio-economic or foster care homes and similar) to pursue further education and realise their potential. Although even that definition doesn't capture the essence of Spark. With Spark, YWB created the space we felt was missing, a place for students who wouldn't make it to the kind of engineering camp that Yasseen or I had gone to. Maybe they lived too far away, didn't have the money, didn't know about it or wouldn't have felt comfortable there. The engineering camp I went to in high school was snow-white and while there's nothing wrong with snow, it's definitely not every kid's natural habitat and can make for quite an intimidating and off-putting environment.

YWB was keen to hire an intern through AIESEC, a large student organisation that offers international interns and internships, but we didn't have enough money. We approached the Dean of Engineering to see if that faculty would sponsor us. This was the first time I'd set up a meeting with the explicit purpose of asking for money, and it made me uneasy, but it was necessary for our success.

I walked into that meeting prepped, and after a minute of small talk, launched into fifteen minutes of the hardest pitching I had done in my nineteen years. When I took my first breath, the Dean simply asked, 'How much are you looking for?'

He instantly gave us the seven thousand dollars we'd requested and I glided out of that room on cloud nine. Now to get the remaining twenty thousand with that same level of ease.

Unfortunately, we weren't so lucky with the rest. Who knew getting cash for a good cause was going to be so difficult? But in the meantime we had enough to employ ourselves an intern, so the real work of setting up the camp could begin.

We hired a lovely Sri Lankan student who believed in the vision of Spark. She seemed perfect to me because she got *why* we were running the camp and shared the values of the organisation . . . except she had no idea how to run a camp in a foreign country. She didn't understand the systems and we didn't understand that she needed more support. There were mismatched expectations all round. Nobody communicated to her what was expensive and what was cheap – so we spent thousands on polo shirts and didn't get enough butcher's paper, for example. It was a lesson in cross-cultural differences: this was not a person who was moving to Australia and trying to integrate; this was someone who wanted to learn how to do business in Australia but who came from a completely different world.

I hadn't even realised then that different people need different levels of support, of encouragement; that they sometimes need to be *led* in different ways. YWB could have got so much more out of the placement, and could have made our intern's experience so much richer, but we wasted the opportunity. It would be a long time before I admitted to myself that I had failed in this respect and that I would need to learn to provide more support for people, instead of expecting them simply to succeed because I had given them an opportunity. I was too young and inexperienced to recognise this, so our intern became another piece in the puzzle we didn't know how to put together.

We had begun contacting schools, building the program,

our general expectation being that fundraising would be easier once we had the foundations organised. We thought the money would come naturally, but as the date of the camp neared, people started asking us to pay invoices that no amount of fundraising barbecues were going to cover. We were eventually saved by another wonderful supporter from Engineers Australia, and the company of one of my previous mentors, after we begrudgingly started knocking on the doors available to us. It turns out people love being part of a successful, empowering journey once you frame it to them appropriately.

All our fingers, toes and appendages were crossed as we focused on sorting out the actual logistics of the camp; we had never done anything this big before and weren't sure how it would work out. Planning the camp activities was a little easier, as we were completely youth-led; we just thought about the activities we would like to do and made them part of the schedule. Bridge-building competitions? Check. Excursion to the CSIRO? Check. Creating your personal mission statement? Check. A day at the theme park to demonstrate the reality of engineering? Check. The best part about being a couple of eighteen- and nineteen-year-olds designing a camp was that we didn't have to think about what the 'young people' would want – we *were* the young people. When we needed help with the training, culture-creation and the details – like how to organise meal times and the best way to manage big groups – we asked some of our friends who had staffed other high school camps to give us some advice, crowd-sourcing the solutions.

The weeks leading up to the camp coincided with my demanding fourth-year exams, which made for a hectic month. I was running from one meeting to the next, missing most of my morning lectures, trying to keep the UQ race team going, scamming rides to uni from my best friend because, to top it all off, my car had broken down and I couldn't afford to replace the snapped timing belt!

Forty students had registered from around the country, and even though only twenty-two walked in the front door, as they arrived we knew we had created something special. They came from around Queensland, and all were ethnically diverse, or from the 'wrong end' of town. They were kids who had potential but who had never considered coming to a nerd camp before. All in our care, believing in us and the experience we had created. They changed our lives as much as we did theirs. They went from being students who didn't want to be at nerd camp, nominated by a teacher or parent who believed they had potential, to proud, confident ambassadors. The people who staffed the camp were other university students who stepped into the role of mentor. They were all friends from engineering who came from similar backgrounds to these school students or who understood and believed in the mission of the camp. We had an extremely high ratio of students to staff, almost two to one, meaning that each student got the connection and attention they deserved.

We were a small team, but the sleep deprivation, the excitement and the sheer insanity of it all brought us closer together, and we made it happen. Our planning had a few holes, so every night I stayed up with a couple of other team members to create the daily schedule and outline the roles for our mentors, printing off programs in the mechanical engineering computer labs and deliriously singing to hip hop tunes. During this time, I realised that even though I could get away with making up things on the run, that wasn't good enough if I wanted to take my team along with me. I needed to communicate where we were going so people felt like they were part of the journey, not just being led blindly.

The feedback at the end of the camp made the exhausting five days all worth it.

We knew we were onto a winning ticket with Spark, but the following year I was working so I asked a colleague if they would be willing to take over the planning. The experience ran smoothly, but messages were coming back to me that the culture of the camp had changed. I should have known that we were heading for a showdown.

Out on the rig, I woke at 3 pm for my night shift and switched on my computer to find an email saying that YWB was ill-equipped to handle Spark and that I should take a step back from my position.

I was sitting at my 'desk', a plank of plywood wedged between the bed and the side of the donga, and my stomach literally dropped. What was happening? I kept reading the email. It seemed to me that the person wanted to take the project away from the organisation. For the first time in my life, someone was making a move on something I had built, and it wasn't a nice feeling.

Oh, was I furious. This was not the point of Spark, not at all. It wasn't about who got to run it, or who got the credit – YWB was created to *avoid* this kind of fighting and competition. I was furious because Spark was meant as a safe haven. It was a place that was inclusive and supportive, a place where people felt as if they could be themselves, broaden their horizons and realise that their world could be so much bigger than they ever imagined. Spark was able to be that way because it was imbued with the values of YWB, and it made the students – all of them, not just the ones that 'fit the mould' – and the wholesome, inclusive experience the absolute priorities.

This email felt like it was trying to turn Spark into 'any other science camp', the beginning of the end of our dream. I was not going to let that happen.

Over the course of the next months, and eventually years, it was determined that Spark would stay a YWB program, but it was a relationship that needed careful management. We had brought in people who were used to a different way of operating. The culture these volunteers were from was the older, science and engineering camp atmosphere. We then realised how crucial it was for all the staff to understand why Spark existed.

I learnt the importance of ensuring I provided the right kind of support for my team rather than expecting them to know how to do everything involved with a job. After all, YWB is about empowering people and building their capacity, not just hiring people who know their path and potential already. I learnt how to fight for the project, as I truly believed in the original purpose of the camp. Spark is about empowering young people to see that they are valuable, and helping them realise that they are capable of doing things, even if they have never been told that before. It is about building capacity in the mentors while creating a safe space for all students. The camp is a melting pot of culture, language, belief and ability, and although that does make it a tough job, it's also what makes it worth doing.

Spark was also the first YWB project that my father believed in. Up until that point, he was in 'wait and see' mode, unconvinced our programs made a real difference. However, with Spark, I finally secured his approval: 'Ah, Yassmina! This is how we create change: we coach, we mentor, we *empower*. It's all about empowering.'

No matter how much I try to deny it, the approval of my parents means a huge amount to me.

Spark now runs in two states in Australia and changes the lives of more than one hundred students every year, with attendees from over forty different towns and cities. It has become a professional initiative in its own right, and the Spark-YWB team has taken it much further than I ever could have. The ability to take something fledgling and make it fly is a special skill. I owe it all to the likes of Lucy Shaw, Liam Nolan, Bianca Goebel, Avrithi Misthry and the others who drove Spark to magnificence and believed in it when nobody else quite did.

Chapter 17:

Why Should I Care?

As I waited for my colleague to let me into his apartment building where the drilling crew was having dinner, I looked down at the food I had brought: Sudanese lentils in a plastic container. It was the recipe my grandmother had taught me, a hearty meal, but in that moment it crossed my mind that it was a dish people would associate with refugees.

'Sorry, Yas,' the voice squawked out of the intercom. 'We'll come down to get ya now.'

It was the day before my TEDx talk and we'd just gone sailing as part of our work competition. A group of five to ten of us regularly went out on the boat once a week in the summer months, competing against other corporate teams from around the city. We would knock off early and cycle across the river to the little surf-cat store where the boats were moored – a true slice of heaven. Then, depending on who was in town, we would all head back across the river and grab dinner. Oilfield folk, particularly those in drilling, tend to blur the lines between work and friendship. Not many 'regular' folk understand the fly-in-fly-out nature of the rig life, or the expectation that you are always on call, no matter what, during operations. The intensity of the lifestyle brings people together, and in some ways they become your best friends, even your family.

There were spectacular views over the river from the apartment, and after a quick tour of the house I returned to the dining table and grudgingly pulled out my lentils.

The thick soup had been agitated in the container as I'd cycled from my house and some of the burnt-orange liquid had seeped around the outside of the seal. I sighed.

'Why don't you have some of this food, Yas?' the friend next to me asked. 'There's plenty and the butter chicken is the best!'

I smiled and thanked her, saying it likely wouldn't be halal – many take-out places in Australia aren't – but it turned out they'd checked before ordering and it was! I was fortunate in this situation, because one of the beauties of working in the oil patch – particularly with those from offshore – is that many of the people there are thoroughly multicultural and have either lived in a country with a completely different culture or worked closely with folks from around the world. There is less ignorance about day-to-day differences in an environment like that, so everyone sitting around me knew what the halal deal was all about.

Never one to pass up a free meal, I tucked into the butter chicken, and as the conversation ebbed and flowed, I joined in the way I often do when faced with a group of people who have different perspectives to mine – I started asking deep philosophical questions to find out how they think. The reasoning behind this isn't necessarily to change people's minds. My questions come from a place of curiosity and from a desire to understand people. I see it more like amateur anthropology –

using my social time to really get to know people and the environment around me and to hear different perspectives. The answers to my questions tend to either change my perspectives or enhance the understanding I already have.

When it comes to whether I try to convince people of my own perspectives, it depends on the situation. Changing minds takes time and I respect that other people have their own opinions. Asking certain questions, though, can sometimes plant a seed of doubt. Over time, that seed can grow depending on whether it is fertilised or poisoned . . .

The role of women on rigs is always fun to bring up, to see people's reactions. I ask guys what they think about it, women in leadership roles, how they feel about feminism, their comments on violence against women – anything controversial. Why not? It's a tailored sample group. The guys just tend to roll their eyes, although some answer and others ignore me. I've been called 'radical' for wanting to know so many things and asking so many questions. I simply say to them, 'Mate, please don't call me radical; people will get the wrong idea!'

That night, my mind was in a different space. I had yet to test run my TEDx speech in front of anyone to see if it would connect with audiences. I didn't feel ready to share it with my crew, so when I finished my butter chicken portion I started to make a move to get some more practice in front of the mirror at home, but a colleague jumped up before I could walk out the door. 'Hey, hey, hey! Didn't you say you were going to do your speech for me? You can do it right here!'

Doing the speech there was nerve-racking. I usually avoided bringing my rig life together with my world of community advocacy. I was also uneasy because unconscious bias – the theme I was speaking on – is a sensitive topic. Audiences that are not in the right frame of mind can easily go on the defensive and accuse you of calling them racist. But I was curious to see if I had framed my speech convincingly enough for oilfield folk, so I reluctantly nodded.

'Who is it targeted to?' another colleague, our host this evening, asked. He was a long-time oilfield drilling supervisor, and I wasn't at all sure how he would react to the speech.

'I guess the type of people who would listen to a TED talk?' I replied. 'The general public?' I hadn't thought about the audience explicitly at this point, but I put that out of my mind, took a couple of steps back from the dining table and began the speech.

I can walk down the street in the same outfit and the way I am treated and the world's expectations of who I am depends on the way I arrange the piece of cloth on my head. However, more broadly, it is not about focusing on the hijab per se, because Muslim women are more than the cloth that they choose to wrap – or not wrap – their head in.

This is about looking beyond your bias.

I threw out a few stats about the great impact unconscious bias has on our lives, before getting into my favourite story, which is used to illustrate that bias in our everyday thinking.

Take this example: A young boy and his father were in a horrific car accident. The father dies on impact, and the severely injured son is rushed to hospital. When they arrive, the surgeon looks at the young boy and declares they cannot operate.

Why?

'The boy is my son,' the surgeon says.

How can that be?

Of course, the surgeon is his mother. This is only an anecdote, but the reality of unconscious bias is backed up by evidence – how many of you initially pictured the surgeon as a man? If you have heard it a million times before, think about this: the number of female doctors and surgeons who have heard this story but also made the same assumption of a male surgeon would blow your mind.

Ultimately, the behaviours associated with these assumptions are a product of unconscious bias or implicit prejudice. This has been proven to have a significant effect on the diversity in our workforces, particularly in places of influence. Think of our current Australian Federal Cabinet.

The question to ask is: how can each and every one of us work to counter the effects of this pretty common phenomenon?

Now, one thing must be set straight from the outset. Unconscious bias is not an accusation of conscious discrimination, or saying that in every person there is a racist, sexist or ageist lurking within. We all have our biases, and these are the filters through which we take in the world around us. Bias is not an accusation here. Rather, it is something that should be identified, acknowledged, and mitigated against. The thing is, if we want to live in a world where the circumstances of your birth do not dictate your future and where equal opportunity is ubiquitous, then each and every one of us has a role to play in making sure unconscious bias does not determine our lives.

Remember to acknowledge your biases so you can look past them.

One of the most famous experiments around unconscious bias with gender was done within orchestras in the 1970s and 1980s. Prior to those decades, female musicians were quite rare, making up no more than five per cent of the top orchestras in the United States, and that was put down to the fact that men played differently, presumably better, or so they say.

The change was brought about through the adoption of a blind audition process. Rather than a face-to-face audition, the Boston Symphony Orchestra introduced the concept of playing behind a screen, in order to eliminate any bias. Interestingly, there was no major immediate change registered – until they began to instruct auditioners to take their shoes off before they entered the room. The click clack of the heels against hardwood was giving the ladies away.

With the introduction of this system of auditioning, the results of a study showed that women had a fifty per cent increased chance they would progress past the preliminary rounds and the move almost tripled the chance a lady would get hired.

What does this tell us? That although we may not know it, we do unconsciously exhibit cases of bias, no matter how forward-thinking we may think we are. I do it all the time myself; the trick is to consciously look past it.

Quite a lot of research has been done in this space going some way towards explaining why there are fewer women in senior positions and in the fields of science, technology, engineering and maths.

One of the solutions offered is a target or quota, and that is super divisive. Often, people resort to the idea of merit.

'I don't want to be hired because I am a woman, I want to be hired on merit. I want to know I am the best applicant for the job.' This is a pretty common sentiment that is shared among the female engineers I have worked and studied with. Yes, it is an understandable sentiment. However, if life was about merit, why would identical resumes be treated differently, such as in the case of the 2012 Yale study showing identical applications for a lab position still had the female applicant being deemed less competent and less likely to get the job?

I always sighed when I read this part of the speech. Some people still think that merit is what gets people jobs when in fact it is also about networks, connections, who you know, who knows you, and their subconscious and conscious impressions of you.

Funnily enough, there may be some research that provides an answer: something known as the merit paradox. In companies that talked about 'merit' being important as an organisational value – for gender and for race – men were more likely than women to be selected, and awarded salary increases. Ironically, this only occurred in companies that emphasised merit as a basis of selection.

Interestingly, the fact that I'm a woman who works on the rigs is way more remarkable than the fact that I'm brown or Muslim. To be fair, most of the guys just can't believe a woman would *choose* to work on the rigs. But it is entertaining. I remember when I told one of the guys I wanted to learn how to surf.

'You won't be able to surf with all that gear you got on. I don't know any women-only beaches either . . .'

'Nah, mate, all good,' I told him. 'I've got an outfit that I wear to the beach.'

'Oh, you could start a new clothing range – beach and surf wear for Muslim chicks. You run that youth organisation, yeah? You could change it. Youth without board shorts.'

I also remember once being asked if I'd eaten some of the yoghurt from the fridge: 'You should keep eating that! It's the only culture you'll get around here!'

Unfortunately there is a little bit of truth to that, and particularly at tables where influential decisions are made.

In 2010, the Australian National University sent out over four thousand identical job applications for entry-level jobs. In order to get as many interviews as an applicant with an Anglo-Saxon name, someone with a Chinese name would need to submit 68 per cent more applications, someone with a Middle Eastern name an extra 64 per cent and someone with an Italian name, only 12 per cent, but still more.

If you look at the top tech companies in the States as another hub of influence, they're not doing great either. Google's ethnicity data released this year indicated their US workforce is 61 per cent white, 30 per cent Asian, and the other 9 per cent a mix of others. The rest of the tech companies who released data are no different. Although those numbers might seem decent, a recent study by Green Park – Britain's leading supplier of senior execs – shows that these numbers don't trickle up.

More than half of FTSE100 companies have no non-white leaders at board level, whether executive or non-executive; and two-thirds have no full-time minority executives at board level. Also, the study says, minority leaders feature disproportionately as non-executive board directors: as a consequence their true level of influence is far smaller than their numbers suggest.

We've identified there is a problem. What do we do about it? Interestingly, the author of the gender resume experiment offered a solution of sorts. 'If you look at the paths of successful women, there is one thing they have in common by and large: they all had good mentors.' Aha. Mentoring, sponsoring . . . we've heard it hundreds of times before. But let me offer this as a solution. I challenge each and every one of you to mentor someone different.

Think about it. We are attracted to mentoring people who look like us, who are familiar, who remind us of us. You might meet a number of people at a networking event, but if someone went to the same school as you and supports the same footy team, you're probably more likely to connect and offer advice that will help them on their way. For the individual in the room who has no shared experience, it becomes a little more difficult. The idea behind looking for what isn't always familiar is to open doors for those who don't usually have access to that hallway. Part of the challenge with diversity is the fact that there is lack of equality of opportunity.

People like me aren't born with the opportunities. I was born in one of the globe's poorest cities, Khartoum. I was born brown, a female, and a Muslim in a world that is pretty suspicious of us for reasons that have nothing to do with me at all. Yet, here I am, talking to you.

Yes, I've had my share of privilege: amazing parents, education and the blessing of migrating to a country that gives me all the opportunity I can grab. But I've also had the blessing of mentors who have opened doors beyond my wildest imaginings.

I'm not the only one either. There are many examples of men and women who have been given a break by a mentor from a different community. A young man in Sydney for example, whose mentor showed him how to set up the Bankstown Poetry Slam event, which has grown and become a big part of the cultural scene. Or a fellow Muslim lady, who arrived as a refugee from Afghanistan and with the help of mentors became a doctor, taking out the Young Queenslander of the Year award in 2008 for her efforts.

Would you have picked me as someone to mentor if you'd seen me in another version of who I am or another presentation of myself?

I challenge you to pick someone who seems to sit at the opposite end of your spectrum. Structural change is going to take ages – history tells us this. I don't have that level of patience. Mentor someone different. Rather than thinking the issue of diversity is someone else's problem to fix, understand that you're part of the system and can be part of the solution. If you don't know where to go to find someone different, go to the places you would not usually find yourself.

If you usually enrol in private high school mentoring circles, try offering your services at a state school or visit your local refugee tutoring centre. Go out for coffee with that new graduate who looks out of place, without it being a tokenistic gesture but because you truly want to open doors and learn about their way of seeing the world.

Diversity is where the magic happens.

> And remember to always look past your first impression,
> because I bet you, it's probably wrong.

As I closed it out, silence rang in the air.

'Okay . . .' tonight's host said, looking at me sceptically while the other drilling engineers in the room applauded lightly. 'It was okay, yeah, but why should I care?'

'Yeah,' another engineer nodded. 'You know, I used to be like you, idealistic and doing all sorts of things, but you got to realise that people just are the way they are, you know? You can't change everyone 'cause a few people are a little bit selfish.'

'Yeah, Yassmin – why should I go out of my way to help others and open doors for them? I've got my own problems. I've got my divorce, we all have bills to pay . . .'

I looked at my colleagues as they questioned not my arguments, but the very premise of my value system. I was actually at a loss for words.

They were asking *why*? *Why* they should help others? Why they should go out of their way to make a difference in this world? Dumbfounded, I struggled to formulate a response. 'Because we could? Because we have the ability to?' I tried different options, but none of them resonated.

'Then why should I help someone else who is really different? Why not help someone who I can relate to, who looks like me?'

'But diversity is good!' I interjected.

'Says who?'

They thought I was being too idealistic. I needed to pick an alternative angle and so I put up my hands in front of me, holding back the barrage of criticism. This was what I had needed to hear, but I hadn't expected it to be quite so vehement.

I thought I would try a different tack and use language that appealed to their good ol' Aussie values. 'Guys, gals. Do we live in a country where everyone gets a fair go? Do we want to live in a world where everyone gets a fair chance? If we want to live in that world, we all have to be a part of making that happen.'

My colleague sat back in his seat and his expression softened slightly. 'There you go. Right, I can see your point there. Make sure you put that in, okay? You gotta show me why I should care about some people who have nothing to do with me and who will give me nothing back.'

I made some notes on my script, thanked the crew and wandered out, slightly readier to tackle the challenges ahead.

Every now and again I am reminded by moments like this of the battles we still need to be fighting.

University researchers from Carnegie Mellon in the United States found that Google's ad-targeting had in-built bias. Male web users were six times more likely than female web users to be shown ads for high-paying jobs. Isn't this terrifying? Computers aren't biased but the programmers are, due to their demographics, which – no prize for guessing – are overwhelmingly white and male. Without even realising it, programmers are unconsciously embedding their own personal bias in the code and arbitrarily reducing opportunities for those who don't fit the norm. That is the insidious nature of bias.

Are these norms something we want to entrench or change? It comes down to thinking about the structural and institutional biases that exist in our systems. The status quo doesn't exist because that is the natural order of things; it has evolved this way because of historical reasons and the beliefs and biases both men and women have about gender roles.

We simply expect women to be less ambitious, and trust men to do the job. So often people don't see the need to change anything. There is a need for change, because the world isn't perfect. Whether we like it or not, whether it is easy or not, we need more diversity (or, in the words of Shonda Rhimes, we need to *normalise* our leadership) because that makes for better, fairer more equal societies. Those who deny the power of diversity usually somehow benefit from the status quo and don't want to see change. Change is happenin', baby. Brace yourselves.

But perhaps that is uncharitable. Perhaps people who aren't interested in change, simply don't care because they have never needed to. What the experience with my colleagues taught me is that you can't just expect people to care. Different people have different capacities for charitable thought; and in the West, caring about each other is seen by many as a luxury and not the standard expectation. This is one of the reasons a cousin of mine said she would never live in Australia after she had spent a few months visiting here. She said, 'It seems like no one cares about anyone else at all in this country.'

It's true and it can be both freeing and limiting. Caring about number one makes decisions easier. With only yourself to think about, you can technically do whatever you want without considering the consequences your actions have on anyone else. Caring can be exhausting – taking on the burdens of others isn't always easy. That kind of individualism has the potential to create a lonely space, though, and a lonely country.

That's not to say that people don't care about each other at all, but the level of care and affection that you see between strangers in the street in Sudan is worlds away from the way strangers interact on the street here in Australia. The public space is much more 'interactive' in Sudan; people greet one another and prioritise making friends with each other instead of efficiently 'getting down to business'. If someone needs help with something like a flat tyre, men will come running out of cars and buildings nearby, scrambling to help out. It's like one giant family.

The challenge is then to not only convince people they should care about others, but to convince individualistic societies that they should care – particularly about those who are different, marginalised and most in need of help. Large-scale movements of people around the world are happening everywhere and we have to adapt with empathy. Whether it be for asylum seekers or for those who suffer from violence in their homes, we need to care about each other to make the lives of each and every individual the best it possibly can be and to give every human the fair go they deserve.

Chapter 18:

Grindin' My Gears

Right before I started university, someone told me that engineering was full of cute guys. What they failed to mention was that my classes would be almost entirely full of guys, cute or not.

First year was manageable; there were about 160 women in a class of almost 1000. Coming into second year in mechanical engineering the number of women dropped from 16 per cent to 5 per cent, then down to only 2.5 per cent in my graduating class. I was always the odd one out; university was no different. So what does a teenager do when she is once again in the minority?

She adapts, all over again.

I remember walking into the first lecture for ENGG1000, the foundation engineering course that everyone had to take, and thinking *daiiiiim*. I wasn't frightened or awed, but just aware that there were *so many guys*. The next thing I did was scan the crowd – were there any other brown people like me? A couple. Were there any other hijabied girls? Nope! Were any of them engineering camp kids, or kids from my school that I could become friends with? Yaaaaaas!

I found a few lads from my school who had chosen the same course, so my crew for first year was a mix of engineering camp friends, school mates and the other brown people in the class. There were so few people of colour (POC) doing engineering at a Group of Eight university in 2008 that we only made up one crew. That's changing now, partly due to the Youth Without Borders engineering camp we created, and also because Brisbane's demographic is shifting. By the end of our degree, everyone knew the POC engineering crew: we were loud and unapologetic and sat up the back, occasionally causing more disruption than we were worth.

First year was my most disciplined year; I would try to get to class early, sit up the front and listen to the lecture. As the months and years went on, I migrated further and further away, until eventually I was one of the back-seat bandits, graffitiing the desks and talking trash – quite a change from the academic character I was at school. I liked the idea of being a 'rebel' (as much as I could be as a non-drinking, non-smoking Muslim chick), particularly when I'd been such a well behaved student all through high school; I was trying on a new identity. I became 'one of the boys' whenever I could, expecting jokes about making sandwiches and doing the ironing, sometimes even cracking them myself – because hell, you have to work with your audience, right? I had no idea what being an engineering feminist was about; the concept of feminism hadn't really entered my radar.

Mechanical engineering only had a few women – six to be exact, and we were all such different characters.

One was the classic tomboy – cool, because she always seemed so sure of herself. A super hard worker, great dancer and quick with a retort, she was also dependable, and the person with whom I always checked over my answers, because we approached questions in different ways but learnt well from one another. She was the first person I met at uni after she offered me a lift at the end of a pre-uni UQ race team meet-up. As she babbled about her love for cars, it was obvious we were going to be friends; then, as we buckled up, she said something that cemented our relationship: 'Uh, so, just to let you know, I'm kind of into hectic tunes –' T.I. burst out of her speakers as she turned the ignition, the rapper spitting rhymes that went a mile a minute, bass pounding out of a subwoofer I hadn't even noticed. I looked over at the slim white blonde girl in the driver's seat and thought, *Well! Can't judge a book by its cover!*

Another was an unexpected friend because she was more typically feminine than my usual mates, always up for a laugh but totally committed to making it as an engineer. A lot of the guys seemed to want to ask her out, so she probably broke more hearts than she realised. She was the person I commiserated with over life's problems, who was happy to vent or talk about feelings; she wasn't a stereotypical engineer but rather an example of how there's more than one type.

All the girls were whip smart; I'm pretty sure they got top marks. And even though we had our own tribes, we congregated to share common frustrations as well as solutions. Different rules to those of the rest of society seem to apply in the world of engineering studies, and we were left to figure out how to negotiate this masculine world. There were no networking events for women to talk about how to handle kitchen jokes and whether you should laugh at a rape gag. There was a prevailing view that we 'weren't like other chicks' – that we could 'handle ourselves', a viewpoint I've since realised can be damaging because it creates a divide between women that serves no positive purpose. At the time, it was how we survived and it played right into the character I wanted to be: the strong woman who could handle herself.

Feminism just didn't seem like something that applied to my situation. I talked about representing women on boards, but in the world of engineering? I wanted to get a job and have friends; I didn't want all the lads to think I hated men. This was an attitude I think us girls shared: we just wanted to fit in, and didn't need the guys to think of us in any other way. There have been studies that show that is how most female engineering students cope. The struggle was real, but even so my UQ days were special and once I made the decision to do engineering, I never looked back.

University life was just as much about developing YWB as it was about engineering. I brought some of the engineering lads and ladies I was friends with into the organisation, and co-opted even more into helping us fundraise for our projects. Working on a community based not-for-profit was new for most of them and was a chance to develop different skills, although ironically it led to an organisation with slightly less diversity. At one point, the YWB board was made up of three Johns, a Jason and a Yassmin, and we were all mechanical engineers!

YWB regularly organised fundraising barbecues – a practical, volunteer activity that anyone could get involved in and thus brought together a wide range of people. The engineers handled the logistics: they had utes, the barbecue equipment and always knew people who were hungry for a snag. Then the various humanities and science students would sell our delicious wares and ensure the customers had some idea of who we were and what we did.

I learnt a lot about the different types of volunteers we could depend on – vital information when you're involved in running a not-for-profit. Some people like being part of the planning; they get satisfaction out of organising an event without necessarily being part of its execution. Our work with Kamar Buku worked that way: YWB helped organise the library, and although our contribution wasn't direct, the pay-off came in knowing the result of our planning had changed lives. Most YWB projects require an enormous amount of this type of volunteering: the behind-the-scenes work that can make or break a project.

The second type of volunteer was the kind who liked to help organise as long as they could be part of the pay-off, and these people had to be constantly engaged in local activities so they could participate directly. We would lose them quickly if there wasn't something they could get involved in.

The third type just liked to be called up on the day and told to be hands-on; they are the kind who enjoy a working bee. All of these were well catered for by a YWB barbecue.

It was often hard to focus on study when so much else was going on!

I remember at times thinking the workload was the worst thing. All my friends who did degrees like arts, law, psychology or science had at least one day off from lectures; they always seemed to be chilling, enjoying the weather on the Great Court, while the engineering students were in labs, working on computer modelling that wouldn't function, problems that couldn't be solved and group assignments that people didn't contribute to. Well, that's what it felt like at the time.

It could also be fun. Yes, it was hard, but it wasn't impossible. In fact, studying engineering is quite different to actually working in engineering in that they train you in the principles first, then show you the easy way to do it afterwards. It was like studying fashion design by first learning how to make cotton; then you get to a fashion house and realise you can just *buy* cotton!

During my initial lecture for a basic first-year subject, the teacher displayed Schrödinger's equation, which, according to wiki, is a 'partial differential equation that describes how the quantum state of a quantum system changes with time'. WTF, right?

Time-dependent Schrödinger equation *(general)*

$$i\hbar\frac{\partial}{\partial t}\Psi(\mathbf{r}, t) = \hat{H}\Psi(\mathbf{r}, t)$$

Time-dependent Schrödinger equation
(single non-relativistic particle)

$$i\hbar\frac{\partial}{\partial t}\Psi(\mathbf{r}, t) = \left[\frac{-\hbar^2}{2\mu}\nabla^2 + V(\mathbf{r}, t)\right]\Psi(\mathbf{r}, t)$$

I remember looking at the projector screen and thinking, *Oh, my lord, I am going to fail this course. There is no way I can do this.*

Fortunately, it was just one of those tactics lecturers use to scare people off, like the massive workload we were given in first year that saw a lot of people drop out. By the time you get to second and eventually third year, all who are left are the few students who actually want to do engineering.

Perhaps because of its intensity, studying engineering was like adopting a family; comradery and banter kept us tight. After five days of classes a week together, pretty much everyone had reputations and nicknames; there were the ethnic kids, the race car crew, the rugby shorts boys, the grammar school boys.

Everyone also drank a lot. I've never drunk alcohol and never will because of my religion, so the heavy drinking culture could have been excluding. I was fortunate because I didn't need alcohol to socialise; having a loud, outgoing personality helped. But generally at university, if you want to engage with any of the big organisations, like the student societies, it seems you have to be able to drink – and drink hard. Your 'piss fitness' is a sign of your masculinity, an indicator of your worth. I remember the organiser in engineering camp saying to us, 'If you don't drink beer, you can't be an engineer!'

I don't judge others for drinking; as almost the entire Western engineering world drinks, it would be pointless to criticise. I would be curious to see what engineers in majority Muslim countries do to socialise and whether I would have thrived in those groups.

Maybe that's partly why I loved YWB and the UQ race team – neither group was formed around alcohol, so the environments never made me feel uncomfortable. When I first started engineering my father warned me there would be many spaces that weren't suitable for me: 'Find your own space, create your own clubs and environments that fit for you. People who share the same viewpoint will come to it.' Without thinking, that's what happened with YWB and, eventually, the racing team.

I ran the UQ race team at university – and by race I mean race car – competing in the Australasian Formula of Society of Automotive Engineering Annual (F-SAE) Competition. The F-SAE is the local chapter of an international competition where all the universities around Australia and the Asia–Pacific region build a car and then participate in something called a 'comp'.

Comp was a combination of static and dynamic events. The static event involved various presentations about the design, cost and marketability of the car. The dynamic element was a series of challenges including acceleration and endurance, among others.

The year before I became the leader was the first time UQ had competed in three years, and we came last in a field of twenty-seven. Our plan in 2011 was to better that – our stretch target was to come in the top ten, but we knew that was optimistic. Either way, our aim was to get the car to comp and to finish every single event without breaking down and being disqualified. The previous year they'd been close to completing all of the events, but didn't quite make it. We wanted to change it up.

I got involved in the team in the first year of uni, left for the second year to try out other things but was drawn back to contributing in the role of marketing lead in the third year. By fourth year, I was the boss, although I hadn't planned to be. I was handed the position of Team Principal when the outgoing one asked me to take over the reins. I wasn't ready to demand the right to lead in that technical space, so I don't think I would have put my hand up for it, but I relished the opportunity when it was given to me. In the race team, leadership and respect had to be earned. Positions of authority usually came if you were technically brilliant and the smartest car person in the room (which I openly admit I wasn't), or by being selected by the predecessors. It was a unique chance to lead a technical project with a rowdy bunch of lads and the occasional rowdy lady.

It was not my technical prowess that landed me the job but more my ability to bring people together around a common cause. I was focused on building a legacy for the team rather than simply winning in my year, and that was recognised by my seniors. It was a chance for us to set the team up for years of success to come, and the success of recent years is testament to that work.

The cool thing about being the leader was that I could shape the team the way I saw fit because I was the boss – and I wanted it to be an inclusive space. The year I ran UQ racing we didn't have huge piss-ups like they did every other year – and sure, some of the guys might have found that boring and didn't like the fact they didn't have crazy stories to tell, but I have no doubt there were some folk who didn't mind the simple pleasures of just hanging and working on the car.

They called me Mum.

I didn't mind it; it was better than 'bitch', 'oi', or a bunch of other names that I could have potentially been called (some unprintable). In a way, 'Mum' was endearing. The team wasn't used to being led by a woman and the last female leader in their lives could very well have been their own mum! They associated me with a motherly figure and I guess the only shame is that they didn't have in mind a female leader other than their mother to draw on. I chose to take it as a compliment. They showed me respect, which I needed in order to lead the group well.

My acceptance of the term could also be linked to my recognition that mothers in Sudan hold a lot of power in the household and in the private sphere. You're often not considered a real woman until you are a mother (which is problematic but that's another conversation), so there's leadership potential in embracing the role of a mother figure. It becomes an issue when women are only allowed to access a leadership position through this motherhood lens, reinforcing traditional gender roles.

I got so used to the nickname that a few weeks after the competition when I was in a shopping centre and heard someone yell out 'Mum!', I looked around.

Women were accepted in the race team, but often joked about. Occasionally, if you weren't paying attention, one of the guys would flip his testicles out of his fly and continue to walk around casually until someone clued onto it: 'Oh, man – put it away!'

Everyone would spin around and get an eyeful then instantly turn back, groaning loudly. Weird, right?

I was never a fan of the old 'flipping out the balls' look, usually swearing at the offender and walking away. Fortunately, my teammates kept their balls to themselves most of the time, which I like to think was out of respect for the girls in the team. They were boys learning to become men, refining their attitudes towards women, but taking their guidance from their peers, pop culture and porn. They were good guys, and they continue to be some of my best friends, but it was an environment where jokes about women were pretty common. I'd often use the same jokes to make a point or to register my outrage with humour. 'I ain't making you a goddamn sandwich, boy, get it yourself!' is what I would often say when asked to do something associated with traditional gender roles, like cook or clean. It was a technique that would always get a laugh while subtly pointing out the disparity.

I'm not sure if joining in was the optimum way to deal with this masculine world, but I did the best I could at the time. My parents had grown up in a different culture and so I couldn't apply their advice directly. There were no female mechanical engineering lecturers or professors I could ask for guidance. I learnt to survive and thrive in the environment in the only way I knew how and figured it out along the way. I did my best to lead like a woman, creating an inclusive environment, ironing out arguments before they became fights and generally treating the boys like my big extended family. I was the matriarch, and kept everyone in line. It wasn't about being overbearing; it was about ensuring every person enjoyed their experience and felt valued. If you weren't on board, you would have to deal with Mama Yassmin.

I took no prisoners. Sure, I was happy to joke around and banter, even if that sometimes strayed into objectification, but I wasn't afraid to shut it down and have a difficult conversation, usually about work (or lack thereof). Around the engineering boys, if I wanted respect I had to keep my language logical, systematic and rational. I also had respect from the university for my community work and decent grades, which helped give me more authority. It was common knowledge that if you joined the race team you would probably fail a few subjects, but that wasn't an option for me so I ran the team and still got top marks. Just because they said it hadn't been done before doesn't mean it couldn't be done! Like with anything else, it was about having priorities.

I had a limited social life, meaning I didn't go out every night and partayyy; not only would my parents have killed me (I am still a Muslim, after all), but there was just no time for it. I let myself have Friday night off from uni work, and usually Saturday as well, which meant that I could have some social life, and it gave my mind a rest.

The other breakthrough was realising that to get high distinctions I only needed 85 per cent. My father pointed this out to me in first year after I spent ten minutes venting about not being able to get something perfect.

'No matter how perfect it is, no one will care whether you got 85 per cent or 100 per cent. Either will get you a high distinction, so you only need to learn up to 85 per cent and then move on. You don't have the time to learn everything to 100 per cent.'

It was a revelation! Yes, I could work super hard and try to consistently get 90s, but then I wouldn't have enough time to do everything else I wanted to do. So I studied enough to get me up to 85 per cent, which may sound unethical to some people but it worked for me!

I also made good use of my time. Don't get me wrong – I binge-watch TV shows, love chatting to people, and can waste time with the best of them. I used to joke that I only ever went to uni to socialise because I did almost no work when I entered a lab; I'm sure I pissed off quite a few people that way. Actually, I know I did, because I was once referred to as a 'loud-mouthed-bitch' by someone who I had obviously annoyed with my laughter and terrible jokes. Luckily, I had friends who quickly corrected that individual's language. The offending lad was in the lab looking at a computer I had been using and left logged in. It gave him the opportunity to start venting about me, until a couple of friends sitting nearby took it upon themselves to tell him to stop, because 'Yassmin's got more mates in here than you realise'. They relayed the story to me with pride; the same guys who would spend all day 'hanging shit' on me, now had my back. That's how engineering worked. How good is it having mates who stick up for you?

People must have thought I did no work, but I had a secret studying technique that I used way before it was cool. I would break time down into half-hour blocks and during that half an hour, no distractions were allowed – no Facebook, no phone, no walking around, nothing. At first, it was hard to concentrate for more than fifteen minutes in a row, as we're all so used to being distracted and multi-tasking. Eventually you start making the most of the time, and when your time is used efficiently it leaves more space in your life for whatever else you want to do.

Part of the respect from the team also came from how I presented myself to the guys. At no point did I doubt in my mind I had the right to be there, and I also never involved myself romantically with any guys in the team or in my grade. I wasn't going to mix business with pleasure, and being a Muslim was definitely a helpful factor in that equation. Perhaps because I was off the table as a sexual conquest, they were able to see me as their peer. I asked a few of them recently why they thought I was able to lead the team and be given respect and, after a couple of conversations, some themes emerged.

One was my commitment to the actual team and the work. It seemed, rightly or wrongly, that some of the guys felt like girls would come in, 'window shop' and leave. I came in obviously wanting to get involved, putting my hands up to do things; I didn't complain and I seemed interested. I wasn't shy, and I immediately started asking questions. I jostled for my position in the pecking order. Because I was willing to be engaged and get amongst it, I soon became known by the others in the team and started being part of the family rather than that strange cousin who just rocks up to occasional family get-togethers. As one of the boys said, 'You acted like a newbie guy.'

I also worked hard, and people could see that. I designed the chassis, and also organised a specialised TAFE course that was just for the F-SAE students that included the basics of hand tools, TIG welding and all sorts of skills. I convinced the university to provide us improved levels of access, I worked on increasing the team's professionalism, and I kept the guys in line. The guys could see that I cared about the team and they respected that – and they also respected that I could do things that they didn't even know were possible.

Another bloke told me I seemed like a career woman, which actually made the guys feel more comfortable in my presence because having a relationship with me was off the table.

When it came to balancing my uni work with YWB and the

race team, it made an enormous difference that I didn't drink and was living with parents who expected me to be home at a reasonable hour every night. Not drinking meant that my Saturdays and Sundays were actually useful. I would wake up relatively (relatively – 10 am!) early on a Saturday, do my part of the weekly house cleaning and then chill out with the family on Saturday afternoons. I would usually begin uni homework on Saturday night, attend a YWB meeting Sunday morning, then come home to do the rest of my university study and YWB work. I had a fairly solid routine, and it made my time pretty effective. I loved it and knew no different.

I write this chapter not to criticise the environment of the race team or engineering; politically incorrect, occasionally casually racist and only slightly misogynistic, but because I was there and at the time, enabled and legitimised it – even perhaps had fun with it. This is simply a reflection and record of what that culture was like. Perhaps it is changing, or perhaps I was able to get a real insight into what life is like in a boy's world.

My reflections don't give the boys the credit they deserve. There was a reason that my brother says that I had no life apart from the race team in my last couple of years at uni. These were the guys I could call at any time of the night to help tow a car, who would offer to beat up a guy if he hurt my feelings, who would give me a place to crash if I needed somewhere to sleep. They would never pay attention to my accolades, but would respect my ability to design a chassis. These were the type of guys who would probably bail me out from jail if I ever needed it, but then mercilessly take the piss for years to come.

Some of the best laughs and adventures I had at uni were with the race team. We learnt to weld together; they taught me how to rip skids, tie-wire bolts in place, and take a corner perfectly.

We'd hit the mountains together in the dead of night; convoys of souped-up and not-so-souped-up cars and bikes snaking their way up Mount Coot-tha, Mount Nebo and, once in a while, all the way to Maleny.

They may have taken the piss, but I somehow earned my place. They made me feel like I belonged, no questions asked.

Chapter 19:

For the Love of Speed . . .

It was a Rotary Club badge that gave me my next big break.

I was in my third year of university when the Head of the Institute of Mechanical Engineers from the UK came to visit the University of Queensland. He was an older man, exactly how I imagined an English engineer – distinguished and proper.

This guy was motorsport gold. He had contacts with all the cool companies in the UK and I knew he would be my ticket to a job in F1, if I could somehow try to approach him. I'd been invited to a lunch panel with him along with a few other students, my prime chance to make an impression, but I just couldn't seem to find a way in. I was starting to lose hope by the time the session was winding up, until he stood up to leave and I realised he was wearing a large familiar badge.

'Oh, are you with Rotary?' I asked.

His demeanour changed almost instantly. 'Oh yes, I love Rotary!'

The nearby Rotary Club had sponsored me to attend a conference in Sydney and I said I'd be happy to connect him when he was next in town. I then mentioned I was interested in coming to the UK to work in the automotive sector, and he gave me my golden ticket: 'Here's my card, get in touch and we'll see what we can do.'

Oh, did I get in touch: I emailed his team, on and off, for almost nine months, trying to secure some work experience until my polite harassment worked, and I was placed in a *paying* vacation job in February 2011 with a company called Ricardo in the south of England. It was the perfect gig and I visited their website almost daily, unbelievably joyful that I was going there. I saved up my tutoring and scholarship money, flew to the UK at the end of January and got ready for the best experience of my life.

It was the best half-day of my life.

My new boss was personable and excited to have me, and as he was telling me about the cool projects I was going to be working on, helping develop new technology for more environmentally friendly systems, mate, I walked past two McLaren F1s! I had made it – I was nineteen and had somehow hustled a real job in one of the best motorsport companies in the world, and I'd done it almost entirely off my own back. Excited doesn't even begin to cover it.

It wasn't until after lunch when HR called me that things began to unravel.

'Yassmin, do you mind bringing over your work visa?'

I told her I'd thought the company had sorted out my visa.

'Oh no, we never look after visa applications,' she informed me. 'It's always the employee's responsibility. Well, if you don't have a work visa you can't be an employee, and if you're not an employee we can't have you on the premises. You're going to have to leave.'

They kicked me out.

It was the most embarrassing, humiliating, wretched experience I had ever had. I was certain the person who organised my contract had assured me there was nothing more I needed to do. Somehow, I had missed out on a crucial part of the whole process and just came in on a tourist visa. Ironically, my dad was studying to be a migration agent at the time.

I slunk back to my uncle's house in Southampton, an hour's train ride away, miserable and defeated. I tried to find a way around it but the only option was to fly back to Australia, get the visa and return, and I just didn't have enough money.

So I sat on my uncle's couch for about a week, watching *EastEnders* and feeling sorry for myself while my uncle tore me a new one. 'You didn't even sort your visa out? What is this! Why are you sitting on the couch wasting your time! Do you even want to work in this industry! Go out and do something!'

I was trying to find other things to do, but I just needed some time to feel miserable. There was no sympathy from my uncle, who didn't think I belonged in the automotive world anyway. He didn't buy it as my true passion.

I was racked with shame, anger and frustration that I had got so close to my dream to have it thwarted by something so innocuous. A visa! I couldn't believe that no one at the embassy could help me, that no one even seemed to care. I wondered whether it would have been different if I'd been someone with 'connections'. It was probably the first time I had messed up so badly, and I had nothing and no one else to blame but myself. I kept kicking myself for not paying more attention, or asking the right questions. I couldn't believe it was a situation there was no quick recovery from. My parents didn't seem to think it was as catastrophic as I did and had little pity – they just told me to 'find a way around it' and take it on the chin.

I decided they were right and that I needed to do something about the situation. Who could I meet in the UK?

I had a few contacts from the *Age* article – a documentary filmmaker who wanted to chart my story (if only there was a story to chart) and someone who ran a race team in the USA, who'd told me to meet up with his friend who taught the motorsport Masters at Cranfield University, if I was ever in the UK.

I emailed around and organised times to meet, but when I told my uncle I was meeting people I only knew through the internet, he was worried and wanted me to cancel the appointments. When I disobeyed and met with people anyway he called my mother and told her that I was out of control, that I was immature and a danger to myself.

'The thing is, Yassmin,' he said to me in frustration, 'I sit at work fearing I'll get a phone call from the police telling me they've found you dead in some gutter. You're causing me so much stress!'

My uncle's fears were based on his own experiences in the UK, which had often been far from happy. Apparently, people in the countryside weren't fans of African migrants, particularly educated ones like my uncle, who would fight back, verbally and physically. He'd suffered from some dangerous racism in the 1980s and 1990s, and at one point had almost been killed, so it's no wonder he was worried for me. But he didn't explain this at the time, or perhaps I just wasn't able to hear him. I couldn't understand why he didn't see I could handle myself; I thought he was just trying to control me. I was used to the trust and relative freedoms my parents had allowed. He had a different view on how young women should act and I didn't quite adhere to those principles.

Don't get me wrong, my time with my uncle was otherwise thoroughly enjoyable. We would have nights sitting on the couch, watching Michael McIntyre make ridiculous jokes – we both loved stand-up comedy. When the rest of his family returned from overseas, we went to restaurants for dinner together, a little bit of normalcy.

Family problems aside, I made something of the trip.

The contact from Cranfield University was a great person to meet, and he helped me for years thereafter to make my way through the industry. He linked me up with a whole lot of contacts so for the next few weeks I travelled hundreds of kilometres by train, meeting people all around the UK: small race team business owners who manufactured their own cars; the CEOs of big companies like Protech and Triple Eight; influences in Williams F1; the Head of the Institute of Mechanical Engineers; and some of the best chassis and F1 designers in the world. By the end of the trip I had actually constructed a better network in the motorsport industry than I could have ever hoped for. I got accustomed to waiting at random stations around the country, hanging out at Milton Keynes and getting taxis into country towns that were more than a little *Midsomer Murders*. Sure, I was dirt poor and still didn't have a job, but I had contacts, and that was important. I accomplished a lot, but I think I'll always wonder: what if I had just got that damn visa?

On my last morning in England my uncle asked me a simple question: 'You say you want to dedicate your life to motorsport, huh. When you wake up in the morning, what's the first thing you think about?'

'People,' I replied, without hesitation. 'Working with people, helping people –'

Then I realised his point. 'Oh, and motorsport, of course!' But the damage was done, and it was a thought that sat in the back of my head for months and years to come.

★ ★ ★

I went back to do my final year of university at UQ and enrolled in the Masters in Motorsport at Cranfield for the year after. Most of the Cranfield graduates ended up in F1 teams so this was my in.

I got a call from the university at the beginning of 2012, offering me another once-in-a-lifetime opportunity – work experience as an engineer and designer with Mercedes F1 that would lead into my Masters and would help me secure a job with them after I graduated. It was a chance to work in a real F1 team, at the cutting edge of technology and designing stuff that would actually go on to compete in – and hopefully win – races.

This was before Merc started winning and they were still finding their way, so it would have been the perfect time to join. But it was unpaid work, and I couldn't afford to live in England while I did it. My parents hadn't financially supported me since I finished school and I wasn't about to change that now. I had been living at home while I was at uni in Australia, but I had covered all the rest of my expenses with tutoring and scholarship funds. I would need more than that kind of money to last a few months in England and my parents would not have been able to afford that.

Motorsport is a prohibitively expensive sport in which to compete. Many people who are able to enter it come from money; if not, their families make the financial sacrifice to support them. My parents had sacrificed a lot, but this was the level of support they couldn't provide – and I would never ask them to either.

After saying no to Merc, the reality of the opportunity in front of me – going to study a Masters in motorsport in the UK – suddenly became much more real. *If I'm going to do this,* I thought, *I have to be completely and utterly honest with myself. Is this what I want to do with my life?* I'd worked towards it for so long!

I gave it a red-hot go. Instead of throwing in the towel after missing out on a scholarship to pay for the Masters, I took a job as a field engineer in the oilfield with the goal of saving enough money to fund my year of study and my living expenses. Once I'd got to the end of that year, I had saved enough money and was ready. I had picked the college where I would stay, started collecting the books – yet something didn't feel right.

I was so close to my goal, but something was off. I began to realise that two things had happened. One was admitting that the reality of working in F1 was different to the expectation, and the second was that I was no longer sure this was the path I wanted to take for the rest of my life.

It was the most confusing, debilitating state of mind and I didn't feel like I could admit it to anyone. I just couldn't. I'd invested so much time in this world; it was part of my identity, part of who I was! My social circles were all about cars, my contacts and the network that I had so carefully cultivated were about motorsport; I had developed great relationships with people in this industry in the UK. People had sponsored me into this role. I would be letting more people down than just myself. However, at the end of the day, I couldn't bring myself to leave the work I had begun in Australia – empowering others through Youth Without Borders – for an ultimately selfish pursuit. The hardest call I've ever had to make was telling the university that I wasn't going to study motorsport that year, or any year after that. Part of me wishes I'd stuck by it, just to be able to say that I had made it in the industry and to show other girls that they actually could too, even if they were Muslim. But I couldn't bring myself to do it.

I was lost. But then I went back to the rigs and tried not to think about it.

★ ★ ★

Even though I'd decided to not work in motorsport as an engineer, I wanted to keep a finger in the pie and an opportunity came from a different angle – by writing for *Richard's F1* website, now called *MotorsportM8*, as a correspondent. Richard was another person who had emailed me when the *Age* story came out, and has since been an amazing support, allowing me to write for the website even though my personal schedule is always a bit of a mess.

I began writing for the site as the V8 correspondent in 2012, but it wasn't until 2014 that I got a big break when Richard asked me to go to the Monaco Grand Prix as an internationally accredited journalist. Monaco! Who was I?

The Monaco Grand Prix is one of the most glamorous events on the global motorsport social calendar; 'A sunny place for shady people', with multimillion-dollar yachts, billionaires making deals and supercars the norm. I arrived in the French Riviera, exhausted but pumped, the Friday before the Grand Prix weekend, after driving three hours from a tiny place in the Netherlands to the Hague and then on to Amsterdam, where I'd dropped off the rental car and caught a flight to Nice.

A friend had told me I could stay at her apartment in Nice,

but when I logged on to the airport wi-fi the girls had changed plans and were staying at a villa in Monaco. Armed with the new address and instructions to message them on arrival, I picked up my new chariot, a turbo Astra. The two gentlemen helping me with the hire car were lovely, but very quick to correct me when I asked if they were from the area. 'Oh no no no, I'm from France,' one said. 'Monaco is weird. The people are weird, their cars are weird, the lifestyle is weird . . . you'll have fun, though. Enjoy your time here!'

My thoughts were joyful as I sped off. What a drive! Honestly, television does not do that circuit justice. Driving to Monaco that night gave me a tiny taste of the adrenaline rush the drivers experience over their seventy-eight laps. The course of winding streets and tiny lanes is almost entirely on the edge of the cliffs; the blind corners and fast cars are an intoxicating combination. I drove the hell out of that Astra and thought to myself, *Welcome to Monaco, girl. You've made it!*

It was only when I arrived at the villa that I realised I'd need to find a place to park. I did a couple of laps of the suburb looking for a spot and eventually capitulated, parking a couple of kilometres away.

Walking back to the villa, I got completely and utterly lost. I eventually started going up random streets in the hope I would see something I recognised, and up and down stairs for the faint chance of a spark of inspiration. I couldn't find any wi-fi for a map, and didn't want to ask someone, convinced that people up at that time of the night would be shady. At one point I tried to retrace my steps but didn't want to pass by a bunch of guys who were lingering outside a shop . . . I'd passed them once and if I walked by again it would be obvious I had no idea where I was going.

After a stroke of luck and a healthy amount of internal praying, an hour later I stumbled across the right street. Success! I skipped to the door ... and stopped. There were eight different villas for the one address, and I had absolutely no clue which one the girls were staying in. I perched on the steps out the front, eventually found a wi-fi connection and sent off some messages, confident that I was now minutes away from a shower and a comfortable bed.

Nothing.

I made a couple of calls via Skype and Viber.

Nada.

By this point, it was the early hours of the morning and getting quite cold. People were starting to return from their night's entertainment, and I was running out of viable solutions. I googled the nearest hotel, glad to see it was noted as an 'affordable option'. Trundling over, I pressed the doorbell and the guy at reception reluctantly buzzed open the glass door.

'*Englay?*' I asked, hopeful.

His face grew even more unimpressed. 'A leetle.'

'Is there any chance you have a room for the night, sir?'

He looked at me, eyebrows up. 'Miss, it is impossible! 500 euros a night, but we have nothing. Very, very busy until Sunday.'

'500 euros! My goodness. 'Can I use your phone then?'

'Oh no, miss, impossible, impossible. Try Olympica, they may have a room.'

I picked up my luggage and shuffled out. No way was I trying another hotel. I was running out of phone battery, so the only thing to do was head back to the car to charge that baby. A seed of thought formed as I made my way to the silver beast. I sat in the driver's seat and pushed the back all the way down. There was enough space, I thought.

I slept in the car.

If my mother and father could have seen me in that moment! It was something we just didn't do, and I had never expected to do anything like that in my life. It was ironic that I was slumming it in the ritziest place on earth.

Three hours later I woke up, freezing my rear end off. Heater on full blast, I scrubbed my eyes and contemplated the next step.

I needed to be at the media centre in a few hours so I made my way back to Nice. Again, I wove through the crazy awesome roads – stopping briefly to check out the view – and found a parking spot right out the front of a Nice bakery that was actually open! It was in this shop that I happened upon a lovely French woman.

I remembered that in French, shower was '*douche*'.

'*Douche*?' I asked the lady hopefully. She nodded, though she looked slightly perplexed. A conversation in broken French later, I was invited in for breakfast and a shower. Phew!

★ ★ ★

Reporting in Monaco was everything it was cracked up to be – glamorous and fast-paced. I rubbed shoulders with the drivers, the team bosses, the journos and occasionally the engineers. I was on smiling terms with Fernando Alonso and actual greeting terms with Hamilton and Button. The trip was a whirlwind of press conferences, filing reports, trying to find out juicy F1 gossip and reading between the lines. F1, it turns out, is less about racing and more about money and power. The journo friends I made looked after me, and I learnt how to ask questions from the best. I walked along the track during qualifying, standing at the exit of the tunnel, closing my eyes and letting the noise and vibration run through me as the cars sped by. Breakfast at McLaren, lunch at Ferrari and afternoon drinks at Red Bull; I had somehow made it into the world of F1, just not in the way I had expected.

My forays in the world of motorsport have had their incredible highs and deep lows. I've made more than a few mistakes along the way, most of which I have to take responsibility for, and they have reminded me that not everything happens the way we want – or expect – it to. If anything, I've learnt more about myself, and started to understand how to deal with situations when they don't quite work out. *This too shall pass*, and something else is just around the corner. I may have felt at times that my world was falling apart, but you know what? It all worked out at the end of the day, *Alhamdulillah*. Happy days!

Chapter 20:

The Romanian Painter

'Oh, Baba, do I have to?' We were finally getting our house walls painted, something Mum had been saving up to do for years. It would have been a cause for celebration, except Dad was asking me to stay home and keep an eye on the process. I was on my mid-year break from fourth-year mechanical engineering and all I wanted to do was go for coffee with friends or hang out at the race team garage.

My father introduced me to the painters – two Eastern European lads, youngish and stoic.

'Gentlemen, my daughter will be around while you're working.'

I smiled toothlessly at the gentlemen. 'I'm just going to be there,' I said, motioning my head to the right. 'Let me know if you need anything.'

I wandered over to the desk and switched on my laptop. Might as well put this time to good use, catching up on the last season of *The Wire* . . .

It wasn't until the third day that I had a conversation with them. The lead painter was working on the entrance doorframe when I walked past.

'Excuse me,' he said, interrupting my train of thought.

'Who – me?' I asked stupidly as I stopped and turned to look at him. 'Did you want me to get you something?'

'Oh no, no.' He pulled a rag out of his back pocket and began to wipe his hands. 'I'm from Romania, you know, and I'm pretty religious.'

I nodded, unsure where this was going.

'I see that your family is doing very well; you guys have a lot of trophies?'

He pointed through the archway to the living room. The back wall had a stack of bookshelves and the top half was dedicated to our family achievements: my father and mother's graduation certificates, my younger brother's soccer trophies, and in the centre, the large Suncorp Young Queenslander of the Year award.

'Ah yeah, we like to keep busy,' I said, suddenly nervous. I didn't like talking about our achievements with strangers; it feels too close to boasting.

'Usually I wouldn't ask someone so young, because we haven't always had much life experience. But you've clearly done some things, right? That's why you won that award. Okay, here's my question. What's the most important lesson you've ever learnt?'

I was bowled over, my mind suddenly wiped blank, as the painter walked back to the entrance doorframe and began working again, waiting for an answer.

'Oh, wow, I don't know,' I said, after a pause. 'There are a lot of lessons I have learnt. A really important one is to listen to those around you, to learn from others.'

This often came up in conversations around the dinner table when we talked about how society could do better and what we need to do to make the world a safer, fairer place. I continued the train of thought, talking to the painter as he coated the doorframe in smooth, even strokes. 'When you listen to people, they often tell you what they want, which is so much better than telling them what you think they need. There have been *so many* people before us, so we'd be arrogant to believe we're the first to think of something, to feel a certain emotion or think a certain way. If we can learn from the past, and also recognise that we are ultimately a small, temporary part of a big picture we can barely understand, maybe we can discover more.'

He smiled and nodded, apparently ready to close off the conversation, but I wasn't quite ready to walk away. I was spiritually hungry now, my appetite unsated. 'What about you, then? What's the most important lesson you've ever learnt?'

'Oh, that's easy,' he said. 'Mine is that you should always have faith in God.'

My stomach clenched. *That should have been mine*, I thought. *I should know that!*

'Trust in God, because he always has a plan for you. If something has not happened the way you want or expect, it is because God has another story written for you. Everything is as it should be, so we should just have faith.'

I nodded. 'Thank you.' *He was right*, I thought. *Everything is as it should be.* Given that I had just come back from my error-ridden trip to the UK, it was a fitting reminder to have faith.

* * *

This conversation resonated with me, so I began to ask those around me the same question. People replied with all sorts of lessons: 'Age does not bring wisdom,' said one taxi driver, his beard as white as Gandalf's. 'Be honest and be yourself, because then you won't have to remember what you said,' was the response of an impressive-looking sailor when we met at lunch with the Queen of England. 'Believe in yourself and your own capacity and the capacity of others,' said Gary Turner, an award-winning teacher I met at another event.

Some of the most profound answers came from people without official titles. 'Do not resist change,' said a lady named Eleanor, who sat next to me at a friend's birthday party. 'Learn to serve – do things for others without expecting anything in return,' was another from Brody, a friend's partner.

Every now and again, I remember how temporary this life really is, and how humble we must be. There is an arrogance that we can sleepwalk our way into something, thinking we deserve it, when in many cases what we have achieved can be traced back to an accident of birth.

Time and time again, I would come back to this idea of listening to others. My life has been shaped by mentors and sponsors, from casual acquaintances who gave the smallest pieces of advice, through to those who have given so much of their time and more. I don't think I can ever give the mentors in my life enough thanks and recognition for all they have provided. We are the product of the people around us.

★ ★ ★

At the ceremony for my 2010 Young Queenslander of the Year award, one lady warned me to stay connected with the community, to ensure I have support and stay grounded.

'I think you'll be all right,' she said. 'Look how many people came with you.'

I had invited my family and friends, my old principal and school teachers – everyone who had played a part in my journey.

'They care about you and support you. Your community is here! Treasure that and make the most of it.'

Her advice still rings in my mind. Today I would be reluctant to invite so many friends to such an event, which is partly about ensuring I stay humble. One of the downsides of the nomadic life of a rig-worker is that you don't spend very much time in people's everyday lives, so the number of those with whom I have daily interactions has decreased significantly and my inner circle has become smaller. It's a price I pay for the life I've chosen, but I make an effort to stay in touch with others who have supported and mentored me.

My mother was the OM – Original Mentor: the one who taught me to read, write, add and subtract before I started school. My father was my ideological mentor, who taught me never to trust the news and who constantly reminds me to stay true to my heritage. Mama and Baba are my weathervanes. I think I will always depend on them in one way or another, even though I now realise that some of our opinions differ.

I didn't have a teacher who was a significant mentor until grade nine, when Mr Carlil, the cool English teacher, taught me about critical literacy and gave us flexibility to choose our own work. I couldn't get enough of it. 'If you want to do something different to the task that has been given, show me why it's relevant. If you can prove its relevancy to me, then you'll probably be able to do it!' This style fit me perfectly. My design and technology teachers also played a big role in my early years.

The true mentoring started when I began university, because to be mentored effectively I needed some idea of where I was going and the ability to connect with the right people.

I met my appointed BHP Billiton mentor for a lunch at a café in the city, and I remember being awed by the fancy restaurant and by the luxury that, because he was paying the bill, I could order whatever I wanted. This was a new world for someone from a family that considered fish and chips a decadence. He had no idea how to deal with me and said as much. I was a loud woman with lots of opinions and ran some youth organisation, yet I wanted to do engineering?

I loved having someone to bounce ideas off who would tell me whether I was totally barking up the wrong tree; someone to give me perspective. Brendon gave me a viewpoint I couldn't have accessed any other way, and it was invaluable.

Sometimes I wasn't so lucky with finding and securing the mentor I wanted. In second-year university I attended a three-week engineering course in France (my first overseas trip alone!). It was a university-sanctioned event, which was the only way my parents allowed me to go, and even then it was *a huge* deal. We went on field trips to different companies, including UNESCO, L'Oreal, Coke and even a defence outfit. I couldn't believe my luck when I met a woman in an engineering-based role in UNESCO, who did some pivotal innovative work with groups in developing nations. *I need this lady in my life!* I thought. I walked up to her at the networking event and simply said: 'I admire what you do and would love to learn from you. I want to explore whether there would be any possibility that you could mentor me.'

There was not even one iota of a chance she was interested. Her face said it all. Perhaps I didn't look like an accomplished person – I was going through a weird hijab phase, for sure. I felt small in that moment and, sure enough, I never did hear from her. But that didn't stop me trying that technique again. It may not have been successful with that individual for a number of reasons – she had no idea who I was, and I was simply being opportunistic, which may not have appealed to her personally – but sometimes that approach works!

Other times, finding a mentor or sponsor can happen organically, and those occasions are special. One of my favourite people is a lady named Julie McKay, executive director of UN Women Australia. She was a fellow participant at an event that I attended in Malaysia – my first 'diplomatic' conference (called 'Track II diplomacy', so cool!). We were part of a leadership program and I didn't speak to her much during the official events, but remember admiring her eloquence. Things changed when we decided to go for a wander around town together, just to leave the hotel and check out Malaysia.

We bonded through tea and conversation in Chinatown in Kuala Lumpur. I had just met one of my most vocal sponsors. A few weeks later, Julie suggested I find someone to nominate me for the inaugural 100 Women of Influence Awards run by Westpac and the *Australian Financial Review*. I didn't rate my chances but I ended up being one of the two Young Leader winners, and the youngest woman on the list. Julie then introduced me to my current mentor, Michael Rose, a lawyer who tells it to me like it is, who is more than happy to introduce me to people who can make things happen and who always reminds me to stay grounded. I owe a lot to these people.

Mentoring and sponsoring is also about opening doors for others, which I suggested in my TEDx talk. All my mentors and sponsors who have opened doors for me are people who come from completely different demographics. If I had stayed within my community I wouldn't have had the same opportunities, because people in the Sudanese community have yet to reach those highest levels of penetration and influence within the wider Australian society. By connecting to people with levels of influence in the existing structure, I am able to find my way through it.

There is a difference between mentoring and sponsoring. Mentors will guide you and provide advice, whereas sponsors are people who will put themselves on the line on your behalf – recommend you for a job, advocate for your pay rise, introduce you to the right people. Sponsors are gatekeepers. I find that it is useful to have both, sometimes in the same person.

Not only have people opened doors for me for the sake of work and progress, but also to give me the chance to meet some random and interesting folk. I've played soccer with Cathy Freeman in Suncorp Stadium; she was lovely and the grass was *so* green and springy, even in the middle of the drought! I wanted to ask her if I could borrow her running suit – it was semi hijab friendly – but I chickened out in the end, telling myself that it probably wouldn't fit.

I attended lunch with the Queen once, and when William and Catherine came to town, I was one of those invited to a reception with them at Government House. Mum dropped me off at the event but she got lost on the way there, so we rocked up within a minute of the doors being closed. I was the last person to enter the room, so when the speeches ended and the prince and duchess walked over to start chatting to people, I was standing nearest to them, right near the door. I was the first person who Kate approached, and so *all the cameras were on us*. Images of me talking to her were beamed around Australia and the world. I got messages from friends saying things like: *OMG, we saw you with the duchess. WTF, who are you?* Hilarious, right?

Even though I'm not a monarchist, when Kate complimented my necklace I almost gave it to her – almost. Both Kate and William were able to make you feel like you were the only person in the room, and they asked questions that showed they 'cared'. They struck the perfect balance between being grounded and being royal, and were all round very likeable. That said, I was reluctant to like them because they represent a system that someone like me can never hope to penetrate. The unearned elitism rankles.

The last encounter I will mention is with the Big O. Obama! I had the opportunity to shake his hand when he last visited Australia, and I was stoked because he is certainly the coolest POTUS. I don't know if he has been the most effective. Do I think he delivered on his promises, particularly when it comes to the Middle East? Perhaps not, but there is no denying he is one of the great orators of our time and he has a unique ability to bring a sense of humour to the presidential office. I definitely feel he was a little surprised to meet a 'sister' at the event, because he took an extra few moments to chat when we met. Me and Obama are tight, is what I'm saying!

I would have loved to have met Madiba. Although it is fantastic to meet Western leaders, there is something special about meeting someone who was able to transcend the troubles of the African nation, move past the colonial hurts and bring people together in a way that no one believed was possible. It may sound corny, but I don't think it would be a stretch to say every single African, whether living in Africa or in the diaspora, has a special place in their heart for Madiba.

Go talk to your painter. You don't know what kind of wisdom you will hear.

Chapter 21:

The School of Life

Have you ever had your fundamental beliefs about your role in society challenged? I never thought it would be so confusing. I've been trying to reconcile what I saw and experienced there with my experience growing up in Australia as an Aussie chick, but I'm definitely still figuring it all out . . .

This is an excerpt from a diary entry I wrote in 2011, shortly after returning from a four-month stint in Sudan. I'd never been a victim of the identity crisis issues that were said to plague third culture kids; I considered myself 'Straylian through and through. From the way I talked, to my mates and my choice of sports, I never had to think about whether I identified as Aussie until someone asked me if I did, post 9/11. I loved that I could walk into a workshop at a mine site in central Queensland as a hijabi-wearing, Sudanese-born gal and, because I grew up here, I could instantly relate to the old mates working maintenance. *This is my country, these are my people.* Right?

I felt comfortable with the choices I'd made and that gender played no part in my role in society: my degree, career, and even my sport (boxing: as feminine as they come). My father never seemed too concerned, although he was delighted whenever I went out in a dress – he'd grin and pinch me on my cheek, his one true sign of affection. He let me do what I wanted sports and career wise, as long as I showed that I cared about it and was doing a good job.

Boy, was I in for a treat when I got to Sudan.

★ ★ ★

'This is the perfect time for you to keep an eye out then.' My aunt smiled at me. We had met by coincidence in the international terminal of the Brisbane airport, both waiting for Emirates flights.

I was reclined on a couch with my feet up on the table, an act of disrespect I knew my parents would have rebuked me for, making it all the more enjoyable. My white 'Soul' by Ludacris headphones covered the cotton headscarf draped over my afro while I read a fantasy novel on the Kindle I'd received for my twenty-first birthday just a few days earlier. My legs had dropped instantly to the ground when my aunt sat down opposite, as I unconsciously assumed the form of an attentive young Muslim girl.

'Perfect time for what?' I asked, slightly bewildered.

'Now that you've finished your engineering studies, you can find someone in Sudan to be your husband. It's about time, Yassmin; these things become harder as you get older.'

I cringed, realising this did actually look like a trip to find a husband. That couldn't have been more wrong. I had always planned to spend time in the land of my birth, but it wasn't until I submitted my final year mechanical engineering thesis that it occurred to me to take a break before I started my job, to enrich my understanding of who I was and where I came from.

It was the beginning of summer in Sudan, the worst time to visit, as I was repeatedly informed by family members, but it was the perfect chance to spend a few months there studying Arabic before this next chapter of my life. This was an opportunity to rekindle a relationship with my extended family and immerse myself in the language that would have been my mother tongue. This trip wasn't just about hanging with my cousins; this was about connecting to my roots, my parent culture, and proving to my father that I hadn't become too Western. It was the Muslim-girl equivalent of finding yourself backpacking around South America.

The only university I could find that had a website with a functioning phone number was the International University of Africa, so I signed up to study Arabic at their campus, fortunately only a short walk from my grandmother's house.

* * *

It had been more than three years since my last visit and I'd still been relatively naive then, my decisions dictated by my parents as I learnt what it meant to be an adult. Now I was a university graduate with a job waiting for me back home. My relatives hadn't seen me in that time – it was far too costly for them to visit Australia – so that first month was a bit of a readjustment for all of us.

At first, I found the cultural differences funny. I loved being the odd one out, flying in the face of what was acceptable – just being me. I wasn't accustomed to the cultural expectations placed on me, even though I understood and accepted the bare bones of it all, like how to dress, how to behave when we had guests, how to make good tea and serve it to the family after meals, how to speak to elders. It was the discrepancy between the roles of men and women that frustrated me and the unwritten rules that I was expected to adhere to without being told why they existed. Apparently, the way I walked, sat, talked and laughed was unfeminine and undesirable for a respectable Sudanese woman, as were the issues I wanted to discuss – *politics isn't for women!*

My family couldn't understand why a woman would want to do sport or be physically strong. 'Isn't that a man's thing?' they asked. 'Are you trying to be a man?'

I used to joke to my aunt that someone should write a rule book on how to live as a Sudanese woman, and she and Habooba Saida, my maternal grandmother, would just laugh.

'Yassmina, you might think you are all educated with your schooling, but I'll teach you about the school of life, *Madrasat Al-Dunya*,' Habooba Saida would say. This was one of the relationships that defined my trip. My grandmother gave me a true schooling in being a Sudanese lady. Even with the cultural differences between us that arose, I deeply admire her. She epitomises the strength and wit people assume women who come from villages in Sudan don't have. How wrong they are.

Much as I enjoyed it, my time in the school of life was frustrating. I couldn't understand why I was being judged on things that had nothing to do with my true character, and I found it perplexing that my cousins weren't fighting for their rights as women. It wasn't as if my cousins were oppressed; they were all studying or working and my aunts all had higher level degrees.

Their command of both English and Arabic was exemplary; they were educated and well read. In fact, one aunt was running one of the biggest businesses in Sudan. I just couldn't understand how they were happy living under these cultural restrictions. We seemed to value such different things, which was strange because in Australia I'd always believed I had Sudanese values.

My Sudanese relatives also had a different reaction towards the community work my parents and I have so much passion for. My family in Sudan seemed to put more importance on getting together and doing things for the family, rather than helping those we weren't related to. Perhaps giving back to the community was more linked to my parents' migrant experience than I had thought.

When I asked them why they didn't get involved in community projects like YWB in Sudan, one cousin's perspective shed some light on how they viewed this kind of work:

'It's so cool that you're travelling and doing all this stuff, Yassmina, but that's your world. We have accepted our world and how we operate in it, and it's not as bad as you think! We know the role we have to play to be a good woman, a good wife, a good Sudanese person and a good Muslim, so we do that. We don't want to make our lives harder by looking for things that we don't really need.'

My cousin saw my involvement in advocacy as something that also challenged accepted gender roles in society, and that wasn't something she was interested in; her perspective was to accept her lot in life and just enjoy it within its limits. I didn't know how to feel about that, or if I was even allowed an opinion. It may frustrate me that Sudanese culture dictates how to be a 'good woman' but if I approach the topic with the attitude that my way of seeing the world is 'right', I'm no better than any

British colonial. After all, the gender roles in Australia can also be restrictive, just in different ways.

My aunt echoed a similar sentiment to my cousin. 'You might look at me and say, "She has a degree but she's sitting at home – how oppressed is she?" But I love taking care of the house, cooking, and being there for my family. I work, but I do hours that will suit my family. *You* might disagree, Yassmina, but the woman is better suited to bringing up a family. You can't have a home without a mother.'

By and large, the women I talked to *wanted* to be caregivers and homemakers; they were happy in that role. These kinds of conversations bothered me. I started to wonder if the West really had corrupted me, and if it was crazy to expect my path in life to be whatever I wanted it to be, despite pre-existing gender roles and expectations that have been built over centuries. It was the first time I considered the idea that as a woman, my role as a procreator and a homemaker could be just as important, if not more so, than my career.

I was told Sudanese women consider it their Islamic duty to be the caregivers and the homemakers. I would later find out that wasn't necessarily true. Some people believe that attitude came from a patriarchal reading and interpretation of the source texts. At the time, however, I had no one I could ask except those who had grown up in Sudan and thus absorbed the values around them.

If fulfilling the 'traditional' gender role of a woman was an Islamic duty, my fundamental beliefs as to who I should be were being challenged, and I was lost! How did I reconcile my faith with my Sudanese heritage and my Australian cultural upbringing? Travelling back to Sudan as an adult had unsettled my way of seeing the world. I wasn't sure which direction was north. It was the only time in my life I ever called my mother, homesick and in tears, born of frustration and confusion.

I was torn between forgetting everything I'd learnt in Sudan so I could continue to live in Australia as I always had, disregarding gender in my decisions, or following the path of my cultural background, making choices largely based on society's gender roles. With religion thrown into the mix, it became soul-wrenching. The school of life set *hard exams*, yo.

Back in Australia, I had considered myself Australian with Sudanese values. I was different from the white kids at school and that gave me some connection with Sudan and with the migrant and Muslim communities. Get any two brown (or third culture) kids together and they will start comparing notes and laughing at the times their parents did 'migrant things' while they were growing up, like staying up all night to tell you off if you were home late, giving you curfews, sending you to parties with your traditional food, or expecting you to spend the weekend cleaning the house or being with the family because relatives were visiting. A white friend might ask you to skip the family get-together to come and hang out, but an ethnic friend never would, because they knew how it worked. Family was always number one.

So I thought I knew what Sudanese values and communal living were. It wasn't until I spent real time in Sudan that I realised my version of communal, what I thought were 'Sudanese values', weren't actually that. I had always told people 'straddling cultures' was great because you got to pick the best of both worlds, and in a way you do, but it can also be uncomfortable when you realise your two worlds aren't always compatible. With the acknowledgement that it wasn't as easy being from both worlds as I'd thought, came the realisation that I might not be able to have it all as a woman, either. So is it possible to be truly African-Arab, communal and Eastern while also being Australian, Western and individualistic?

Damn skippy, it is. Whoever said we had to do the done thing?

There is a middle ground, and that is the path I choose to take, *Inshallah* – one that is informed by the fact that I'm a woman but isn't limited by it.

Chapter 22:

Family and Marriage

'Who exactly do you think you are?' My mum's voice was cutting.

I'd just asked if she would let me move out with some university friends. She looked at me with her I-can't-believe-you're-asking-that face, an expression I saw every time I stretched the boundaries of my Sudanese-Australian household.

That was the end of that conversation for, well, ever. It didn't help my cause that I had asked to move out with a couple of Aussie guys, engineering colleagues. What was I thinking?

In Sudan, people don't leave home until they're married, and even then the newlyweds will often stay in the same building. Sudanese families always live close to each other, which is why FIFO (fly-in-fly-out) work seems insane to most of my extended family. I actually still don't know how I get away with it.

In Sudan, an individual is seen as no more than one cog in

a larger machine, be that machine the family or the tribe. In that community-centric culture, your actions do not reflect solely on you, but on your entire family and tribe, which changes the way most people approach their decisions.

This creates an intersection between the great respect given to education and the equal respect that is given to marriage and the importance of being a 'woman' who knows how to hold a house together. The strength required to run a household successfully is as highly valued as that required for a successful career.

This means that even though many of my cousins are well educated, they are equally valued for their ability to be excellent homemakers. It's an accomplishment they're proud of. These are women who have travelled around the world, some choosing to live in Western nations like Canada and Australia, but who still felt strongly about fulfilling their traditional female gender role while also following their careers.

I have often reflected on this attitude. In many Eastern societies the role of a woman as a mother offers her a level of social status that men have no access to. At times, that value becomes skewed or hyperbolised, like the tradition in some parts of the Gulf of calling women by their connection to their first son – using 'Um Ahmed', meaning the 'Mother of Ahmed'. But women are appreciated in this role of the mother and as the leader of a household, while in the West there is a common perception that a woman who stays at home for her family has less power than one with a successful career. I have often wondered what my mother 'could have done' had she not given up part of her career to focus on motherhood. Does that imply I view one path as more valuable than the other?

The issue for me is choice. While it is important that women are respected in the family if they choose to be a mother, the choice to aspire to something apart from motherhood should be equally valued, and I don't think the East or the West has this balance right yet. Motherhood in both types of society is still wrapped up in the concept of being a 'good woman' and what that entails. Do we end up in a situation where women are pressured into motherhood by society's expectations – and if so, is this something we are okay with? Am I barking up the wrong tree?

One of the fundamental differences between my Sudanese-bred cousins and me is our mindset. Despite being brought up in a Sudanese household, I had absorbed some of the individualistic characteristics of Australian society, something I had begun to recognise after my extended stay in Sudan. Being a Caramello egg changed my approach to making decisions.

On my trip I struggled to understand why my cousins didn't want to do anything too far outside the norm.

'Would you do what Sudan and Sudanese people think is right even if you don't really want to or don't agree with it?' I asked my cousin, trying to understand her perspective.

'It's not really like that,' she said, searching for a way to explain. 'If I want something, but if the family thinks it's a bad idea, I will probably go with what they think because they're older and wiser than me. They know what is best, and they might understand things that I don't yet. It's like, if you loved someone and wanted to marry them but no one in your family approved, would you still marry them?'

I actually might, I thought, surprising even myself. My parents had always accused me of doing what I wanted to do regardless of whether or not it matched their expectations. I didn't act maliciously, but my decisions usually came down to what I wanted. I once tried to tell my mother that I was driven by duty and obligation and she laughed at me, saying, 'No, you're not! You don't do anything out of duty!' When I'd protested, she'd pointed out that if I didn't want to do something, almost nothing would make me do it – and certainly not a concept like duty.

I was having a similar moment of realisation now, in response to my cousin's question.

'I would be quite stuck, I think,' was my eventual reply to her.

'I wouldn't. Why would I be with someone who would damage the relationship between my family and me?'

The opinion of her family, her tribe, mattered to her beyond my belief. Initially, I dismissed her response, thinking that it indicated a lack of agency, a lack of strength of character that made her unable to make a difficult choice, but as I spent more time with my cousins as an adult, I started to see it in a different light. Rather than viewing these decisions through the lens of my personal, individualistic understanding, I learnt to see them from a community perspective. If the most important thing was not the fulfilment of your own personal desires but the safety, security and fulfilment of your family and tribe, your decisions had a different meaning. The most important factor is no longer your personal desire, but is how your choice affects those around you.

Naturally, not all women in Sudan fit into that mould. Some of my other cousins were more similar to me in personality and drive and were not impressed that they were meant to settle down early and live an 'acceptable' life. These were the cousins I could most relate to – the Mac-owning, squash-playing, backpacking cohort that still somehow exist in the Sahara Desert. However, if my family at home in Brisbane is visited by another Sudanese or Arab-African family, my Sudanese breeding immediately kicks in and I go from a terribly outspoken, opinionated, sassy chick to a relatively demure housewife-in-training. I sit politely and listen to the conversation, but only after I have served each guest with a cold drink, brought out the biscuits, neatly arranged on a plate, and then prepared and served the tea – made with cloves, cardamom pods and just a little cinnamon. When a few families come around, the women and I automatically peel off into the kitchen and the second living room so that we are separated from the men. So, even in the Australian-Sudanese community, there are strong gender roles that I find myself adhering to, so that I don't attract criticism for acting outside the social norm. In these situations I also conform because otherwise my actions would reflect badly on my parents, as well as on myself. I owe it to my parents to show people in the community that we were brought up 'well'.

★ ★ ★

The pressure for women to have it all is intense. In Sudan, having a family as well as a job isn't just an option but is an expectation, although there are some structural mechanisms that make parts of this journey easier to achieve than in Western societies.

In Sudan, if you are part of the wealthy classes and wish to work, typically your extended family can help look after the kids while you pursue your career. This is made simpler because you usually live quite close to each other, if not in the same building. However, there are also class and socio-economic factors at play, and although that choice might be available for Sudanese upper- and middle-class families, for the lower classes, the options for women are much more limited.

For women in any society, difficult choices have to be made around family and work. But the stakes are often higher for those living in a communal society, as your choices are not deemed yours alone; they reflect on your parents, your extended family, your upbringing. The power of tradition and 'not wanting to bring shame to the family' is strong. The fact that women in collective societies often go along with societal traditions does not make 'all Muslim women oppressed' or 'all Arab women pushovers'. When a woman in Sudan chooses her own path, this is often 'claimed' by the West as a 'win against the barbarians'; this is insulting to her and to her culture, because the culture is something she most probably still values.

Yes, there are women around the world who are oppressed and some of them happen to be Muslim. But *their Islam* is not the cause of their oppression; the cause is usually the regime they are in, their economic circumstances, or the patriarchal environment and culture. To me, this is very clear, but it is something that seems to be difficult to communicate. The women I grew up with – my mother and the other women in my family and community – are nothing like the images of a 'Muslim woman' that are sold to ignorant audiences. The public commentary about Islam (and Africa!) is so far removed from my actual experience of it that sometimes I find it difficult to believe the commentators are talking about the faith I hold dear and the values by which I live my life.

Western societies need to appreciate that there is more than one way to do things and more than one way to be 'right'. There needs to be a move away from the idea of the implied superiority of Western civilisation. The choices women from the East make are not anyone's to control or dictate.

I often ask myself: is it wrong to continue partaking in traditions you know are based on patriarchal or potentially problematic historical contexts, in order to keep the peace? I don't know the answer to that question just yet.

Chapter 23:

On the Rigs

'Alllllllahhhhhhhhhhhu Akbar, Alllahhhhhhh–ahhhh–ahhhhhhhu Akbar!'

I looked around me, stunned. Where was that coming from?

It was 4 am and I had just walked into Cobham airport, Perth, to check in for a flight up to the oil and gas rigs. The small terminal was packed to the rafters with men in high-vis clothing and steel-capped boots and I fit right in with my faded tangerine number. Threads were trailing off the silver reflective strips on my arms, adding legitimacy to my outfit.

'Alllllllahhhhhhhhhhhhu Akbar, Alllahhhhhhh–ahhhh–ahhhhhhhu Akbar!'

I swore as I realised the sound was coming out of my bag. Dropping the fifteen-kilogram duffel, I began searching for the offending equipment: my phone.

In an effort to encourage myself to wake up on time for the morning prayer, I had downloaded an app called Never Miss *Fajr*, which would play the *Adhan* (call to prayer), super loud until the person answered five Islamic-based trivia questions to confirm they were awake. Brilliant, right? Except that I'd forgotten to switch the app off before heading to the airport that morning, and it just so happened that prayer time coincided with my passage through security.

Bloody perfect, I thought, as I searched through the bag, cursing myself for having packed in a rush that morning. The other rig and mining guys started looking at me from the corners of their eyes, although some were less subtle and just blatantly eyeballed me. I was holding up the queue to go through security and nobody was impressed. I could only imagine what they were thinking. There were no other people of colour in that airport that morning, and definitely no one who looked remotely Muslim, even though some rigs are actually quite diverse. It wasn't my lucky day . . .

In typical Aussie fashion, no one said a word.

Aha! I finally grasped my phone and poked at the screen, trying to answer the trivia. After a couple of moments with no success, I decided I needed out, and switched the phone off.

Silence, finally. I breathed a sigh of relief, and the security guard lifted one eyebrow at me. 'Step forward, please.'

Just another day in the life of an Aussie Muslim chick rig-hand.

★ ★ ★

So here I am, squished between two dudes on the long drive to the rig. It's quite cold in the car, and there isn't much conversation – none at all, actually – and so half an hour and a short nap into the trip I've put the headphones on and am listening to Eminem. In typical fashion I don't know what to expect, but am quite looking forward to whatever comes next! I've got bright orange nail polish to match my high vis and clothes so new they still have the creases. I'm keeeeen :)

I'm gonna focus on following Avs's advice.

This is taken from a diary entry, day one on the rig. My best mate, Avrithi, who had been my friend and colleague through YWB, Spark and university, had sat me down right before I left to give me a stern talking-to:

'Don't kid around with these guys, okay? You have to be strong. You don't have to be their friend. You don't have to let them treat you poorly. Be a boss and channel Beyoncé. Don't let them in your room, don't add them on Facebook. Watch yourself!'

Avs was a strong woman who suffered no fools and she knew I would make friends with anyone. She wanted to protect me, but sometimes I just needed protection from myself. She was half right – I would have to adjust – but I also found ways to make friends on my own terms. A little bit of Bey, though, never went astray. I would have to be the one to make the effort and set the tone.

A few hours later, we drove onto the lease. It was a cleared piece of land, about 100 metres by 100 metres, on which sat the rig, with all the equipment required to drill the hole, the dongas (converted shipping containers), which are used as offices and a 'crib room' (the cafeteria). On a land lease there were generally about thirty to fifty workers (two weeks on, two weeks off, usually), and on an offshore rig between 100 to 160, depending on the size, working month on, month off. There's also accommodation on the lease for some of the personnel, usually the geologists and the company representatives, while the rest of the workers sleep in a camp a short drive away.

We parked up near the main equipment, jumped out of the truck and grabbed our hard hats. The new kids on the rig wear green hats, but I was not a fan of being singled out as a newbie, so I'd bought my own white hat and pre-decorated it with tags and graffiti, based on what I'd seen at the mines during vacation work and on TV, so I looked like I belonged. Graffed hat on top of my rig-friendly hijab, which just looked like a Rastafarian cap tied down with a bandana, I mentally donned a tough persona, channelling my inner Alanna of Trebond, and walked with the crew to sign on and meet the boss of the rig, also known as the Company Man (gendered profession alert!).

It was at this rig I met my future rig-bestie, an awesome young female geologist who taught me how to be friends with the guys without being seen as a sexual object. She warned me what to watch out for, and told me the Golden Rule: 'Don't screw the crew.' *Well, there's no chance of that happening!* I thought, chuckling internally. I felt super lucky to have this friendly, experienced woman for my guide into the rocky wilderness.

I knew what it was like studying with a bunch of male engineers. We had been the same age, learning the same content, and had enough shared background to be able to relate to each other, and the 'success criteria' for respect was the same for everyone: get good grades and you earn respect. I quickly learnt it was nowhere near as clear-cut in the 'real world'. The men I would be working with came from all over the globe, meaning varied ages, generations and social expectations. This was now my reality and I had to learn the ropes as fast as I could.

I had assumed that my religion would be the biggest barrier out on the rigs, but apparently working with a Muslim is not as surprising as working with a woman. Although, to be fair, the guys don't always realise I am a Muslim. My hijab on the rig is less obvious and not as obtrusive, convenient to combine with the hard hat. In true Australian fashion, religion is the one topic that is studiously avoided in this workplace. People also don't always realise the significance of my head covering. This makes for some interesting conversations over lunch, starting that very first week with: 'When's that tea cosy come off?'

I turned around to my colleague, already grinning inside. 'Nah, mate, it doesn't come off. I was born with it, hey!'

He looked up from his steak, jaw dropping slightly in confusion. 'Wha–?'

I laughed out loud. 'It's a religious thing. We call it a hijab, and I guess this is the abbreviated, hard-hat friendly version.'

'Oh yeah, righto . . .' He nodded uncertainly, then shrugged and went back to his meal.

When I told my family at home, Baba couldn't get enough of it. 'Let's call you Tea Cosy now!'

Sia's 'Breathe Me' was my soundtrack for that first trip; it spoke to a kindness and a gentleness that I couldn't get in my new environment. I would curl up on the top bunk of the beds in the donga, willing myself to sleep as the words wrapped around me, cocooning me safely away from this place I was yet to understand. Although I was getting along well with my new colleagues, it really did feel like a big change. I needed more than colleagues, I needed friends. This was my first time away from home for real, which probably added to the feeling of loneliness. Spending all day being strong came naturally to me, but with my new life built around that persona, there was very little room to be small, which I needed to be once in a while. That vulnerability stayed between me, Sia and the darkness of a small, cold donga.

It's a lifestyle I'm pretty used to now, and when I'm back home, in some ways I miss its simplicity – just work, sleep, meals and small talk to fill the hours. There are many moments, though, that draw on your personal reserves. Moments when you're the only woman in a group of guys and you find yourself arguing against calling the duct tape 'rape tape'. Moments when engineers are yelling at you because you've made a mistake that will cost hours and tens of thousands of dollars, or when you don't know what you're doing but you just have to figure it out because you are literally unable to walk away from the place. At moments like these, the rig feels as if it's a dream that you can't wake up from, because this is your *life*, the life you have chosen.

Some people call home to talk to their partners and family about their day, but it's quite hard to explain what life is like on a rig if you haven't been on one. It is even harder to explain what life is like on a rig as a woman, even to a man who works with you, because they can't fully understand the constant balancing act. It's during casual conversations that I find myself most challenged, and I've gathered dozens of examples during my time on various rigs.

One afternoon during a typical shift, I went to the rig floor to shoot the breeze with the lads. The topic of conversation was graphic; they were discussing their masturbation habits, particularly crudely. I dithered, and then decided to sit and listen, figuring it was an interesting conversation from an anthropological point of view. I couldn't leave every single conversation with which I felt uncomfortable, otherwise I'd be walking in and out of chats all day! How else was I going to make mates?

After a good few minutes on the topic, the lads save the driller left the rig floor for a smoko and I hurriedly changed the topic to the pecking order on the rig, curious about how people fit into this strange world and keen to get onto safe ground.

Later I wondered: did the fact that I sat and listened mean I was implicitly condoning their conversation? What did this say about my character? How was I meant to navigate this? Can I participate in this type of chat with my morals intact?

The topics I liked talking about – cars, racing, boxing – were things the guys would be interested in and happy to chat about. Often, though, the conversations ended up a mixture of dirty jokes and worse. Where did that leave my dignity?

The kicker was the realisation that the same banter that makes 'men men' on the rig, is not open to women. Too much backchat and your value is 'diminished' (too difficult, thinks too much of herself, doesn't shut up); too little, and you're perceived as uptight and hard to work with. A fine line.

My willingness to stay and put up with awkward conversations stemmed from a desire to want to be friends with people, no matter who they are or what status they are perceived as having. The currency for someone like me, someone who is constantly an outsider, is the ability to communicate with a group and be accepted – just enough that you are allowed in the 'tribe'. Sure, I will never be a man, so I will always be inherently different and may not quite fit into the existing pecking order. However, if I am able to effectively communicate and understand the tribe's language, I can exist and contribute to that space.

Perhaps it is about being adaptable, but there is a difference between adaptability and submitting. I will never give up my values in order to gain credibility with a group. That's not what a group demands, anyway; the group dynamic requires respect and a genuine interest in what the tribe cares about. If I want in, I need to make the effort, and if the gateway is learning how to shoot the shit, that's something I can do. I just have to be careful not to cross my own boundaries. But the more ways we learn to communicate, the better we can connect and see how others view the world, and that makes this work worthwhile.

It's not all rough on the rigs, and the industry has changed significantly, even in the past few years. Despite the traditional male dominance, there are strong factors forcing welcome change. Two catalysts for change are the increasingly strict Occupational Health and Safety regulations and the growing presence of women on rigs.

While there are relatively few women in the physically demanding rig environment, there are increasing numbers of women working as geologists, engineers, and in wireline, and drilling and measurement services. When companies also hire women as drilling supervisors it tends to have a significant impact on the group dynamic.

The transition has not been easy and reactions from the rest of the rig workers vary from acceptance and encouragement to fear of the change the presence of women might bring. 'It makes it feel more like the real world,' several rig hands have said to me. 'When there's a woman around, people argue less, talk about different things and it doesn't feel like such a strange place to come to.'

To be honest, that perspective was slightly surprising and also encouraging. The more common opinion is shaped by fear. Although some men enjoy having women as part of their workforce, they still believe it's their domain and that women are 'more trouble than they're worth', or are promoted before they are ready, in front of men with more experience.

'We gotta suss the chicks out,' an assistant driller commented. 'You don't know if one of them's going to report you just for a joke you didn't even realise you made. I don't want to lose my job, so I just stay quiet.'

This view is not uncommon; a lot of men have said the same thing in different ways. On one hand, it is heartening to see the system working, to see that women's rights in the field are taken seriously. On the other, it instantly causes an 'us and them' rift. The men band together; their view is that 'all women are the same and out to get them' or that they are 'too sensitive' and won't understand the men's banter. Unfortunately, on most sites there are not enough women to form their own gangs (yet).

The banter is not always gender-related. I once had a sixty-eight-year-old directional driller grin at me when he finally decided he could talk to me, and his first words were, 'Oh yeah, I have some blacks in my family tree!' I was naively impressed (and surprised) that we had some shared heritage, because Charlie looked like an average 'Aussie battler'.

'Oh yes, yes I do. I think they're still hanging there, out the front of the house!' His wizened face creased into a smile as he began to chortle. I laughed as well, mostly in shock. 'Charlie, you're a terrible man!' I replied, shaking my head.

'I know! It's great, isn't it?'

★ ★ ★

I am constantly asking myself, even today, if I should adopt and accept the mannerisms of the rig to fit in, to become one of the boys, to accept the status quo and not cause waves. Or should I, and other women, stick to our guns and demand change, insist that the men working in these isolated and testing environments change their culture and mannerisms to incorporate women?

Even as I write this, I feel I should apologise and add a disclaimer. Not all the oil and gas fields are like this. Or is that just me explaining away behaviour that is common on rigs so I don't rock the boat and become unpopular? Am I just being nice? I haven't been able to answer these questions yet. Working on the rigs has, however, forced me to reinterpret my understanding of what it means to be a strong woman.

'I'm going to kill 'em with kindness!' I announced to my boss after more than a year on the rigs. I was an older hand now, with a little more experience under my belt, but I was having particular trouble connecting with a driller and the crew kept playing practical jokes on me, like calling me over the PA and sending me to random parts of the rig for no reason or putting my equipment where I wouldn't find it. I figured being the nicest person I could possibly be would be a good response.

'Who?' he asked, perplexed.

'Everyone!' I grinned, thinking it was the best solution ever.

'Right.' The boss looked over at me. 'You're on the next chopper!'

There was no room on the rig for being kind. He was joking, of course, but there is another, similar word that the women *are* expected to be, and that is 'nice'.

For a long time, I went with 'being nice'. I had taken on the suggestion of an older, very successful woman I had met on a women's issues panel event who said I should 'always be charming' because 'you can't lose if you're always nice'. It was great advice, or so I thought at the time. *We won't reach equality if we're always on the attack*, I reasoned. Being on the offensive always puts the guys offside and makes for a difficult working environment. Rigs, in that respect, were no different to university.

'Nice' is playing by the rules – fitting into what is expected of us as women and not demanding change, be it quotas on boards or separate sleeping quarters to the men. 'Nice' is assuming that everyone around us wants what we want – equality of opportunity and a free and fair society – when that is often far from the daily reality. 'Nice' is fine if you don't want to rock the boat. But is the reason the women's movement is the least violent movement for social change in history because women are better at negotiating what they want or because they were told to play nice?

Being nice can still be a pretty good negotiating tool, a useful weapon in my life arsenal. At times, it allows you to make changes without getting people offside – being charming while challenging the status quo so that people don't even realise change is occurring until it has happened. That definitely works for some people, but it doesn't always work either. What is the alternative?

Sometime during the first year after university, as I entered the workforce, I started to care less about not rocking the boat. This was due to the gradual realisation that if I never made people uncomfortable, there would never be any reason for them to examine their beliefs and actually change. If I was nice, I was working *around* the system to make it functional, and while that made it work for *me*, it didn't change the structural expectations of society or make it easier for anyone else.

If I didn't speak out on behalf of women, especially women of faith and women of colour, in spaces where those voices are not heard, then there was little point in having me at that table. I was not only wasting an opportunity, I was being disrespectful to those who had entrusted me with the responsibility. Challenging the status quo openly is not 'nice' – although the delivery sometimes can still be. But it is important.

As women, we are taught to conform to social expectations. We are taught that it's important to be liked. We all like to be liked, generally speaking. So to fight that instinct takes a little gumption, a little concentration, and a capacity for more than a little work. But let's be real – women have all those talents in spades. The rigs are the frontline of the 'picking your battles' war zone. Sometimes, you have to roll with the punches and kill 'em with that kindness, and other times you have to put your foot down and channel your inner Beyoncé. If anything, this job made me realise that I am proud to be a woman, and being 'strong' doesn't necessarily mean being 'masculine'. It's ironic that it took a world renowned for its toughness to make me appreciate my femininity.

Chapter 24:

#ThingsRigPigsSay

'He's tighter than a fish's asshole.'
'Don't forget, hygiene is all about cleaning the back, sack and crack.'
'That guy's so irritable, we call him "Thrush".'

Being on the rigs is an interesting environment for your backyard, wishing-they-were-a-real anthropologist. It's an opportunity to hear perspectives that I don't usually hear, either because people make a judgement about my values and omit certain topics and expressions out of respect, or because I don't always get exposure to people with opinions vastly different to mine.

One situation during our weekly safety drill caught me unawares. At every rig there's a weekly muster drill during which everyone practises assembling, simulating an emergency. I always look forward to standing in the muster lines, as much as you can look forward to standing in a life vest and full Personal Protective Equipment (PPE) in the beating sun. You never quite know who you will end up next to, and as the drill drags on, people tend to chat to the folk around them. Although I try to meet as many people as possible on each rig, I don't get to chat properly with everyone if our shifts don't line up, or just because some people don't quite want to talk about life and love at breakfast, our main gathering time.

This particular morning, an older English bloke was the recipient of my chatter. I asked him about his history and where he had worked. He'd been everywhere, like most older blokes in the industry – had done time in Angola, the North Sea, Brazil. You name it, he had probably been there. So I asked him how he'd enjoyed working in Africa – both Nigeria and Angola.

'Oh god, it was awful!' he said, disgust colouring his voice. 'The people in Nigeria were just . . .'

He went on to describe all the stereotypes Nigerians hate being associated with – that nobody would like to be associated with. I stood there, taking in the barrage, internally aghast.

'It couldn't be all bad . . .' I countered, trying to draw out an alternative narrative. I'm not sure whether this guy realised I was born in Africa or not; perhaps my mocha-latte complexion gave him the impression that I just had a big booty and a tan. Either way, I thought I could use this opportunity to offer an alternative perspective, so I tried a different tack. 'But you can't blame people over there for being resentful, right? A lot of African nations are still dealing with all this post-colonial stuff [Yep, I dropped an academic word into the middle of a debate with a rig guy, that's right!] and . . .' I trailed off as he started shaking his head.

'No, darling, it's not that. It's just that their culture is corrupt. I mean, look at what's happening to England. London is full of people from other places. Where are we meant to go now?'

Ah, I thought. Here comes that anti-immigration spiel.

'Don't get me wrong – I definitely think we should be helping folk,' (I nodded approvingly), 'but they need to work hard and understand they have to earn their place. We can't just open our doors to anyone. I mean, they kill their daughters for being raped!' He swore. 'And those Muslims treat their women so horribly –'

I sighed. 'Hey,' I interrupted his tirade. 'C'mon, man. It's not like you white lads are all that great to your women either!'

'Yeah, well, at least we don't kill them in the name of honour!'

My retort, if I had been quicker, would have been 'No, in Australia, men just kill women because of underlying gender imbalance. More than one woman a week dies at the hands of a partner, yeah?'

This is not about having a fight to the bottom, though, and I was busy trying to understand why men like him had such toxic views of the cultures I identified with.

I listened some more, probing to make sense of his attitudes. Admittedly, he'd experienced discrimination and resentment at the hands of those from a different culture, but he refused to make the connection between the wider context and himself. He was unable to see that he was most probably being treated as a representative of a system that was exploiting those same people.

By the end of the muster, only twenty minutes later, I was exhausted. No manner of reasoning was going to change this man's mind and I had decided this was one of those battles I just didn't need to fight so when we were given the signal to head back to work I took long strides away towards my shack. The man followed, still talking at me, not taking the hint, so I started up the stairs.

'You see, Yassmin, these Muslims, right . . .'

I paused, turned to listen to the last of what he had to say.

'I've worked with lots of good ones. But there's something really wrong with the way they treat their women. You know they circumcise their women? How awful is that? Female genital mutilation is a thing for them, they have to do it –'

'I didn't think that was a religious thing; I am pretty sure it's a cultural one,' I tried to cut in.

'Oh no, it's definitely in the religion. They do some messed-up stuff and they're taking over England. Think about it – how would you like to be forced to wear a burqa and have your bits removed with a rusty knife?'

'Wow, really?' He must have somehow interpreted my thinly veiled sarcasm as innocent ignorance. 'It sounds like that would be terrible. Anyway, I've got to get back to work,' I called, as I walked up the stairs.

'Talk to you later!' he called from below.

Maybe . . . I thought. Maybe.

That conversation played on my mind for the remainder of the day. It saddened me that although he'd lived and worked with Muslims, his experience was not positive. I could understand why – the issue wasn't the religion but the practices of the people and how he was treated. There are so many other facets to his experience – socio-economic, educational, postcolonial – but it still made me dejected that some Muslim countries had retrograde attitudes that flew in the face of Islam. I was also frustrated that, for some reason, this had legitimised the superiority of the West. 'We aren't like that' was not a new sentiment, but it grated – oh, how it grated – because people like that guy had no problem highlighting negative issues in less developed countries, even though they got sensitive when similar problems in the West were pointed out. The hypocrisy is galling; people are unwilling to recognise problems in their own backyards – the effects of violence against women, of conscious and unconscious bias, and the current violation of international human rights. The peak of this hypocrisy is that other cultures, with the same kinds of problems, are rendered unworthy of respect when viewed through a Western lens. Why won't all cultures learn from each other?

There are no easy answers, but those of us who grew up on the cusp of two worlds don't get the luxury of claiming any one culture is better than the other. While this puts us in the unenviable position of disentangling each culture's attitudes towards the other, it does remove the mysticism surrounding the 'other', and translates it in an authentic way.

The second reason this particular conversation played on my mind was because the man had obviously not associated me with Islam. He had taken my abbreviated hijab for a health-and-safety item: some of the guys also covered their hair under their helmets, to soak up sweat or keep dreadlocks out of the way. My external identity felt disconnected from my internal one. Although the way I was wearing my headscarf was not traditional, to me it was still a hijab. In addition to spiritual reasons, I had always worn my hijab as a visible expression of my *Deen*, my faith. To have it be interpreted differently or ignored completely was disconcerting: was that my fault for not being more 'typically' Muslim and not dressing in the manner traditionally associated with a Muslim? A Company Man had once accused me of being an 'undercover Muslim', someone who didn't announce their religion and just flew under the radar.

This made me distinctly uncomfortable, like I was cheating. I was getting away with not being discriminated against because I didn't look like the women traditionally associated with Islam.

Did that make me an impostor? Perhaps not, but it did give me an unknown and perhaps unfair advantage. By wearing the hijab in a way I felt comfortable with – and it helps that the uniform on the rig is loose coveralls, so my clothing was also hijabi-friendly – I was able to satisfy my religious requirements and also find a way to fit into my environment. I would not face the same attitudes as a woman who wore the traditional hijab to work on the rig. Did that mean I was letting down the sisterhood?

In moments of confusion like these, I would reflect on what Islam has to say. There are numerous verses in the Qur'an that talk about Allah lightening the burden on humankind, and Hadeeth (sayings of the Prophet [SAW]) that describe Islam as a religion of ease: *'Allah wants to lighten for you [your difficulties]; and mankind was created weak.'* (4:28)

There is also the story of the Bedouin who passed urine in the corner of a mosque. People caught him, but the Prophet (SAW) ordered them to leave him and just pour water over the spot. *'You have been sent to make things easy and not make them difficult,'* the Prophet (SAW) was recorded to have said (Bukahri, Volume 1, Book 4, Number 219).

Islamic tradition is replete with stories like these. People are to live their lives within the tenets of Islam, but allowances are made to enable you to choose the easier path, as long as both paths are right, because Islam was not meant to be a religion of toughness and extremes.

So I continue wearing my abbreviated scarf, which performs the function of a hijab but does not take its traditional form. Then, when I do put on my 'civvies', or my 'going home clothes', at the end of the hitch and the men realise that my beanie or tea cosy was not just a health-and-safety measure but actually a representation of my faith, the benefit is that they've already got to know me as a human, rather than ignoring me because I am Muslim. A small win, perhaps.

Sometimes life on the rigs provides me with unexpected nuggets of golden happiness that remind me of our common humanity and desires. One such experience occurred on a night shift, the gift arriving without any fanfare.

I was sitting next to my colleague, a guy who had worked on the rigs all his life and had excelled in the tough environment. He was the typical masculine rig bloke: a Kiwi, hefty and opinionated, an ego as large as his biceps – and they were sizeable biceps. He'd been working in the industry for decades but was only in his mid-forties and had climbed the ranks quickly. With that came an assurance that bordered on arrogance. When he was right, he was right. Until he changed his mind, then he was still right. Kapeesh?

We had a mixed relationship because he would rarely back down, particularly when he thought he was right – and neither would I. He had experience, while I was young and new to the game but had theory and years of debating practice behind me. I treated him like my dad – I kept discussing (or arguing) until he either saw my point or got so exasperated that he walked out and I got what I wanted. Admittedly, maybe not the smartest way to go about making friends.

This guy's voice pulled me out of my work calculations that evening. 'My wife has taken up singing lessons again!' he said proudly, as he swiped his finger up his phone screen, scrolling through Facebook.

'Is that right? That's awesome,' I replied. I was tempted to turn back to my computer but sensed there was more coming, so I slid my hands off my keyboard and swung my chair around to face him. As I absent-mindedly scratched at a grease stain on my coveralls, he told me how a teacher's comment when she was young meant that his wife had spent two decades believing she couldn't sing, even though that's all she'd wanted to do.

'Now, we found a teacher who believes in her and she's singing these songs amazingly! It is only now she's seeing what she is really capable of . . .' The deep, authoritative voice I was used to hearing command attention and frighten roughnecks was thick with indignation, but swelling with pride at what his wife was now achieving.

'Ha!' I laughed. 'It's amazing how words have the power to change the direction of our lives. Apparently Einstein was told he was useless at maths, did you know that?'

He scratched his head before replying. 'You know, Yassmin, I think what you do is actually really inspirational.'

I did a double take. Wait, what? Where had this come from? This was the last guy on the rig I had ever expected to utter the word 'inspirational', let alone to me, the only woman, and the one person on the rig who constantly challenged him. 'Huh?'

'Well, think about it! You're a Sudanese-born Muslim woman, but you decided you wanted to work on the rigs and do it well. People probably told you that it wasn't the place for you but here you are – even with all the other stuff you do outside work. I mean, your dad probably didn't want you to do this and no doubt there are a lot of people who don't expect someone like you to be out here. Even with the attitudes of the guys out here you have to deal with. You do it anyway. I wish I could do what you do.'

I was shocked by this admission and said so.

'You know,' he continued, 'all I've ever really wanted to do is be a mechanical design engineer.'

'Oh really?' I asked, and it made sense as I thought back on the times he'd described inventions to me, and the strange reactions he would have when I asked about the design details or whether he had begun to prototype it.

'I wanted to when I was young, but that's not what men in my town did. We went and got a trade, then got a job. I joined the rigs straight away and that's where I've stayed.'

I wondered how different his life would have turned out if he'd been sent to Spark when he was a young man.

'Well, it's not too late. Study it now!'

His voice took on a wistful quality. 'I've got all these ideas, I just don't have the engineering knowledge to make them a reality.'

'Oh you should!' In the back of my mind, I registered surprise at the idea that my engineering degree was something prized, a skill that I had that others on the rig didn't. The experience of those around me meant that I constantly felt like my skill set had a lower value, but my engineering degree offered me a level of authority I had not yet even begun to understand clearly, but which others saw. It was a bizarre feeling because I still had so much to learn.

The door to the shack opened, and the surreal, almost soppy feeling in the air was instantly cut.

'What's going on in *here*?' Three day guys filed in, taking their seats around the office.

'Oh, I was just telling Yassmin that what she does is inspiring!' He threw the sentence out and it hung in the air, as the men who'd walked in looked at him, bewildered.

'I mean think about it. She's a Sudanese-Muslim woman working on the rigs, even though everyone around her says she shouldn't! She decided that she wanted to, and just made it happen!'

'Yeah, well, I guess that is pretty cool . . .' one of the others replied and looked at me, a quizzical frown on his brow.

'Okay, so now I've told you – you're an inspiration. Enough of that. Now shut the f*** up and do some work.' He spat the words across the desk at me with a grin.

'Ahhh, there's the lad I know and love!' I smiled, closing the conversation forever.

What on earth just happened? I wondered. Who knew? Ultimately, we all want someone to believe in us, and sometimes that person just happens to be the toughest bloke on the block. When someone asks me why I spend time in places like these, I think of moments like this.

Chapter 25:

Why Do You Care What I Wear?

I was running late to catch my flight out to the rig when the lady standing at airport security stopped me and asked me to remove my head covering. 'What do you mean, it's because of your religion?' she asked when I refused.

'Uh, it's what I wear for a hijab,' I said, confused. 'I'm a covered Muslim woman and I have to wear this because it's compatible with my field engineering job.' I was getting frustrated; this was holding up the entire line and causing an unnecessary scene.

'Yeah, look, it really isn't religious enough. Aren't you guys supposed to wear the . . .' She trailed off as she looked at me.

'You mean the full veil, the hijab?'

'Yes, that. You have to wear that for it to be religious. Guys who wear turbans can't come in with a baseball hat covering their hair and say it's religious. Do you have a veil with you to prove that this is for your religion?'

I looked at the lady, incredulous. 'No, I don't carry an extra scarf with me in my hand luggage.'

She didn't seem to pick up on my tone. 'Oh, okay then. In the future, carry a scarf with you so you can show security.'

'Wait, wait a minute.' I had started collecting my bags and was ready to leave, but I just had to clarify. 'So you're telling me that what I'm wearing isn't religious enough for you, and I need to bring a "proper scarf" with me to prove to you that I'm really Muslim?'

'Yes. Do you get where I'm coming from?'

'No, not really. But I'll just go with it so I don't miss my plane. Thank you *so* much for your advice.' I shook my head with exasperation and ran towards my gate.

How am I meant to feel about that kind of encounter? Should I understand how difficult it is for people to discern what is and isn't religious, particularly when we live in a world where a few people might use a hat or a hijab to conceal something dangerous? Or should I be outraged? I just can't believe I have to use brain space thinking about these kinds of things. But, in the West, not having to deal with people's internal biases and expectations in every single interaction of your day is a privilege that belongs to those who aren't hijabied.

* * *

Covered women are the battleground for society's attitude towards Islam – and I am sick of it.

This frustration is one shared by many Muslims and other marginalised groups. It is the feeling that stems from constantly being silenced. Often, someone else tells 'my' story, through their filter. The conversation we are now having, through this book, is a privilege: I can talk to you directly, share my unadulterated views and, hopefully, provide an insight. That doesn't happen very often for people like me.

You may disagree with my opinions and that is well within your right! In fact, I encourage disagreement, so long as it is backed with the open-mindedness to accept that there are other views in the world. We can coexist, peacefully, in disagreement.

'*We have made you into nations and tribes so that you may know one another,*' the Qur'an says (49:13).

For me, this is about the acknowledgement of our differences. However, there is also an implicit encouragement for us to come together despite – or in fact because of – our differences. So we can learn from each other, develop, grow, see the world from alternative perspectives and understand that our lens is not the only one that exists.

* * *

There are not many things that annoy me greatly. Sure, when I was a kid, my little brother touching my property would send me into a possessive rant ('Yasseen! Did I say you could take my special pen? Did I?'). But I grew up and got a hold on my temper, as most people do. It's a matter of pride that I can keep my cool, particularly in times of pressure. If you're in the business of negotiation, or you are in the minority – both of which I often am – it does not pay to be seen as angry. I've also found that, as a woman, any anger I show is attributed to my gender rather than accepted as a genuine emotion about the topic at hand.

'You should have *seen* her. She was hysterical!'

'She is one messed-up bitch, hey. She just had these crazy eyes going.'

So I find it important to stay calm, particularly in disagreements, but especially when people talk publicly about why they think the hijab isn't progressive, or how it is connected to the patriarchy, or that they think it is some sort of 'religious arrogance and subjugation'.

Stop! Just stop it. Don't we have more important issues to be concerned about? Why is this symbol so challenging?

It's hard to believe that people think they have the right to tell me how to dress. This applies to everyone who has an opinion on whether an individual Muslim woman should or shouldn't wear the hijab, niqab, jilbab, chador or burqa. We claim to live in a society that allows us to be free, here in the West, where individual choice is supposedly one of the differentiating and defining features of our society. Yet when it comes to women choosing to conceal rather than to reveal, the individual decision suddenly becomes everyone's responsibility.

The salt in the wound is that people make it seem like they are doing it *for my own good*. That doesn't sound like the 'freedom' we are apparently so proud of. Actually, it smells a little like neo-colonialism to me, cloaked in the guise of 'good intentions'. If people *really* truly cared about the welfare of women wearing hijabs or any other Muslim-related covering, they would take their cues from the women themselves and ensure that their intersectional reality is respected. Rather, whether consciously or unconsciously, people apply their own cultural lens and project their broader prejudice onto another ideology – Islam – and in doing so they lose the respect of the people they claim to want to support.

To be fair, people have less issue with the hijab than they do with the niqab. The hijab has become accepted in Australia. However, it does visibly mark one as Muslim, particularly when it is worn in the traditional manner, and that seems to invite all sorts of people to make their opinions known to you. The issue some people have with the niqab runs deeper – they feel a fear and discomfort, perhaps due to an unconscious acknowledgement that these women are choosing to do something that they themselves wouldn't do.

The solution is simple: respect people's choice to make their own decisions about how they dress themselves. If you have a problem with it, check yourself.

I sometimes feel like I'm banging a drum no one wants to hear, because the discussion makes them uncomfortable; to my mind this highlights that their attitudes can be a smokescreen for bigotry. Denying people the right to wear the hijab or disparaging its legitimacy is definitely more about reducing the visibility of Islam in the community than about 'protecting women', and it comes from a place of fear, ignorance and bigotry.

There are many ways this bigotry is framed. Sometimes, people make it about themselves and, by extension, national security. 'The niqab makes me feel uncomfortable. I want to see their face! How will we know who they are!?'

National security is not a legitimate reason for this conversation. Beneath that attitude is fear – fear of difference and fear of 'the other', an ideology and a 'people' they know nothing about. Niqabis are, like your everyday Jane or Jannah, law-abiding people, and have said time and time again that they are happy to show their faces to a female identifying authority for the sake of security. Why should we make allowances, you ask? Because that's how an inclusive society works! In the same way that we make allowances for people with dietary requirements and preferences, why shouldn't we make similar adjustments for people with religious requirements and preferences, and ensure there are female authorities available for the identification process? Lots of majority Muslim countries seem to be able to do that without an issue. And if we somehow can't find enough female authorities for the job, is there a deeper problem around gender equality that we are also ignoring?

It strikes me as strange that there is such fuss when the veil as an item of clothing is not something new. Christian and Jewish women have been wearing veils for centuries. What, then, is the issue?

The issue is that the custom is at odds with the socially constructed norms of the West today, and that difference is seen as threatening. It almost seems as if some people think that a person who is covering themself is demanding others do the same and judging the choices of other women in Australia. My choice to cover has nothing to do with your choice not to cover.

It is not always as simple as it sounds. Remember, some Muslim populations have emerged from decades of colonial oppression and have framed their identities in relation to that move. If you take a long-oppressed people and try to make them see sense in the arguments of those who have victimised them, it should come as no surprise that there will be pushback. Hating on the hijab gives Muslims who are feeling the colonialism hangover more of a reason to believe in an 'us versus them' narrative. We can't continue to let any discussions about Muslims in the West be pitched as 'us versus them' battles of civilisations. Why? Because that is utterly destructive. We have to do everything we can to ensure the language we use respects and acknowledges the history we share.

There is a famous story in the Qur'an, when the Prophet (SAW) was driven out of Taif by the locals. It hadn't been a good year for the Prophet (SAW). His wife and main supporter, Khadija (RA [May God be Pleased With Her]), had passed away and shortly after, his Uncle Abu Talib, the man who had protected him from the angry tribe, also died. The guy who succeeded

Abu Talib as the leader of the tribe, Abu Lahab, was quite the hater. He hated the Prophet (SAW) and his beliefs so much that he would throw dirt and stones at him in the markets, yelling at him and warning others against following him. Eventually, when the Prophet (SAW) was visiting a town called Taif, children were instructed to throw rocks and curses at him until he was driven outside the city limits and found refuge in an orchard.

The story goes that the Angel Jibreel told the Prophet (SAW) that he had the Angel of the Mountains ready. 'If you wish, I can bring the two mountains at the opposite end of the city together and crush them.'

'No, they should be spared, [for their descendants could be believers].' The Prophet's (SAW) words were clear.

These were people who had stoned the Prophet (SAW) out of their city because they disagreed with his beliefs. He had the compassion to forgive them and show them mercy. There was no 'us and them' or a desire for vengeance and to right past wrongs. No, there was leadership and mercy. Regardless of motivation, there was mercy.

This is what we must constantly remember. At some point, there has to be forgiveness. Yes, there can be immense frustration that we have to continually explain ourselves. Yes, there can be anger at past wrongs. Yes, there can be recognition of pain and hurt. Yes, there is a responsibility for those in the majority and those in power to recognise past wrongs, to realise the value of doing things differently – to actually *lead* and not simply hold on to power.

Even after recognising all of this, at some point everyone needs to set an example and be the bigger person. Every community has to shoulder the responsibility of educating and re-educating people. The conversation really comes down to respect. We live in an individualistic society. And okay, yes, you might not like what I choose to believe in. But even if you don't like it or wouldn't choose it for yourself, you must respect it, because that is how we build civilisation. That is how civilised societies and people behave – by respecting each other's agency and beliefs and the right to uphold their values. After all, that's what living in an individualistic society is about, right?

Chapter 26:

We Gon' Be Alright

So there you have it. Twenty-four-and-a-bit years of third-culture-kid ups and downs, figuring out how to be strong, which battles to fight and how to have a laugh along the way.

It hasn't always been a straightforward journey and, *Inshallah*, I've still got a way to go, but reflecting on these experiences has allowed me to reach a few conclusions.

Coconut or not, I'm proud to be Australian.

Even if the world keeps asking me to define what that means, I'll continue living it and let the rest figure itself out along the way. Australia is my home, my place to own and improve and to strengthen where possible, just like it is for every other Australian, and I relish that privilege.

My journey so far has also taught me that there is great strength in kindness and compassion, although every once in a while we have to make a stand for what we believe in.

There may be worlds of difference between where I was born and where I am today, but bringing the value systems of my faith and heritage to the culture that I grew up in has allowed me to understand more than one way of seeing the world, and I hope has enabled you to, as well.

Occasionally, I am overwhelmed by the vastness of the challenges that lie ahead. Lying in the dark on my single bed, the room swaying with the swell rocking the rig, it is easy to think of myself as insignificant and unable to make a difference.

But that's not true, is it? It isn't true of any of us, and knowing that is immeasurably powerful.

There is great inequality in the world, and there is injustice that drives me to tears of frustration. Turn on the TV or check out your newsfeed; I'm sure you'll understand what I mean.

So how do we find our way out?

I don't have the answer, but I do know something has to give. We have to believe that things can change – otherwise nothing ever will.

In the meantime, we have to learn to check ourselves: to challenge the implications of everything we read, eat, buy and think, because when we are uncomfortable, we are learning, growing and changing. We have to hold ourselves accountable, because sometimes no one else will.

Once we are aware of the systems we are operating in then we can improve them.

Is it going to be easy?

I doubt it. Is it going to be worth it?

Most definitely, *Inshallah*.

Chapter 27:

And Now?

Habooba left us in the first week of Ramadan, the ninth month of the Islamic year. She had been ill for some time, not even able to pick up the phone when I called. Frightened that my strong grandmother could become so frail, I resigned myself to sending voice messages my aunt could play to her. The reality of her condition was difficult to reconcile; I avoided looking at photos on the family Whatsapp group – her sunken eyes made her spirit looked crushed, and I couldn't bear to have these images as my final impressions of the great Habooba Saida. I hadn't seen my grandmother since Aya's wedding two years earlier, and even then her health had been faltering. Our time together that visit was short, but her voice was bright and familiar. She smiled as she held my hands in hers, skin soft and grip firm. 'I love it when you call me just to see how I am,' she said, and my heart lifted. I had planned to sit with her and record her childhood story, but we didn't have time. *Next visit,* Inshallah, I remember thinking. Alas.

When the news came I was on my way to Brisbane. I had wrangled a few days of the holy month back home, a rare treat.

This would be my first Ramadan with my family in years – the last four had been spent on the rigs – and I was looking forward to throwing myself on the couch next to Mum while she watched trashy TV and chatting about future plans and politics with Baba, just like old times. No matter how independent I became, coming home was grounding.

I arrived late and suspected nothing until the family car pulled up. I'd asked Mama to collect me and my too-many bags but she was sitting in the passenger seat, face ashen, and my father was driving. 'We're dropping Mama off at the International Airport,' he said warmly – not the tone I was expecting. A grin with a pinch on the cheek, maybe. A half-hearted barb about not visiting enough, definitely. Dad hadn't been impressed by my move to Melbourne a few months earlier and was even less excited about my decision to take a year's sabbatical.

'What's going on?' I asked as I loaded my suitcases into the car.

'Habooba isn't doing so well . . .' Baba's hand gripped my shoulder, briefly, awkwardly. The meaning was clear.

★ ★ ★

My mother called us from Sudan with the news the next morning. She had reached Habooba before she passed and the ritual cleaning of my grandmother's body and her burial were incredibly quick – a good sign, I was told by my aunt: 'If it only takes a short time to wash the body it means most of their sins have already been washed away, already been forgiven.'

My few days in Brisbane blurred as friends from the Sudanese and Muslim communities called to pay their respects. *She left us during Ramadan*, we reminded ourselves – one of the best times possible. It is said that during Ramadan the angels are out in full force. *Pray for strength, pray for her forgiveness, all we can do now is pray* . . . Across the ocean, Sudan kept my mother and her sisters busy – hundreds visited to mourn with the family, filling the house with love and memories.

I felt far from the shared mourning in Sudan. There was no real language for grief in our Australian home beyond prayer: my father, like many Arab men of his generation, wasn't one for tears. Mine would sometimes spill over despite my best efforts, but I was quick to wipe the traces from my face whenever I heard Dad approaching. 'Are you crying?' he asked once. I shook my head. 'Good. We don't cry now.'

I soon returned to my life of constant movement, back to a world that demanded all of my attention. Grief was not an emotion I knew how to process, and I was even less certain about how to perform it publicly; the world only knew the joyful, optimistic Yassmin. Was there space for anything else? I limited the public announcement to a single, heartfelt, Facebook post.

I was looking forward to my trip to Sudan – to time with cousins loosening my tongue with Arabic, to the chaos and confusion of Sudanese existence. My life had changed significantly over the past year: I was almost always on the road away from family, friends and language. The separation had left me feeling unmoored, so I was keen to get back to my roots but anxious about going back to a land that I knew would feel completely different. Sudan had always meant family to me and I dreaded seeing Habooba's unoccupied bed in the Arkaweet home; the country of my birth would feel empty without her. For the first time, I was seeing Sudan not just for its people, but for its true landscape: hot desert sands, a tough, unchanging political climate and an increasingly conservative populace and government. Strange how the loss of one person reshaped the way I saw an entire nation.

* * *

The flight to Khartoum had a stop in Dubai. After passing through immigration I stole into the women's bathroom, got my old ibaya out of my hand luggage and waited in line. The double-denim outfit I had worn on my flight from London might have been trendy-yet-modest in the UK, but it did not send the same message in the airport in Dubai and most certainly would not do in Sudan. As I unfolded and refolded the ibaya in my hands, the soft polyester pouring through my fingers, I thought about how much my presentation to the world had changed over the last few years. Had I made the right choices, or had I strayed off the right path – as my father occasionally suggested – and normalised what wasn't 'true' Islam? I wasn't sure. Sometimes I didn't know how to tell the difference between pushing the boundaries and drifting.

I was the woman who spent most of her life in hi-vis orange coveralls and steel-capped boots, whose only make-up was a few sticks of lipstick. At some point I had started to have fun with how I dressed, playing with colour, material and character to tell stories with my outfits, and not just the story of my faith. My appearance began to reflect who I was as an individual, my intersectional clothing mirroring the growing complexity of my life: hipster ghetto, preppy tradie, on-trend traditional. I had realised there wasn't just one way to look like a 'good Muslim' and I was embracing it. Sure there was tradition and expectation to live up to, but culture changes with the times – or that's what I told myself, anyway. And yes, culture does change, but when you're the one evolving it, who checks whether you've changed it for the better? My answer has always been to look to Islam, but in areas where there's so much room for interpretation, religious certainties are harder to come by. I was struggling to find a way to interrogate my beliefs without feeling blasphemous. How does finding the right path work when the religion encourages questioning and growth, but the environment does not seem to allow that?

If the Whatsapp messages my mother sent admonishing me for the tightness of my jeans and the new piercing in my nose were anything to go by, she didn't think the way I was dressing aligned to our values. So even though I was having fun, was my behaviour appropriate, Islamic, right? I had to hope so, *Inshallah*.

As a woman vacated the cubicle in front of me her eyes travelled up and down my person, clocking the ibaya in my hands. I could see the cogs of judgement whirring. In that moment I realised that to her I had become one of 'those women' – the ones who were derided while I was growing up. The stories were well known both in the Arab Muslim communities and outside of them: women who wore ibayas in their home country and then changed into Western clothing as soon as they got on a plane. 'Those women' were used as pawns on any side of an argument about the hijab: proof that Muslim women were losing their way, proof that Muslim women actually wanted to live like Westerners, proof that Muslim women were oppressed, that they needed to 'be saved' . . . Had I become one of 'those women'? I wasn't sure. Things were far simpler when I didn't challenge my own attitudes. I could challenge the world around me but challenging *myself*? That was trickier. Sometimes I wished I could settle for seeing the world in black and white, but I knew that unquestioning certainty lent itself to a blinkered view. I was certain about one thing: my belief in Allah, *Alhamdulillah*. But on how to dress? I would have to live with the uncertainty and pray, *Inshallah*, that I was making the right choices.

It's ridiculous that our bodies are constant battlefields anyway, I thought as I changed in the cramped cubicle. The ibaya was about twenty centimetres too short, so the bottom of my jeans were visible above my shoes. The blue of the denim juxtaposed against the black ibaya reflected my dilemma – no matter which way I tried to dress or speak, either my Western or Sudanese identity would intrude.

When I left the bathroom I was no longer a striking brown woman who garnered attention, either positive or negative. Last time I visited, that hadn't even been a consideration – one of the many ways my life had changed. I had grown up not caring that people thought I was different. I knew I stood out – because I was tall, or wearing the hijab, or laughing loudly – but it wasn't something I thought about. These last few years standing out had become something I was *rewarded* for. People wanted to feature my style in magazines. They invited me to fashion events. They re-grammed my Instagram photos and they remembered my name. My inability to blend in had become a strength, and it felt good to have people compliment my scarf style when it had been a lightning rod for ridicule for years. And it felt good to gain access to the world of fashion; a world that had been well and truly sealed off to the nerdy, large-framed Sudanese-Muslim engineer version of me. I had never been considered beautiful as beauty was defined by an Anglo-reality I could never achieve. And yet suddenly, strangely, I had been invited into this new adventure and it felt good to not be in tension with one thing that society – and my extended family – implied women should aspire to be: beautiful.

In some ways this rankled: I felt self-involved, ashamed at liking rewards that had never been part of my self-narrative. Even though I enjoyed the cultural and societal capital gained, I was torn about taking advantage of a privilege I felt shouldn't exist. I also wondered how my foray into fashion fit with the narrative and purpose of hijab. Hijab is not meant to be an object of beauty – at least not the way I was taught about it. So does turning hijab into one defeat its purpose? One school of thought argues that 'modest fashion' is oxymoronic, that if hijab is about modesty then wearing it to be striking and fashionable makes it redundant. This school argues that fashion is focused on the worldly when hijab is about doing something for Allah. I don't disagree, but for me being a Hijabi is about both: about doing something for Allah but also about loudly and proudly proclaiming my identity as a Muslim.

Wearing the black ibaya, I could put that discussion aside for a while. Now my appearance was homely at best – make-up free with a hijab arranged in a deliberately 'fashionless' manner. The eyes of men slid right past me, barely registering my presence: I was invisible. In some ways it felt powerful. Islamically, wearing the ibaya made me feel at peace, but my clothing wasn't the only reason for my sense of calm. In Sudan no one would ask me to speak on behalf of Islam, take my choices as representative of the entire Muslim faith, or ask me to apologise for and justify the actions of other Muslims. I was simply one of the masses. Who would have thought that would be liberating?

★ ★ ★

That sense of peaceful calm was short-lived. 2016 was a year of enormous and unexpected change, both worldwide and personally. I had begun the year scheduling my book tour and advocacy work around my FIFO schedule – I was finally going to earn my stripes following a promotion to a supervisor role on an offshore rig. When that didn't quite go to plan, I decided it was time to take the plunge and focus full-time on 'the other stuff' I did – although I was nervous about my parents' reactions. When I raised the idea of quitting my job, my mum's rebuke was swift: 'You know how tough it is to find a job in this market!' She was right; instead, I took a year-long sabbatical.

My father surprised me, though, when he said I should consider whether this was a good opportunity to start afresh. 'You're too old to keep just trying things for the sake of it, Yassmina. Think deeply about what you want to do – *and it doesn't have to be in engineering!*'

I couldn't believe it. What did he mean? The idea of having a job away from engineering, being defined by a non-technical career, made me feel physically ill. Being an engineer was how I identified and differentiated myself publicly, as well as how I saw myself in the world. More than that, I loved it! As an engineer I found tangible solutions to problems, saw my work being built and felt like what I was doing was *real*. Engineering gave me fluency in another language. I used my experience as an engineer to introduce issues from the social change sector into the corporate world. I could talk to high-level corporate executives around the world about unconscious bias because I had lived experience of it. To get respect as a young, brown, Muslim woman I had to play by some of their rules. And as a working engineer, I did. Beyond the personal love of the profession, being an engineer gave me real credibility in my advocacy work. How could I walk away from that?

Dad reminded me that he had never worked as an engineer

in Australia and yet I still thought of him as one, but moving away from a technical role felt wrong. I was worried about becoming a talking head, about not being able to make a tangible difference through my work. I also couldn't imagine doing just one thing – I had always run on multiple career tracks simultaneously. On top of all that, I knew I would miss the uncomplicated world of the workshop, the field and the rig, and the challenge of making it where I wasn't supposed to. I would miss finding ways to have that human connection around people I was different to.

My identity was still wrapped up in being an engineer, more so than I had previously appreciated. It was a role I was still proud of, still wanted to be associated with, still claimed. But it was good to know that I had the option to walk away.

★ ★ ★

Once I decided to take my sabbatical, I immediately began to make plans to move to Melbourne, to a city with a ready network of friends and connections working in the social impact and non-profit space. If I'm honest, a small part of me hoped there would be more marriage material in Melbourne than in Perth or Brisbane. It turned out all the guys with beards weren't Muslims though, just hipsters.

I thought I would have a holiday, read lots, take it easy, sip lattes and eat smashed avo – ha! I toured with this book to schools, writers' festivals and other events around the country. I hosted a podcast with the *ABC* called *Motor Mouth* on my dream to become an F1 driver. I started a TV career, hosting a documentary on the science behind racism as well as a weekly TV show on the *ABC* called *Australia Wide*. My face, as friends would tell me, was everywhere. The media opportunities weren't part of a strategic move, but having more time and a tendency to say yes meant things started to snowball, *Alhamdulillah*.

I also grew my international presence, doing at least one overseas speaking gig a month, which meant I travelled to almost twenty countries over six months to talk about youth and female empowerment, unconscious bias, the diaspora experience, entrepreneurship and more. From keynoting alongside Kofi Annan in Switzerland to trips through the US, UK, Indonesia, Singapore, Canada, Saudi, Jordan, UAE, Sudan, Egypt, Palestine, Qatar, Kuwait . . .

I also made it onto the world stage after an unusual altercation at a writers' festival blew up into an international incident. In short, I walked out of the keynote opening night speech at the Brisbane Writers Festival, delivered by a famous American author, Lionel Shriver. I wrote about the event and my blog went viral, which means the story is easy to find online, so I will spare you the details.

Many people asked why I decided to walk out of this event: *What pushed you over the line? You often talk about situations in which you have chosen to not take offence when someone has said something offensive, but rather made the person feel comfortable and worked upwards from there.*

And these people are right. My preferred modus operandi is to minimise fuss, to 'wear' it, to weather the storm and then rebuild from the wreckage. That is still largely how I tackle these situations. I have been starting to realise that this always places the burden on the minority, and the weight of that burden was beginning to irk me. Why should I, as the butt end of the joke, also be expected to be gracious when explaining why the joke was tasteless? Does the privilege of the majority and the norm extend a free pass for insensitivity? Do we simply accept that people who don't have to learn about others won't, and that it is our job to educate them? And why does freedom of speech seem to extend only one way – are people free to offend, but not to be annoyed when their words cause offence?

Within Islam we are taught to be gracious to those who seek to cause us harm. But we are also encouraged to have self-respect, and allowed a measure of self-defence. Being gracious doesn't mean being passive and accepting of all treatment. I'm certainly still figuring this all out. You're witnessing a young adult trying to decide the best way to engender change in this day and age, particularly on issues that are swathed in nuance.

It does frustrate me that I now have a public profile built on the assumption that I enjoy outrage. That has never been, and still isn't, my chosen mode of change. I've always been about bridge building, and yet the one time I walked away from the bridge was the time people noticed. I guess building bridges isn't as newsworthy. The Shriver case pigeonholed me as a defender of a single decision, rather than someone offering the first point in a constructive debate. The public response gave me little room to move intellectually, stifling the opportunity for me to learn and grow from the encounter. I accept that my thesis could be improved upon, but rather than using the opportunity to engage, the public response was to howl me down and personally attack me. Perhaps if I had known how it would play out, I would have spent more than a few hours on a Friday night venting my frustration. But I fell victim to the outrage machine. I do wonder whether we would be having this conversation if I had done anything differently: 'I stayed until the end of Lionel Shriver's speech, but I didn't like it' doesn't have the same ring to it.

The actual concept of cultural appropriation itself wasn't something that I had too much attachment to. Cultures change and adapt and borrow from each other, they always have. Sharing, mixing and exchange of cultures isn't new, and that isn't what I took issue with when I walked out of Lionel Shriver's speech. The conversation I'm interested in engaging with is about racism and structural inequality and the power dynamics at play in our world. As far as I was concerned, the freedom to write fiction was a strawman argument for the reinforcement of the status quo, and the anger at anyone who dares criticise the natural order. That's what I understood the talk to be about, and what I took issue with.

My family has had mixed opinions about the event and its fallout. Mum has been totally on board since the debate escalated and has encouraged me to stay engaged in the conversation – I think it's her inner activist coming out. Dad was bemused by the whole affair and paid it little attention. Broader family members, particularly those in Sudan, weren't all on board though. 'It's not fair, of course!' one aunt said. 'But that's the way it is – she can write whatever she wants! You can't change the system overnight and expect to bring people to your side by walking out. You have to do it softly, and in different ways.'

I can understand that notion, and largely I agree. At an individual level I will still meet people at face value, because more often than not their intentions aren't malevolent. From my experience, one-on-one influencing is always more effective when the other person isn't on the defensive. But I think we have to be particularly careful of the language we allow in public spaces, at keynotes and in public discussions. They hold a weight that is different to what is said in an individual discussion. Having a platform changes the dynamic, and in our current post-Trump, post-Brexit, Hanson/Farage/Le Pen-era language matters more than ever.

In need of a constructive way to channel this energy into something positive, I started working on my next project. MUMTAZA, which means 'she's excellent' in Arabic, is a speakers' bureau for women of colour. The many corporates and event organisers the world over who say they struggle getting good diversity for their panels can now come straight to us, and we will match them with a fantastic, fit-for-purpose speaker who happens to be a woman of colour. Tokenism? No. You can't be what you can't see, and the world doesn't see the excellent women of colour around the world talking about issues they're passionate about and experts in. MUMTAZA is about raising their profiles, and it comes with training and support, underlined by the same concept as YWB: building a family. It's one of the practical ways I'm working on paying it forward. Yallah!

* * *

When I arrived in Sudan, nothing was quite the same. Rather than driving to my paternal grandmother's house in al-Riyadh as always, we drove to the apartment Dad was now living in. The small flat my parents had recently bought was sparsely furnished, but it was *our* Sudanese home. It wasn't the Sudan I knew, but I later realised that this was a real moment of achievement for my father. He hadn't owned his own apartment or house in Sudan before, or had a place to call his own for his immediate family. No wonder he was so proud.

Habooba Saida's house had been sealed and was gathering dust. The al-Riyadh house that was always so full of laughter and kids was now a diaspora of young adults, everyone living their own life: going to school or university, planning weddings. We really had all grown up. My cousin Aya was having a baby, and Aalaa, the sister three years our junior, was getting married. This became a source of ribbing. 'Yassmina, *khalas*! When is it your turn, habiba?' my aunts scolded me good-naturedly. I laughed, slightly self-conscious. What could I say? Even in the Muslim community in Australia twenty-five was old to be unmarried. I had passed the age at which I had told my father I would start seriously considering marriage. Weddings, kids and relationships had become a constant conversation around me, both in Sudan and Australia, and I never quite knew how to respond. I usually fell back on humour. 'Oh, you'll have to wait for Yasseen! Give up on me,' I joked when we visited the extended family, but the sentiment went down like a stone. 'What! Why, Yassmina! Don't say that,' they would admonish. '*Inshallah*, you will find your partner soon and have children before you know it!'

The same comment that garnered laughter in my Westernised circles in Australia provoked pity and embarrassment in Sudan. Prioritising family – a value that seemed to have lost its place in the Australia that I knew – was alive and well in Sudan. Once again, the tension of reconciling my Western views with those of my family settled in my gut.

Yet I was happy with my choices, *Alhamdulillah*. What exasperated me was the assumption that I was somehow diminished because I was unmarried, or that I was not a complete adult as a single woman – a reality that would be different if I were male. I had thought I'd be able to ignore the comments and double standard, and perhaps I could at twenty-one. Now it had become a regular feature of discussion, up front and centre, and I wasn't amused. It wasn't as if I had actively avoided getting married. I had no ideological opposition to the institution. I had just focused my attention on my career and assumed everything else would fall into place. Evidently not! As I constantly explained to my family, it was an issue of economics: supply and demand. The demand was high, and the supply didn't quite meet the requirements, particularly in Australia. When I broached the idea of marrying someone outside our Sudanese norms, the familial responses differed wildly but there was one thing that was constant: he had to be Muslim.

I thought about the men who had come into my life during this very confusing year – men who were definitely not Muslim. Men who I walked away from, despite our compatibility, because they were not Muslim. My family's response reassured me I had made the right choice. But my heart still hurt. Had I made the right choice by me? I hoped so. *Allah knows best,* I told myself. But part of my heart wondered if Allah would make exceptions.

I was shocked at some of the conversations I was having with myself this year – beliefs and behaviours I had taken for granted were being deeply challenged. Was this growth or drift? Healthy or destabilising? Probably all of the above. I just had to hold onto my faith and the belief that everything would be as it was meant to be, *Inshallah*.

It wasn't until we were sitting in the living room of the house in al-Riyadh, the same house that I had run around as a child, that I realised how deeply my personal decisions affected my father. Aya had just given birth in Saudi, and the family was gathered to congratulate her dad on becoming a grandfather. Not prone to expressing emotion, that day he beamed with joy. The family then turned to my father: 'What about you, Midhat? You're looking jealous!'

Baba was! His mouth was drawn with a wistfulness I had not seen before, his smile rueful as he shrugged and looked at me. 'I just don't know where we went wrong.'

I almost recoiled from his words. I had known Baba wanted me to get married but I hadn't realised he cared so much, and I was gutted my priorities had caused him pain. Although he had never pressured me to put family first, my dad had always valued his family above his career. In that moment I was reminded that we're from a communal family and that my decisions are not mine alone. In fact, they reflect more on my *family* than on me. That changes the dynamic of my decision making. In a communal environment, my being disappointingly unmarried isn't only my fault, but a reflection on the way my parents brought me up. How can I continue a behaviour that I know is directly hurting my parents, who had given everything up for me and my future? Classic third culture kid guilt.

But when I spoke to my mum about what Baba had said, she was reassuring: 'Yassmina, Baba has lived his life. He's enjoyed it and had a full one, *Alhamdulillah*. Live your own life. We believe that Allah has written for us who we get married to. So don't worry so much! There's no point sitting around waiting for it. Just do you.'

All the marriage drama aside, my time in Sudan was a welcome break from the usual hubbub. I spent hours with my father debating the Sudanese political landscape, American foreign policy and what I was going to do with my life. I began to see Sudan through different eyes. It was no longer the place I came just to see family. It was a country I could have a mature relationship with in a way that was still being cast and redefined. I began to appreciate that I was probably more Sudaniya than I realised – I truly was one of the diaspora and I could give back to this community. I'd always assumed that I wouldn't be able to have an impact in Sudan, through volunteering or otherwise, because my family didn't have a tribe, because my Arabic wasn't as good as my English. But for the first time I brought my change-making identity to the land of my birth. I spoke at Khartoum's *Start Up Grind* event that trip, sharing the learnings from starting Youth Without Borders and bringing the concepts of unconscious bias to Sudan. The response was massively positive, which gave me food for thought. Perhaps there is work to be done here. Perhaps I can make a difference. And although Habooba wouldn't be here to see it, I am sure she would agree, *Inshallah*. Although she probably would want me to get married first!

★ ★ ★

I wore the ibaya back to the airport, blending into the crowds on the way to Australia. Well, blending in until I got on the flight from Dubai to Canberra, where I definitely stood out. I was flying direct to Canberra for an unconference, Junket 2016, and I chose not to change into my Western clothing, savouring the last little bit of Sudan. As I rolled my suitcase into the Canberra hotel, people who passed stared at my outfit – a different kind of stare to the one I usually got. When she later saw a picture of me in Sudan, my Melbourne housemate Cass said, 'I would talk to that Yassmin so differently to the Yassmin I'm used to.'

I smiled at the hotel receptionist, thinking of how this same dress said wildly different things to different people. No wonder I couldn't figure things out. As I took off my ibaya in my room and slipped into an outfit the young attendees of the unconference would find more palatable, I laughed to myself.

Caramello egg, chameleon, or just confused? What a time to be alive.

★ ★ ★

The world is changing around us in ways no expert seems able to predict. We are truly in a state of flux. Everywhere I look, whether internally or to the people, cultures and norms around me, things are shifting. The West seems to be moving to nationalism, isolationism. The MENA countries are increasingly conservative in their religious expectations and practices. Powerhouses like China and Russia are jockeying for position. Australian politicians seem incapable of explaining to my generation where future jobs are going to come from, or how we will ever be able to afford a house. 'Post-truth' is the word of the year.

But on the other hand, I've had fourteen-year-old school students talk to me about intersectionality, using phrases I only learnt recently. Young girls are being encouraged into STEM subjects, youth-led organisations are popping up around the world, and tech is being used to unlock talents across developing countries.

It is an incredible but also deeply uncomfortable time to be alive. There is a Lenin quote that sums up my feelings about the current happenings:

There are decades where nothing happens; and then there are weeks where decades happen.

I think we are living in those weeks.

Now more than ever we have to be engaged, vigilant and ready to fight for what we believe in. I believe in a world of equal access to opportunity. Of reduced inequality. Of respect for one another, of empathy, of the power of human connection to trump difference. I will plant my stake in the ground for these things.

What does that mean for what I do going forward? I honestly have no idea. People keep asking what's next, and I can't say for certain where I will be in the next year, five years, or decade. If you had asked me five years ago whether I would have toured the world, published a memoir, hosted a TV show, worked on oil rigs, moved cities and accidentally picked a fight with a famous author then written about it for the *New York Times* and *still* not have gotten married, I would have laughed in your face. Loudly and boldly, probably with some leg slapping. So I cannot predict where the next five years will take me, *Inshallah*.

Moving forward my choices will be more actively aligned with my value system and the difference I want to make in the world. At the moment my focus is on the empowerment of women, particularly women of colour, and in access to energy. But who knows from here?

All I know for certain is that the world can no longer wait for me – or anyone – to be comfortable with the idea of stepping up to fight for a better world, or to step into our power. There is too much happening, too quickly, for us to wait.

'The standard you walk past is the standard you accept.' The quote popularised by General David Morrison rings particularly true in times like these. It forces me to ask myself: what am I accepting around me, implicitly or explicitly? Am I positively impacting the world in every possible way, *Inshallah*? Am I living with integrity?

Ultimately though, the words of my mother provide me the truest guidance: 'One day, Allah will ask you: "I gave you all these gifts, all these opportunities, all these skills. What did you do with them? How did you use what I gave you to make the world a better place?"'

I hope I have a good enough answer, *Inshallah*.